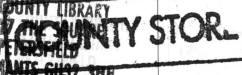

FERTILITY GARDENING

LAWRENCE D. HILLS

CAMERON & TAYLEUR
in association with
DAVID & CHARLES

Published by Cameron & Tayleur (Books) Limited, 25 Lloyd Baker
Street, London WC1X 9AT
in association with David & Charles (Publishers) Limited, Brunel
House, Newton Abbot, Devon.
Distributed by David & Charles.

House editor: Elisabeth Cameron

Text set by Typesetters (Birmingham) Limited, 90 Edgbaston
Road, Smethwick, Warley, West Midlands.
Printed and bound by R. J. Acford, Terminus Road Industrial
Estate, Chichester, Sussex.

First published 1981.
Printed and bound in Great Britain.
ISBN 0 7153 8188 1

Contents

To

CHERRY

Who Weeds my words,
Prunes my Paragraphs,
Feeds our Fertility
And is

MY WIFE.

Preface

All gardeners go on learning all their lives, and organic gardeners learn more than any of their colleagues who go in for chemicals, as Nature's packaging carries no simple directions, and there is a lifetime's pleasure to be gained from the knowledge that grows in the garden. This book is based on facts that I have learned in twenty-five years about what is perhaps the most important aspect of organic gardening—how to maintain the complex recycling of plant foods, trace elements and humus that keeps gardens growing without chemicals.

In 1956 I wrote *Compost, Comfrey and Greenmanure* for the then infant Henry Doubleday Research Association (we sold 10,000 copies at 1s 9d each) and together with over 6,000 members I have gone on learning ever since. Members' own experiences, distilled through our Newsletters, are part of this book, and I would like to thank them all for their contributions. There has been a great increase in our knowledge of soil biology and plant physiology in the past quarter-century, and it is safe to say that even the most orthodox gardeners are rarely as fiercely chemical-conscious today as they were in the past. I would like to thank Dr Anthony Deavin, our scientific Adviser for seven years, for advice and help from his expert and up-to-date knowledge of how plants feed, and Miss Pauline Pears, M.Sc., our Research Assistant, for much searching, scanning and reference-checking.

Because this is essentially a book for gardeners of all kinds who want to grow crops, rather than pass examinations on them, references have been kept to a minimum, but will enable anyone who wishes to delve further into controversial subjects. In the case of trees and herbaceous plants that drink through their leaves, there is a whole bibliography available to those who are concerned with research on plant physiology in tropical and subtropical countries with irregular rainfall.

In this book, I have allowed myself to move from questions of distances between rows, and consider instead the 'why' as well as 'how' of maintaining fertility, the newly discovered aspects of trees and forests, as well as garden crops, and 'the beauty of the wild green Earth and the infamy of man', to adapt Cameron Wilson's 'Magpies in Picardy', from 1914 to an age of pollution.

In the hope that my readers will not need pictures of wheelbarrows and bunches of vegetables to coax their eyes through my words, this book is illustrated only with line drawings where these are essential. They are drawn by Piotr Swierczynski, a former HDRA student with the rare talent of drawing exactly what he sees, for the reader to make what is illustrated. He also drew the cover design. Thank you, Piotr, for a good job well done.

Many of the figures for the tables in the text have been gathered and paid for through the years in the course of the work of the Association. These include almost all that relate to Comfrey, but the majority are from Bulletin No. 210 *Organic Manures* (Ministry of Agriculture, Fisheries and Food, HMSO, £1.10) and are averaged over large numbers of samples that reflect the quality of what can be bought today, rather than in the pre-factory farming Britain of the 1920s, and permission to use them is gratefully acknowledged.

My greatest debt of gratitude is to the late Professor T. Wallace, C.B.E., D.Sc., F.R.I.C., V.M.H., F.R.S. of Bristol University, who wrote *The Diagnosis of Mineral Deficiencies in Plants by Visual Symptoms*, published by HMSO in 1961 at £3.50, and out of print for many years. A new edition of this unique work will be published in several volumes by the National Vegetable Research Station, eventually, with modern colour plates of all the symptoms of trace element shortage, but its cost will be astronomical. Meanwhile I am grateful for permission to quote extensively from it.

With the steadily increasing demand for organically gown produce, it is becoming more and more important to define exactly what may and may not be used by organic farmers and gardeners. The British Standards are given in an appendix, and if International Standards can be agreed, they will be given in later editions of this book. From my experience of Conferences on Organic standards, this may well have to wait until I have learned enough to write a still larger book on Fertility. There is so much more to learn.

Lawrence D. Hills

1 The Organic Way

A fertile soil is one which will continue to produce good crops indefinitely, as the Weald of Sussex has grown oaks and the Amazon Basin has supported the rain forests, where 55,000 species, from mighty trees to humming birds, mesh together, endlessly recycling through the sunlit centuries. Burn the rain forest and you destroy the fertility, which means not only humus and plant foods, but the whole system of cycles, interlocked like the Olympic Games symbol and powered by the sun and rain, to form what almost amounts to a living entity, that today we call the 'biomass'.

About 5,000 years ago, neolithic farmers arriving from Spain burned the beech forests that then covered the South Downs, and replaced them with sheep, wheat and barley. Slowly, the land found a new fertility, that we are learning to rebalance with fewer trees and more people. We shall have to learn how to adjust the balance again and again to allow for still more people and further pollution, as the fossil fuels and fossil fertilizers run low.

The late F. W. Newman Turner, first president of the Henry Doubleday Research Association, wrote *Fertility Farming* in 1951, and *Fertility Pastures* in 1955, both published by Faber & Faber. These books, long out of print, are among the classics of the organic movement. They were concerned with maintaining the fertility cycles in farming without chemical fertilizers, which merely drive the cycles faster and faster, and without pesticides, fungicides and herbicides based on artificial molecules that soil micro-organisms cannot take apart. These chemicals can build up to dangerous levels in the soil and, via the food chains of eaters and eaten, in our bodies. In contrast, the substances containing nitrogen and phosphorus that arise in Nature may be as variously toxic as the proteins of snake venom, the oxalic acid in rhubarb leaves and the alkaloids in deadly nightshade, but all decay safely in compost heaps or by Nature's slower methods.

Newman Turner's basic idea was the herbal ley, a temporary pasture with deep rooting herbs, like burnet and chicory, that reach far down in the soil for minerals to replace the ones that walked off the farm in meat, milk and bone, or fed human beings as grain or potatoes. Always, his aim was to return all the straw, manure and urine back to the land, to keep the fertility cycle going.

This book is about the garden version of Frank Newman Turner's idea, which is more difficult to achieve because chickens and rabbits provide less efficient recycling than grazing animals, and almost every gardener is striving to grow the most food in the least space. He must therefore drive his fertility cycles harder to release sufficient plant foods to allow two and sometimes three crops a year, and so needs to import manure, or its equivalent, and organic fertilizers.

The word 'organic' was first used as we understand it today by the late Jerome Irvine Rodale in 1942, when he wanted a short and simple word that would be easily understood by hundreds of thousands of people to imply the growing of food in accordance with the ideas expressed by Sir Albert Howard in his book, *An Agricultural Testament* (Faber & Faber 1942). Perhaps he chose the best possible word, for today his monthly magazine *Organic Farming and Gardening* has a circulation of nearly 1¼ million in the USA.

Had he called it 'Journal of Applied Ecology', he might by now have been responsible for a more fact-filled and scientifically famous journal, but he would have had far fewer readers, and made fewer organic farmers and gardeners. 'Ecological' has been coming into fashion only since 1970, though it was already being used in the 1950s, but this term is no more accurate. *The Concise Oxford Dictionary* has defined ecology as the branch of biology dealing with the relations of living organisms to their surroundings, their habits and their modes of life. Like 'biological', which is now popular in Europe, this word has the disadvantage that it applies just as much to battery hens and to hydroponic tanks, where tomatoes and lettuce are grown in nothing but chemicals and water, as to what we have taken to calling 'organic methods' because there appears to be no other phrase that covers the meaning so well.

'Organic' of course has its disadvantages. In 1807, Baron Jöns Jakob Berzelius (1779–1848), a Swedish professor who was one of the fathers of modern chemistry, insisted that chemical synthesis of 'organic substances' was impossible, since they could be formed only by the agency of a 'vital force' present in living cells. Urea was synthetized in 1828, followed during the next thirty years by many more substances which did not contain carbon fixed by living leaves. So the 'vital force' theory, like many others, passed away.

It left us the phrase 'Organic Chemistry' to describe that branch of the science concerned with the enormous number of possible carbon compounds, but this is now being replaced by the term 'Carbon Chemistry', which is far more accurate. Berzelius, however, continues to provide a hair for academic minds to split, while 'organo' remains a convenient part-title for a number of pesticides, containing carbon, which are synthetic and cannot be taken apart by living organisms. They do break down in time, but often into products that are as harmful as the original compounds, or worse.

The great advantage, however, of Jerome Rodale's decision, was that he had to make up his mind quickly and finally on which substances used on farms or gardens should be accepted as organic, and therefore permissible in advertisements, and which should be rejected as inorganic. His decisions have been the basis of the 'Whole-food Standards' of Britain and the many other countries in Europe, and the USA. For the basic object is not to preserve the niceties of Chemistry, but to protect the public against deception.

Organic Standards
Anyone who offers 'Organically Grown' produce for sale can charge a high price for it, with the premium on wheat at about 15%. Those who are prepared to pay extra for food that is said to be grown without chemical fertilizers or poison sprays are entitled to have what they are paying for. The selection or rejection of substances for inclusion here is based on the need to provide a satisfactory answer for the Judge who is one day going to ask 'What *is* a Chemical Fertilizer?' in a case brought by some public-spirited member of the public against a Health Food shop that has bought inorganic food cheaply on the open market for resale as organically grown, at a high price.

A number of cases have been fought out in France which were decided on the presence or lack of pesticide residues. It is far easier to make this measurement than to detect whether chemical fertilizers have been applied, for although their use normally means more water in the crop, variations in moisture content also depend on rainfall. Definitions and standards set out in this book are based on criteria agreed some years ago between the Henry Doubleday Research Association and the Soil Association and subsequently modified by the Soil Association's Standards Committee. Gardeners and market growers who abide by them can be sure that they are complying with the highest standards, and that it is perfectly possible to use them commercially—they are reprinted as Appendix I.

There are two entirely different categories of customers involved in the question of standards, and both must be satisfied (even though the most important customers have no legal rights). One category is the shoppers in Health Food stores who are spending about £50 million a year in Britain alone, vastly more in Europe, the USA, Australia, Canada and New Zealand. Demand on this scale exerts enormous commercial pressure on anyone who can deliver well cultivated, well packed, and fresh organically grown produce, to lower the standards, pile on the fertilizers for maximum yield and use every chemical pesticide, fungicide and herbicide possible to cut labour costs and improve appearance in order to serve more customers. But, fortunately, most organic farmers and growers are dedicated, which is why they are rarely rich.

Officialdom regards these customers as faddists and cranks, despite the support gained by many of their ideas from modern medicine and nutritional science but they are really people who have thought out their position. It is their decision, that 'We will not do or encourage others to do anything that will harm the future of our world, where we all have to share one atmosphere and seven polluted seas.' They say: 'Since this may harm our children and their children and the future of all the races of mankind, and endanger our health and that of others, we will have none of it.' Finally, they say: 'There are only so many of these resources in the world. Therefore we shall seek out and find ways of replacing them, so that there will be enough left for the people of the future, since we, the greediest generations known, have spent our share. We will destroy no more, because we refuse to rob the future.'

They impose the limits at many different points, according to the branch of what can be called 'The Organic Movement' to which they belong, but always with roughly the same intention, and nowhere with more agreement than in the fields of food, farming and gardening. At a press conference held by Pan Britannic Industries in 1979, Dr G. H. Hessayon, perhaps Britain's most famous inorganic gardener, stated that one amateur in three was unwilling to use chemical fertilizers or sprays, and explained that their 'Back to Nature' garden products were being launched for this expanding market. Standards are crucial, now that those who cannot beat potential customers have decided to join them.

Plants Have Rights

The second group of customers is even more important: the crops we grow in our gardens and on our farms, whose diets we have changed from those they enjoyed since their first domestication to those based on ideas that began at Rothamsted in 1841, when the work of John Lawes and Joseph Gilbert led to the first Green Revolution. This development caused not only an enormous increase in food production, which nevertheless still lags behind world population in growth, but also the counter revolution which is the organic movement.

The only way in which we can draw distinctions between organic and inorganic plant nutrition is by considering how plants and trees feed. Followers of the inorganic outlook, especially the elderly and orthodox, will argue that all this is mere 'muck and mystery', so for their especial benefit some references are given at the end of this chapter, which is based on recent experimental work in plant nutrition. The object is not to argue with the public relations officers of the chemical industry, but to help anyone who does not wish to use any of their products that do not satisfy the agreed standards. The principles vary from country to country, and it is to be hoped that this account of a very complex subject (which may well need correcting in the light of fresh discoveries) will help the many well-meaning organic movement committees who are devising standards of their own. It would be better still if it helped the International Federation of Organic Agricultural Movements (IFOAM) to agree a set of standards that would be accepted all over the world.

How Trees and Plants Feed

The most important difference between humans and trees is not that we walk about and they do not. It is that plants feed through tiny, transparent root hairs, (which live only for about three days) on their main roots, while we, like every other mammal from whales to weasels, maintain our food supply through hairlike villi on the membrane lining our intestines. The villi, too, live three days, extracting nutrients from our digested food in the same way. We are more like plants than we think, for although they grow in the soil and we in the air, only walking on the soil and cultivating it, we are equally dependent on it for our physical existence.

Our digestive juices are mainly hydrochloric acid; theirs are mostly carbonic acid. Ours stay in our stomachs but plants and trees release theirs into the soil, often from the root tips which erode their way into the subsoil, making minerals available; they are strong enough to etch glass, as shown in a classic experiment by Boussingault. They can also release plant food minerals they no longer require.[1] When our villi wear out, we merely re-cycle them, but plants use the food value in their worn-out feeding roots to support a host of bacterial and fungal allies in what is called the 'rhizosphere', surrounded by a blend of stomach and hunting-ground, where root hairs reach out to absorb the large, watery molecules that hold minerals in solution.

Some of the bacteria fix atmospheric nitrogen, converting it to compounds that can be absorbed by the roots and built by the plants into proteins. Many nitrogen fixers are free living, notably *Azotobacter chroococcum*, which uses the soil's organic matter as its source of energy. These are in addition to the well known nitrogen-fixing bacteria in the root nodules of many pea family (leguminous) plants, which are given a 'living wage' in carbohydrates in return for this service. Other microscopic helpers are the mycorrhizal fungi that live in or around plant roots, making phosphates available through the cell walls in return for nutrients made by the plant.[2] Sir Albert Howard at the Indore Research Station in India (where he fathered the compost heap as we know it today) was perhaps the first to draw attention to these fungi, which are as important in the phosphate nutrition of a wide range of crops as the clover and pea root bacteria are in nitrogen fixing. Today, their value is widely recognized.

The inorganic method of feeding with soluble salts uses mainly the transpiration stream, the force, not yet fully understood, that makes every wood a forest of fountains, with as much as 40 gallons (180 lt) of water flowing upwards through a large oak on a hot, dry day. Some of the water is used by the plant in photosynthesis with carbon dioxide taken in through the leaves, making carbohydrates and releasing the oxygen which keeps living creatures breathing the world over. Photosynthesis has provided all the energy that we use up in fuel (except for a relative trifle from wind, water and nuclear power) and is behind all the food that 'fuels' our bodies.

The rest of the water taken up by plants is thrown into the air as vapour through the under surfaces of the leaves, cooling them and placing trees among the world's best climate controllers. In one sense, this water is merely the 'empties' that have carried up dissolved minerals even from the deepest root to the topmost twig, by way of the mysterious fountain that sucks a film of water from soil grain to soil grain. On the scale of the microscopic life of the living soil, the transpiration stream of a tree can be compared with a mighty wind, picking up dissolved minerals, wanted and unwanted.

Unwanted minerals may be pushed out on the upper leaf surfaces. In a tropical rain forest, they wash away along the branches to supply food for orchids and ferns. In climates like that of Britain, they feed the algae, mosses and lichens on tree trunks, which are not parasitic, but depend for all their essential plant foods and trace elements (minerals like manganese, copper, zinc and boron that are needed only in tiny traces) on material that trees discard. Trees stay in position longer than herbaceous plants, and have therefore to tolerate for longer soils that may be rich in minerals they do not need. The existence of this throwaway habit was firmly established in .1975 by experiments showing that peas discarded unwanted zinc.[3] This new knowledge has been applied by prospectors, flying over forests in northern Canada in helicopters and taking air samples to measure the minerals that the trees throw away. The richer the subsoil in unwanted minerals, the more they discard into the air through their leaves and needles.

In deserts, or in periods of dry weather elsewhere, discarded plant foods are blown away on the wind to be picked up by such trees and plants as need them. The conifers of the Northern hemisphere operate a kind of Giro system, and it was found that pine trees that burned in a fire in Glen Nevis left ashes containing just as much calcium as if they had grown in Hampshire, even though the peaty mountain soil contained hardly any lime. The Spanish moss (*Tillandsia usneoides*) associated with swamp trees in the Everglades of Florida takes all its food from these tiny airborne particles, and grows so well that the Highways Department has to send round a lorry with a tower on it so that the masses of trailing moss can be pushed off the telegraph wires before they break even the poles with their weight.

The system of feeding through the leaves is far more selective than the transpiration stream from the roots. This is fortunate, because the sulphur that blows across to Europe from our tall power station chimneys is merely making some of the Swedish lakes too acid for trout and crayfish. Their pine trees—suppliers of so much timber and paper pulp—are not forcibly fed with our pollution products and are unharmed.

Foliar feeding, making use of this principle, normally with seaweed preparations, is now widely employed as a method of correcting trace-element deficiencies in a whole range of crops, and in some cases pays off by supplying main nutrients as well. The existence of this feeding system, which trees and plants have used since they began on earth, was discovered after World War II, during which the blockade had prevented French wine growers from spraying against mildew with copper sulphate. They used copper nitrate instead and found that it cured nitrogen deficiency in their vines as a bonus.

In addition to the upward stream from the roots, trees and plants have a downward current carrying sugar for energy and cellulose building, and the minerals that their leaves have gathered. The leguminous *Prosopis* genus of trees in desert countries can drink in the dew at night, pumping it out about half a metre below the surface, and one species, *P. tamarugo*, which thrives in the Atacama Desert in Chile, takes in through its leaves all the moisture and all

15

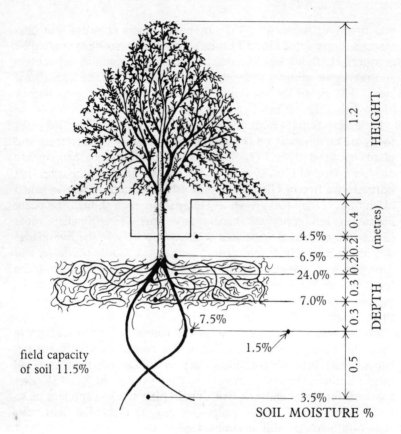

HEIGHT 1.2 (metres)

4.5%
6.5%
24.0%
7.0%
7.5%
1.5%
3.5%

0.4
0.2 0.2
0.3
0.3
0.5

DEPTH (metres)

field capacity
of soil 11.5%

SOIL MOISTURE %

Prosopis tamarugo

the minerals it needs except the chlorides of sodium, potassium and magnesium, because its habitat is a dried seabed with no rain at all.[4]

Harnessing this quality to irrigate the dry hillside and deserts of the world without fuel, pumps, piping, salination or waste through evaporation, would be a greater stride for Mankind than anything in Space.

Organic and Inorganic

The basic difference between the two systems of plant feeding is that the inorganic method aims at feeding the *crop* directly, giving all its calculated requirements as soluble, readily available, plant foods that can be taken up fast along the transpiration stream. However, all soils have, in effect, a balance sheet; if you take out more than you put in of anything, using any system, you must make up the difference. The organic system feeds the *soil* with manures and slowly released materials which the plant is designed to absorb, in forms which will be made available by living organisms of the soil and rhizosphere.

This is not a question of whether the analysis of the crop will be the same by either method. First, it is a question of what the commercial grower is honestly entitled to sell to those who are prepared to pay extra for organically grown produce. Secondly, it is a question of what to use and what to do in your own garden to build up its fertility. The definition of fertility with which we began stressed how important it is to maintain the system of interlocking cycles that will keep the soil producing food of first-class nutritional value with the minimum of imported substances, all of which will, in any case, have to be bought at ever-increasing prices.

This book is not called 'Fertilizers for Organic Gardeners' because this would leave out the manure, and there is a clear difference. A manure is a substance containing organic material that releases energy in the soil when broken down by the action of bacteria, as well as adding to the complex substance we call 'humus', which is responsible for the crumb structure of the soil, plus the watery molecules that are available to the rootlets, and a number of other materials that would be missed if they were lacking in the soil. Manure also contains plant foods and trace elements, all of which could be bought more cheaply in a bag, though plant roots seem stubbornly to prefer the ones from manure.

Manures vary greatly and can be stored well or badly, just as compost may be well made or poor stuff, but all composts and manures are undeniably organic. Among the vegetable substances, such as leaf-mould and peat in their varied qualities and stacking systems, we can count green manures. These are crops specially sown and dug in to decay in the soil, releasing plant foods, humus and energy material. They have the disadvantage that their raw foliage produces a great increase among certain soil bacteria, which take up any available nitrogen and phosphorus at the expense of the crops that follow; it has therefore to be dug in at the right stage (see Chapter 5). Seaweed in all its forms belongs here, as does comfrey, which is to some extent the gardener's deep rooting 'herbal ley', gathering in minerals, especially potassium.

Then we come to the 'Fertilizers' which are substances of animal, vegetable or mineral origin, containing plant foods and trace elements, but no humus and very little energy-providing material. The production of energy is vital for the activity of soil bacteria and all life in the soil that is not fed directly in the rhizosphere or by the plants. Perhaps the most important soil life of all is provided by earthworms, which are powered by decaying vegetable matter in the soil and break down mineral particles from the subsoil with their digestive juices and gizzard-like intestines, spreading them on the surface as a constant top dressing of available plant foods.

Dried blood, for a rapidly available nitrogen tonic in emergencies, hoof and horn chips for nitrogen made steadily available by bacterial action, bonemeal—coarse for slowly released phosphorus or fine for fast—and the ever more expensive fish and meat meals are all obviously organic. The modern problem is that such vegetable wastes as rape cake, made from the residues of crushed rape seed for oil, are all bought up by cattle cake manufacturers, who even buy poultry droppings from laying batteries to add a cheap but unattractive protein to the diet of cows on fieldless factory farms.

Leather dust, if it can be obtained without unbreakable ground plastics, real wool shoddy, free from man-made fibres (also impossible for soil bacteria to break down), municipal compost, and sewage sludge are organic these days, only if they can be found uncontaminated. Municipal compost and sludge are not so much fertilizers as tragedies.

When we farm or garden organically, we break the fertility cycle unless we return our bodily wastes to the soil. Today, industry's heavy pollution of our sewage sludges with such toxic metals as lead and cadmium makes them more dangerous to use in some areas than any pesticides because, though organo-chlorine compounds break down in time, metals remain unchanged in the soil and can poison it for centuries. Municipal compost (dustbin refuse composted with sewage sludge) contains even more toxic metals, which are concentrated from coloured inks when paper, the main compostable constituent, is broken down. In addition they contain undecaying plastics on such a scale that the only Dano compost machine left in Denmark, where this popular system was invented (at Aarhus), will be replaced by an incinerator as soon as it has filled its present hole, for filling holes is the main modern use for what was once a promising source of humus for every garden.

Rural sludges without industrial contamination are still safe. But the wastage of sewage effluents—and, with them, most of the plant foods—by pouring them into rivers, where they grow algae that take up the dissolved oxygen as they decay, and thus reverse the energy cycle, quite literally 'drowns' any fish. The killing of fish in summer and the conversion of clean rivers and lakes into lifeless sewers are relatively minor disasters. The number of seas that dried up with large fish kills in the past to leave beds of rich phosphate rock is limited, yet we are squandering this source as well as polluting the present seas, which release more oxygen though photosynthesis than all the world's remaining forests.

The real challenge of the 'seventies was not space but sewage, but we preferred to spend money on research in fields where it is more profitable to travel expensively than to arrive. As world population doubles and redoubles through the next century, we shall no longer be able to afford to replace fertility with pollution by our present methods of sewage and refuse treatment, and I shall therefore treat this subject separately in Chapter 8 as a campaign to be fought, rather than merely with reference to two good but low energy fertilizers of major long-term importance.

Ground Minerals

It is when we leave the fertilizers of animal and vegetable origin that we come to the difficult questions. We have to satisfy, among others, the judge who asks us to define a chemical fertilizer, the far more common retired schoolmaster who wants to argue, and the inorganic gardener trying to score debating points at a meeting where everyone is impatiently waiting for the speaker to explain exactly *how* to garden organically.

Jerome Rodale's first decision concerned the property of solubility. Rock phosphates are finely ground fossil fish and other minerals, with a composition that varies between 5% and 20% phosphorus, none of which is available either to water or to the solution of citric acid which agricultural chemists use to duplicate the 'digestive juices' of plants. It becomes slowly available through the action of the mycorrhizal fungi, because it is in the form in which plant roots would naturally find it in the soil.

Superphosphate, made by treating rock phosphate with sulphuric acid, is quickly soluble, however. It has produced swift changes in crop production on soils low in phosphorus that is available to citric acid or carbonic acid, or containing almost none at all, as in parts of Australia and New Zealand, where there is normally a specialized wild flora that can manage on the swift recycling of small quantities of phosphorus. Nature's way of economizing on any mineral is to speed up the cycle of use and decay, also taking advantage of the foliar feeding system; it may eventually force the world to adopt a long-term rotation of a hundred years of organic farming, followed by a century under forests.

This principle of solubility applies only to minerals because they are normally made available by the action of micro-organisms and root secretions on organic matter and tiny rock particles in the soil, either fast or slowly, according to the conditions of moisture, temperature and sunlight that rule the growth of plants. A tree cannot move off in search of better 'grazing' for its roots when all the minerals within reach have washed away in wet winters. Therefore, it is adapted to take its minerals in forms that are slowly released as they are required.

Organic fertilizers are derived from organisms, animal or vegetable, that have once lived. They can be highly soluble, like dried blood, or slowly available, like hoof and horn chips, but they are entirely unlike chemical salts, either separately or as part of a mixture. We living creatures repay, with blood, bones, hooves and horns, our debt to the plant kingdom for splitting air and water in the process of photosynthesis that enables us to live, and we pay our daily interest in whatever we excrete, whether we are bacteria, birds or bishops, to speed the recycling systems that keep the world growing and breathing.

Nitrogen Fertilizers

All nitrogen fertilizers are rapidly soluble, as is dried blood. Organic gardeners and farmers use only blood if they are observing the British standards, for they regard nitrogen fertilizers as the 'white sugars' of soil nutrition, which produce fast, soft, sappy growth that is attractive to pests and more subject to disease than crops on a better diet. It is the gain in health from cutting out nitrate of soda, sulphate of ammonia and nitro-chalk (calcium nitrate) that is largely responsible for the firm belief that organic gardeners do not normally have to deal with the pests and diseases that plague their inorganic neighbours.

The ounces per square yard or kilograms per hectare we spread on our gardens and farms are tiny fractions of the vast reserves in soil and subsoil, while nitrogen gas, one of the three main plant food elements makes up about 75% of the atmosphere. To combine nitrogen gas with oxygen, so that plants can take it in as nitrate and link it with other materials to make the complex proteins of life, demands energy. Roughly speaking, it takes six tonnes of oil to make one tonne of chemical nitrogen fertilizer, but the nitrogen fixing bacteria do the job with the aid of the waterfall of power that flows down from the living leaves.

The nitrogen we supply as fertilizers is far less efficient in terms of energy than that which is fixed by bacteria, because it is available all at once, while the supply from the soil and the rhizosphere is released gradually under the conditions of moisture and temperature in which the crop is growing. It is passed from hand to hand like money in a village, so that much less is enough for the needs of the stable community formed by the soil and the crops. On heavy clays that warm slowly, organic farm crops start less rapidly than those fed with chemical nitrogen, which is available immediately, but they catch up later in the season.

Soil Testing

One of the most common problems among organic gardeners is that they continue to think inorganically. They buy a soil testing outfit, or have an analysis carried out, and attempt to add up all the plant foods in the crops they harvest, replacing the ones needed to bring their soil back to an ideal balance, using only organic fertilizers, but piling on far too much. Without skilled interpretation, a soil analysis can be actively misleading, for the nitrogen level goes up and down according to how busy the bacteria have been. Their activity varies from day to day, and analyses on organic farms have been known to show a shortage of almost everything, which has then been corrected in five years without the addition of any fertilizers at all, as Frank Newman Turner found at Goosegreen farm in the 1950s.

The only type of soil tester that is of value to organic gardeners measures pH, using a kind of liquid litmus paper with a colour chart to show how much lime is needed to bring the balance of acidity and alkalinity to neutral, or pH 7.0. Otherwise, analysis can merely resemble a count of the notes in your wallet which ignores your bank balance and investments—in this case in the soil below.

The Capital of the Soil

At Rothamsted Experimental Station, they still have a field called Broadbalk which has grown wheat continually for nearly 150 years and includes plots where nothing but farmyard manure has been used, some with chemical fertilizers added, and some with nothing at all. The last are still yielding a harvest that has settled at the level where the process of cultivation will make available enough plant foods to maintain a crop year after year, for more than a century, once the fertility system has stabilized.

Analysis of the top 9in (23cm) of soil, after a hundred years of cropping with no manures, lime or fertilizers and, as humus, only the roots of the wheat—which would add up to roughly a mile (1.6km) in length if those on a single plant were joined together, and penetrate down as much as 6ft (2m)—showed the following:

	per acre	=	per hectare
Phosphorus	2,750lb		3,090kg
Potassium	6,750lb		7,580kg
Nitrogen	2,500lb		2,810kg
Magnesium	9,000lb		10,100kg
Calcium	62,250lb		70,100kg

This is not to suggest that organic gardeners should aim at minimum yields, using no compost, manure or fertilizer of any kind, but it does show that all good soils contain sufficient minerals to crop for centuries at a level that depends on their fertility—the interlocking cycles of concentration and dispersal, or drawing together of minerals as trees do, and *we* do, returning the legacy of our lives to the soil that feeds us all.

1. DEAVIN, Anthony *The Scientific Basis for Soil Husbandry* Part IV Soil Association, Walnut Tree Manor, Haughley, Stowmarket, Suffolk 1976

2. DUDDINGTON, C. L. *The Evolution of Plant Design* Faber & Faber 1969 pp.64–85

3. BEAUFORD, W., and BARBER, J. 'Heavy Metal Release into the Atmosphere' *Nature* Vol. 256 3rd July 1975

4. SUDZUKI, F. 'Absorcion foliar de humedad atmosferica en *tamarugo*' Phil. Bol. Tecnico 30–1–23 University of Chile, Santiago

2 Concerning Compost

A 'manure', whether it is of animal or vegetable origin, contains energy that can be released by bacterial or fungal action in the soil, as well as plant foods, trace elements and humus. A 'fertilizer', organic or inorganic, may be a source of plant nutrients and trace elements, as are bone meal and fish meal, but will contain too little energy to be classed as manure, even though it may provide a trace of humus.

Though coal dust is of organic origin, it is not a manure because the energy it holds is not available as food for the life in the soil. It is important to draw this distinction because there are a number of deposits of lignite, or 'brown coal' in the USA, France, Germany and in Devon. It looks rather like fossilized peat, and, in the USA, is sold expensively to gardeners as an organic manure, when it is in fact a fuel of low calorific value, high in ash, and therefore no more a food for bacteria than coal is for us. Peat and leaf-mould are sources of humus; they help retain moisture in the soil and have a lightening effect on clay. They are not manures because their plant foods and energy are locked up by the preservative action of the tannic acids they contain, and only slowly become available.

The word 'compost' originally meant a pile of mixed manures—including human wastes and added vegetable matter—in which much of the material been broken down and concentrated, so that the plant food levels were larger in proportion to the moisture (even though much of the nitrogen had gone off as ammonia). Although its quality was far below that of a tractor-turned compost heap on a modern organic farm, its superiority to ordinary fresh manure was recognized in Thomas Tusser's *One Hundred Goode Pointes of Husbandrie* (1557), perhaps our first practical farming book:

'One acre composted is worth acres three,
At harvest thy barns shall declare it to thee.'

Considerable confusion has arisen among gardeners from the incorrect use of the word 'compost' to mean a mixture of soils for potting and seed raising, especially since the invention of the John Innes and Levington Composts (mixtures of sterilized loam and peat with fertilizers) which are used very extensively for potting house plants on a commercial scale. The first is a potting or seed soil, the other a potting peat, since true compost is too rich in plant

23

foods, humus and energy-providing material to use for raising seed or potting plants.

Good compost is the key to successful organic gardening, for though organic farmers can reduce its use to a minimum with deep-rooting herb leys, legumes and livestock, the gardener must increase the turnover of his plant foods and trace elements to gain the maximum yield from a small area. The weeds and plants that go on our compost heaps have all spent their relatively short lives gathering minerals, apart from nitrogen-rich proteins and fast or slowly released energy materials. If they are burnt, almost all the nitrogen is wasted, the potassium and sodium become very readily soluble, while the phosphorus, together with most of the trace elements, is only slowly available.

It used to be believed that plants could take up only relatively simple mineral salts, but recent work has shown that feeding roots can take in quite large organic molecules, which they appear to prefer, gaining an advantage that can be compared with making a chair from a kit of parts rather than buying the wood and shaping it first. This explains why the effect of organic manures on crops is out of all proportion to their mineral analysis, for instead of returning everything to 'square one' with fire, organic manures and compost retain plant foods and trace elements in the forms that plants can use most easily.

Every plant gathers the minerals of its choice, and at the end of its life these must return to the soil and be dispersed. It is therefore an important part of the work of gardeners and farmers to spread the trace elements by composting and other methods, so that they remain as only the traces that crops require, instead of building up to toxic levels.

Zinc is an example, needed by our bodies, but poisonous to crops in the quantities contained in sewage sludge and composted city refuse that has been heavily polluted with industrial wastes. Peas contain 4.0 parts per million, with far more in the haulm, and if the plants take up more than they need they can throw it away on the wind from the upper surfaces of their leaves, as trees do. Lucerne contains still more, and our best sources of supply for a shortage of nutritional zinc are herrings with 100 parts per million (p.p.m.), cow's milk with 17.66 p.p.m. and wheat bran with 14.0 p.p.m. If it were not for the natural recycling processes, zinc would accumulate until our peas and other legumes, our grain crops and our cattle had poisoned themselves with their own wastes, as human beings may yet poison themselves with industrial pollution of their own making.

Though few British soils lack trace elements, the value in composting a wide range of weeds and other material, such as the peel from imported fruit in our kitchen wastes, lies in making sure that we have a full set of these minerals in readily available forms and in the quantities needed, for spreading them in mineral form could well mean a toxic excess in some cases. Stinging nettles, all types of thistle, and chicory are rich in copper, iron, and calcium; fat-hen (or goosefoot) and sunspurge (or milkweed) are both good sources of boron, while rosebay willowherb contains cobalt, and foxgloves gather manganese in relatively large quantities. All have roots that search over wide areas, and some are foliar feeders, especially nettles, which also store quantities of nitrogen, fixed by their rhizosphere bacteria.

The Carbon:Nitrogen Ratio

A compost heap is, roughly speaking, a method of reducing garden rubbish, which initially contains an average proportion of 70 parts of carbon to one of nitrogen, compared with the 10:1 that is level in fertile soil. If there is too much nitrogen, as in a manure pile, then combined nitrogen is released as ammonia or other smells from the breakdown of the proteins in which it is mainly stored. This applies also to the soil, where there are denitrifying bacteria as well as nitrogen fixers, and it is easy (though very expensive) to overmanure. If there is too much carbon in relation to the nitrogen, there will be a vast increase of the bacteria that break it down, and they will take up the available nitrogen and phosphorus to make up their own bodies, causing an extreme local shortage.

Therefore we compost. If we dig our garden rubbish directly into the soil, we can cause a reduction in yield instead of the increase at which we aim. Young and sappy weeds can be dug in, for they contain so much protein that their proportion of nitrogen is already high, while most of their carbon is in the form of carbohydrates, and therefore breaks down fast. So can young green manure crops, but if they are left too long and allowed to grow stemmy and strong in preparation for flowering and seeding, they will contain enough fibre to cause nitrogen robbery.

The table, as a guide, gives the carbon:nitrogen ratios of a number of materials. The most important fact is at the top of the table—the 500:1 for sawdust and shavings. If you dig sawdust into your soil, you will introduce so much food for bacteria and fungi that they will continue robbing your soil of plant foods for many years. If materials this high in carbon are used on the surface, they act as a mulching material, decaying slowly without harm to the soil below, but they must never be dug under.

Material	C:N Ratio
Fresh sawdust	500:1
Old sawdust, dark brown	200:1
Wheat straw	128:1
Oat straw	48:1
Bracken	48:1
Young weeds	30:1
Carrot roots	27:1
Fresh potato haulm	25:1
Ragwort	21:1
Turnip tops	19:1
Seaweed (average)	19:1
Cabbage heads	12:1
Tomato trimmings	12:1
Lawn mowings	12:1
Rotted farmyard manure	14:1
Good compost	10:1
Dried sewage sludge	10:1
Comfrey leaves	9.8:1
Dried blood	4:1

Carbon:Nitrogen Ratios of Compost Materials

Though there are many riding stables and horse owners who use shavings litter today, and will even deliver it free to get rid of it, this is a very bad bargain. The content of horse manure and urine will be used up by the bacterial and fungal action that starts to break the shavings down, but will be spent long before the job is completed, and the result is disaster. To convert the surplus carbon back to heat and carbon dioxide needs just as much oxygen as if the energy had been produced by burning, and unless the material is put through a shredding machine to increase the bacterial working surface and continually turned it will not break down well. The best use for it is as an addition to deep litter for poultry, for there the heat produced will help dry out the poultry manure, and the potassium from the wood will balance the high phosphorus of the poultry droppings.

A measure of the carbon:nitrogen ratio is a good way of assessing the degree to which a compost has decayed, especially one intended for commercial sale (the best proof of a compost in the garden is in the crop), but ask the tester to 'exclude the lignins', otherwise the result will be misleading.

The Black and Wakeley test does not distinguish starches and the sugars, which are both quickly consumed by bacteria, fungi and other soil life, from the celluloses, hemi-celluloses and lignins, which make up the lasting part of humus. Woody materials such as herbaceous plant stems cut down in the autumn are going to leave behind far more lasting energy material in the soil than potato haulms, which are 25:1, but mostly starches and water, decaying to very little. Fresh bracken, cut in July or August, when it will contain 2% potassium rather than the mere 0.2% it has when dead and rust-brown in the autumn, is perhaps the best bargain to collect for lasting humus, and its alkaloid content is broken down by the composting bacteria. All poisonous substances—from the oxalic acid in rhubarb leaves to atropine, the alkaloid poison in deadly nightshade (*Atropa belladonna*)—decay easily in compost heaps, because micro-organisms in the recycling systems of the world have evolved to break them down for the disposal and re-use of their constituents. It is the man-made molecules, difficult for nature to take apart, that cause present and future problems.

The Compost Container
A compost heap is a bacteria and fungus farm. Fortunately, so long as we provide the right conditions, the organisms will thrive and continue their task of recycling indefinitely. They need not only food and the correct carbon:nitrogen ratio; they must also have moisture, warmth and an adequate air supply. These are best supplied, on a garden scale, by a compost container, which does far more than merely keep the pile of vegetable wastes tidy and prevent it from drying out until it becomes only the basis of a bonfire.

Though there is always a temptation to site the heap under trees in dry shade where nothing grows well, that will bring the roots swarming in after the plant foods and moisture. The worst place for a compost heap is beside a privet hedge, because this has the greediest roots of all. The second worst position is on a concrete base next to the coal bunker, for there the worms will be unable to come up from the soil to complete the final stages of breaking down and rebuilding not only plant foods, humus and energy material, but a number of auxins (a group of compounds concerned with plant growth) and other organic substances that play vital parts in disease resistance and healthy development.

The best system is to have portable containers, moving them round the garden, either as part of the rotation or concentrating on the least fertile places in turn, so that drainings from the decaying material seep down where they do the most good. Leaf-mould heaps or peat stacks, which do not lose plant foods in draining, can well stay in the most convenient place, but though the portable heap can mean a longer trek with the kitchen wastes, the finished compost can often be forked straight from the bin for spreading.

The New Zealand Box

Perhaps the world's first group of organic gardeners was the New Zealand Humic Compost Society, founded in 1941, and their idea of a neat compost container for amateurs was named 'The New Zealand Box'.

The version illustrated here is taken from the Henry Doubleday Research Association leaflet *Give up Smoking Bonfires*. When the box was first made in accordance with the directions that follow, the timber cost £5. Fourteen years later, inflation has raised the expenditure to £25. It is still a good design if you can find second-hand timber and for those who have the tools and skill to make it, even with new wood, it holds more compost than bought bins costing the same sum.

A box with compartments 3ft (1m) square to hold 1 cubic yard (1m³) of finished compost in each, takes 190ft (57m) of 4×½in (10×1cm) sawn plank, six 4ft lengths of 2×2in (5×5cm) timber and five 3ft (1m) lengths of 2×1½in (5×4cm) timber, but the dimensions are not important.

Saw nine 6ft (2m) planks for the back and 27 others 3ft (1m) long for the sides and middle. Then creosote everything, including the uprights, and leave to dry for about a week. Other wood preservatives such as Cuprinol or Solignum can be used, but all are more expensive than creosote. If you want to paint the bin green or black, use a bitumen paint (as sold for use on corrugated iron), because it will 'take' on top of creosote, which can then replace costly undercoat with a better rot preventer.

Lay three of the 2×2in (5×5cm) uprights 3ft (1m) apart and nail the 6ft (2m) planks to the upper 3ft (1m) of the uprights. Then nail the 3ft (1m) planks at one end to the upper 3ft (1m) of the remaining three uprights. Dig six holes at the corners of the yard (metre) squares, fit the three uprights of the back into their respective holes but replace and firm the soil round the upright only at one end. Now put the lower foot (30cm) of the upright of the first end in its hole, and nail the free ends of the planks to the upright on the back, holding a brick against it to take the shock of the hammering. Then replace the soil round the upright and firm it well.

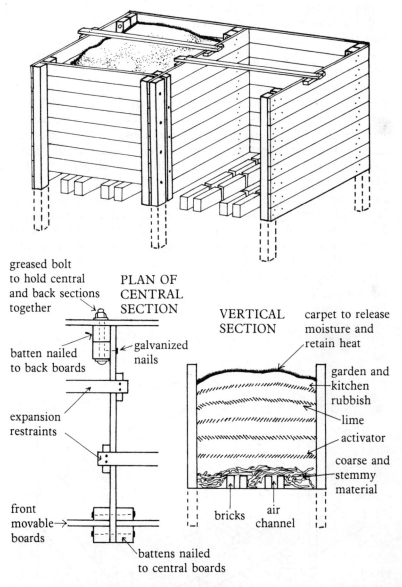

greased bolt
to hold central
and back sections
together

PLAN OF
CENTRAL
SECTION

VERTICAL
SECTION

carpet to release
moisture and
retain heat

batten nailed
to back boards

galvanized
nails

garden and
kitchen
rubbish

expansion
restraints

lime

activator

coarse and
stemmy
material

front
movable →
boards

bricks

air
channel

battens nailed
to central boards

New Zealand box

When the middle and other end are fitted in this way, you have a
strong, wooden letter 'E' in plan. Saw the remaining planks, which
make up the removable board fronts of the compartments, into
lengths of slightly less than 3ft (1m). Fit them into slots made by

nailing the last five 3ft (1m) lengths of 2×1½in (5×4cm) sawn timber approximately ¾in (2cm) from the front uprights. You will need three to make the slots on both sides of the middle divider. Creosote the front boards and their sawn ends and let them dry before fitting.

When you eventually need to move the heap, dig the soil out of the holes for the uprights as far as possible, then lift from both ends and replace the uprights in new holes dug ready 3ft (1m) apart on the new site. Do not try levering up the end with an iron bar, because this puts a great strain on the bin. Those who are better carpenters can nail the free ends of the 3ft (1m) boards to a 3ft (1m) length of 2×1in (5×2.5cm) timber, which can be bolted to the upright with a ¼in (6mm) coach bolt 4in (10cm) long. Smear the bolts with motor grease or petroleum jelly before driving them through holes drilled in the uprights, the 2×1in (5×2.5cm) wood and the planks from the inside, screwing the nuts on from outside, because they will be more likely to rust inside the heap. If well greased, they will screw off easily and the bin will come apart with less trouble. This is especially useful if you move house, as you can then pack your compost bin flat on the van.

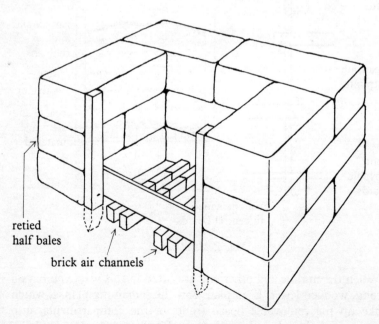

retied
half bales

brick air channels

'Strawbale bin

The Straw Bale Heap

This type takes thirteen bales of straw, one of which you will have to divide, after cutting the binder twine, to produce a 'half brick' effect, so that the bales 'bond' like a brick wall. Bales can often be obtained for nothing in the country, but in towns they can be expensive, especially as the heap will last only two years before it composts itself entirely into humus. It needs no skill in carpentry to make, and its thick walls are such good heat insulators that temperatures of 189°F were reached on the HDRA Trial Ground, where it was first made.

The 'bin' is built as in the diagram, with two bales along the back and two at each side, overlapping at the corners, and finished off with halved bales. Five stakes are required, so that wire or nylon string can be tied firmly across to hold the bales down in the windy, cold gardens where this type of bin has the most advantage. Two posts in front will support a removable board front which, if it is well creosoted, will outlive a dozen sets of straw bales.

The Loam Stack

The New Zealand Box and the Straw Bale Heap both need to be charged and managed in the same way, and both are excellent for the standard Indore composting system, though they also suit almost any activator. With both of them, you also need to take measures against the commonest source of failure in making compost—too many large clumps of grass weeds with solid clay sticking to the roots.

Except in dry weather and on sandy soils, it is hard work to shake all the soil off the grass roots, but it is impossible for any heap to reach temperatures high enough to kill weed seeds and roots if it is filled with mud caked on the grass roots. Therefore stack the grass weeds, roots upwards, as a 'lean-to' heap against the side of the compost bin. They will not heat at all, but will decay slowly to a stack of surface soil mixed with rotted grass blades and roots, that will be ready for use in about a year. Combine two parts of the resulting loam with one part each of sand and leaf-mould to make a seed sowing soil, or use seven parts of the loam, three parts of leaf-mould and one part of sand for potting. A good handful of fine bonemeal used to be mixed into every barrowload—an accurate enough proportion is 1:00 (or, say, 1lb to 1cwt) for what is an old-fashioned potting soil. A richer mixture could be made by replacing half the leaf-mould with well rotted and sifted compost.

Filling the Compost Bin

Both types of container need exactly the same routine as the standard Indore type heap, starting with two double rows of bricks and brickends, about 3in (7cm) apart and 2ft (60cm) between pairs, running from front to back of the compartment and extending beyond the removable board front. To act as effective air channels, the bricks should be covered with short ends of wood, pieces of tile or slate, or anything that will leave plenty of gaps to let the air through yet serve to prevent fine material like grass mowings from blocking the draught.

Spread on top of the ventilation system a first layer of stemmy rubbish, even hedge clippings or stumps of brussels sprouts and cabbage that have been bashed on concrete with the back of an axe. This is a quicker and cheaper means of breaking tough stems than feeding them one at a time into any hand-operated compost chopper. This first layer should fill the spaces between the brick channels and come about 4in (10cm) above them. Next add a first layer of garden rubbish 8in (20cm) thick, bearing in mind that the only value of soil on the roots of weeds is in supplying the bacteria that break down organic matter. As there are so many millions of these organisms in every teaspoonful of soil, the more you shake off the better, for the less soil you include in your heap the better it will heat, and the fewer seedling weeds will grow from the finished compost.

The average carbon:nitrogen ratio of garden rubbish is 70:1, but the more soft weeds there are, the closer the ratio becomes, and the ideal level to reach with decay is 25:1. To bring the level right down to 10:1, the ideal for making available the plant foods combined into slowly released forms and providing a wholesome diet for the soil organisms, you need fast heating and a rapid bacterial increase, which is achieved by feeding in several ways.

The Indore method is to spread a layer of any organic manure roughly ½in (1cm) thick on top of the first layer, add another 8in (20cm) of material and, on this, scatter either enough slaked lime to whiten the surface completely or about ¼in (6mm) of wood ashes. Follow this with more 8in (20cm) layers of rubbish, manure, more rubbish, then lime, and so on, like a giant layer cake.

The manure is supplying nitrogen and phosphorus for the bacterial explosion, which begins by producing quick heat and rapid decay, but the lime or ashes and the air supply have another important function. Every gardener knows that a pile of lawn-mowings on a summer's day will be too hot inside for a hand to bear within about six hours, but that though the mowings heat fast, the result is not compost, but a slippery and smelly mess.

This is a rather bad version of the silage that farmers make by *excluding* air and, to increase the effect, adding rapidly available sugars in the form of diluted treacle (modern inorganic farmers add chemical acids) which ferments to lactic acid, producing a kind of vegetable 'cheese', with the grass or other green crop mixture preserved by its own acidity. Farmers want silage to heat until it is too acid to decay further. Gardeners add lime or the lime in wood-ashes to keep compost alkaline, and supply plenty of air so that the heat can be maintained by aerobic (oxygen breathing) bacteria, which take up just as much oxygen as a fire would to produce the same amount of heat in burning. A compost heap is in effect a slow, bacterial bonfire.

It is also rather more than a waste recycling unit for every garden, because some of the energy in the broken down vegetable waste is spent on fixing nitrogen by the action of a number of bacteria, especially *Azotobacter chroococcum.* One of Sir Albert Howard's heaps at Indore in the 1920s gathered in 26% more nitrogen than he had supplied in the activator and the material, and his average was about 12% extra. If a heap is sheltered to prevent an excessive loss of plant foods through rainwashing, all the plant foods added in the activator are still present in the finished heap.

The Carpet Covered Compost Heap
There is a third version of the New Zealand Box container which has the great advantage of being cheaper than any other system. Choose your site, which should be level and not under trees, and begin by digging two straight trenches 2ft (60cm) apart, each 8in (2ocm) wide—spade width for convenient digging—and 6in (15cm) deep. Reinforce the sides with rough planks (which can with advantage be creosoted), held on edge by stout pegs driven in upright, to prevent the soil crumbling in and filling the trenches. If bricks or odd lumps of concrete are available to hold up the sides they will do as well, and two double rows of empty bottles neck down would serve, but the essential is that the rows extend about 1ft (30cm) beyond each end of the heap, which should be 4ft (120cm) wide at the base. It can be any length, depending on the room you have and the quantity of wood, bricks or bottles available.

Place stout sticks, short ends of wood or tiles, even unbashed brussels sprout stems if they are available at the time of building, across the trenches, and make a foundation of rough rubbish for the base of the heap, exactly as when filling a New Zealand Box. Then build the heap with alternate layers, tapering the sides in slightly so that it slopes in from 4ft (120cm) to 2ft (60cm) wide and finishes 4ft (120cm) from ground level. It has often been suggested that the making of compost in wooden bins should be replaced by surface heaps, built like potato clamps, with 2–3in (5–7cm) of soil piled on and whacked firm with a spade. Apart from the hard work of digging a deep trench all round the heap to provide the soil, or

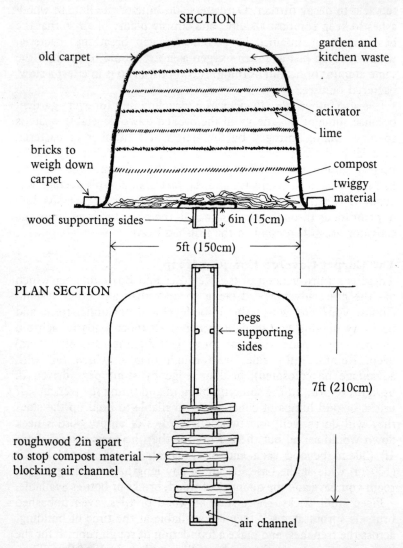

Carpet covered compost heap

wheeling it from other parts of the garden, soil is a poor heat insulator, does not keep out winter rains, and gives as an end result compost that is heavily adulterated with soil.

The best covering for the mound type of heap is old carpet, which can often be found for nothing on skips, refuse dumps, or from second-hand furniture shops and even those that sell new carpets. They are excellent heat insulators and keep off the wind and rain beautifully. Avoid foam backed carpets because the steam condenses on the foam as the heap heats up and trickles back to make the compost too wet. An ordinary wool carpet, however worn and threadbare, soaks up moisture from the condensed steam at night, then dries out during the day. After about three years of this soaking and drying, the carpet is ready to be composted under another cast-off. It seems that the young and modern buy new carpets in ever more striking colours far more often than previous generations, carrying away a steady stream of carpets from carpet shops in every town, so let us gather old carpets while we may. They are excellent heat holders, as the following table shows.

21st August	140°F =	60°C	1st September	122°F =	50°C
22nd	172	78	2nd	120	49
23rd	186	86	3rd	120	49
24th	180	82	4th	119	48
25th	174	79	5th	118	48
26th	170	77	6th	115	46
27th	160	71	9th	112	44
28th	158	70	10th	107	42
29th	153	67	11th	103	39
30th	146	63	12th	104	40
31st	134	57			

Temperature of a Carpet Covered compost heap

The heap was built on 20th August. After 12th September, the fungi and lower temperature bacteria took over from the thermophilic types that heat haystacks, for all compost heaps decay with the help of a long succession of micro-organisms, each generation producing heat that becomes too great for it to bear and giving place to another. No-one has ever produced a complete account of exactly what happens inside a compost heap; to do so would need a larger team of biologists staining, culturing and testing than the organic movement would ever be able to afford. When the heap finally went cold, the earthworms moved in, and it was ready for use, without turning or trouble.

Compost Heap Activators

The first modern compost heaps, apart from the human waste disposal type that kept the Chinese farming for forty centuries, and the British versions appreciated by Thomas Tusser, were built at Rothamsted. There Hutchinson and Richards made what they called 'Artificial Farmyard Manure', described in the *Journal of the Ministry of Agriculture* in 1921.

They established that air supply, temperature, moisture, and a source of readily available nitrogen were the important factors, and considered urine, urea, and ammonium carbonate the best activators, as ammonium sulphate made the heap too acid. The chief bacterium concerned in the rapid breakdown of straw to humus and plant foods, with the release of energy, is now known as Hutchinson's spirochaete in honour of Hutchinson, who was the father of *inorganic* activators from Adco to Garrotta and other mixtures.

Sir Albert Howard acknowledges his debt to Hutchinson and Richards, who gave him the idea that he developed in his experiments at Indore from 1925 to 1931, using organic manures, which have always produced better balanced heaps and greater disease resistance from feeding the soil and its living organisms as a whole. His aim was fertility, and his discovery of, and stress upon, the part played by mycorrhizal fungi in plant nutrition is now fully recognized today, though it was scornfully regarded as 'Muck and Mystery' by the orthodox in the 1930s.[1]

It is now known that there are many micro-organisms involved in compost making, and mixed activators produce the best balance, though Hutchinson's spirochaete is still the best breaker of straw, attacking the hollow tubes so effectively that it can produce enough heat to dry out wet poultry droppings, and is so efficient that it can even break down wood shavings. The dab of white on a poultry dropping is the bird's urine, which consists mainly of urea and ammonium carbonate, the favourite food of this particular bacterium, which is the reason why bird manure is ideal to go with high cellulose wastes.

Perhaps the best of all fast activators is pigeon manure, with an average of 6% nitrogen when weighed fresh—so high that pigeon keepers, knowing it is far too strong to use on their gardens, will often give it away. It pays, therefore, to contact your local pigeon club, for there may well be supplies free for collection. The table in Chapter 7 shows what a bargain it is in terms of plant foods, despite the smell.

Use poultry manure in the same way as pigeon manure, in layers ½in (just over 1cm) thick, although pigeon droppings are lower in moisture and far stronger. The droppings of cage birds of all kinds are worth using, as well as those from rabbits, goats, cows—indeed any that can be obtained. Any vegetable wastes, hard or soft and sappy, will use the excess nitrogen that a stack composed solely of manure wastes in smell to feed the first flush of micro-organisms, which can put heap temperatures up to 180°F (82°C).

Well-rotted manure is not nearly as useful, because it will have spent the fresh nitrogen, and municipal compost is inferior to dried sewage sludge (if you can get it), because you are not seeking humus but the means of getting it from the raw materials. Mushroom compost is also a humus provider rather than an activator and, though it is possible to buy the dried and pulverized waste products of factory farming in polythene bags, they are expensive in relation to what you get. Those who have no objection to factory farming can use them as activators at the rate of 4oz per square yard (180 gm/m²) of layer surface in Indore heaps. Fishmeal or fish and meat meal can be used in the same quantities, as can dried poultry manure; all of them may be kept in a lidded bucket by the heap for use as required with slaked lime from a similar store.

An excellent activator for the use of vegetarians or vegans (who eat no dairy produce or eggs and refuse to use any animal manures in their gardens) is seaweed meal. This is different in action from the normal organic nitrogen supply, which is aimed at starting a layer of material decaying with a 25:1 carbon:nitrogen ratio. Dried seaweed contains alginates, and the scattering of 4oz a square yard (180g/m²) provides, in effect, an impure version of the agar jelly used as a culture for bacteria in hospital laboratories and, in the same way, makes the soil bacteria increase rapidly, taking up the readily available trace elements as they feed, and biting into soft weeds for the nitrogen in the protein.

Seaweed meal is expensive to use at this rate, but, where dried sewage sludge can be obtained, 75% can be mixed with 25% seaweed meal to give an excellent activator with a very fast acceleration rate from a standing start. This combines the two actions and reduces the price for those who are fortunate enough to be able to buy a dried sludge from their local authority. An account of its use by the HDRA is given in Chapter 8 (see the section on Dried Sludge as an Activator).

Seaweed has been used as a manure for centuries in the Channel Islands, the Scillies and Scottish coastal areas without any trouble from an accumulation of salt in the soil. There is of course some on the outer surface of the weed but none inside, just as the body fluids of fish are low in salt. Dr Alain Bombard crossed the Atlantic in 1952 without food or water, catching fish and drinking their fluids, and the late Miss Hilda Quicke of St Agnes in the Scillies managed to grow a full range of vegetables for thirty years using nothing but seaweed to maintain the fertility of her garden. Her beetroot were excellent, as they are salt lovers, but she had very few earthworms, which dislike salt.

There are many proprietary compost activators which exploit the ability of soil bacteria in weed roots to unlock their own nitrogen from vegetable protein, and they work well, provided they are used with green material, not straw or woody wastes. An excellent one is the herbal activator QR. The Fertosan series include spores of bacteria and fungi as well.

Whatever the activator, the compost is improved by turning. Heaps should be watered with a rose can in drought, but the best way to start them into action again is to turn them. This is especially important in a dry year, or in cases where they have been allowed to dry out and become little more than kennels for ants and woodlice. The way to cope with woodlice is to pour household ammonia round the inside edges of the heap and cover it quickly with opened out polythene bags to hold the stink in and gas them out. A square of *foam backed* carpet is a good covering in dry weather, because it will cause condensation of moisture at night as well as providing heat insulation, as was shown by a trial at Bocking in the summer of 1975 (Appendix 3a).

It is possible to make compost without any activator at all, but these heaps do not heat fast enough to kill weed seeds and rarely go over 180°F (82°C), which is the temperature of an electric soil sterilizer.

The Californian Cylinder

This was invented by Captain James Macdonald, late of the United States Navy, an enthusiastic organic gardener on poor, dry Californian soil. The British version is made from a short end of 4ft (120cm)-high pig netting, which is strong galvanized iron, square mesh netting. Look for a fencing contractor in the yellow pages of your telephone book and phone round until you find one with short ends left over from fencing fields measured in furlongs and chains using 55 metre rolls. A useful size is a 9ft (3m) length, which can have the ends hooked together to make a cylinder about a third of that in diameter and 4ft (120cm) high, though these dimensions need be only roughly followed.

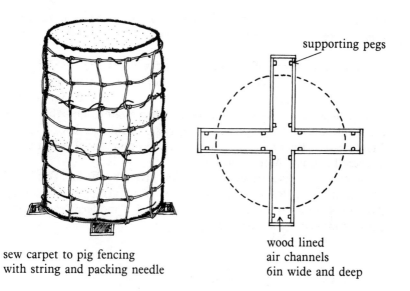

sew carpet to pig fencing
with string and packing needle

wood lined
air channels
6in wide and deep

supporting pegs

Californian Cylinder compost heap

Dig out two trenches 4ft (120cm) long, in the shape of a cross and line them with brick or wood, as for the carpet covered heap. Then set the cylinder upright so the ends of the trenches protrude 6in (15cm) or so beyond the sides. Secure it to three pegs driven into the ground outside, because these cylinders can blow about before they are filled. Line the inside with opened out cardboard cartons sewn in place with thin string and packing needle, or better still with a carpet—foam backed for choice.

Cover the trenches with short pieces of wood and then a layer of rough stout material such as hedge clippings, smashed cabbage stumps, and cut-down herbaceous plants. On top of this, fork in a layer of weeds, then empty in the contents of the bucket that should be under every kitchen sink for household waste. The weeds and garden rubbish are accumulated in a pile, then forked in with each daily emptying of the bucket.

The activator recommended by Captain Macdonald is one known tactfully as 'Household Liquid Activator'—human urine. It is emptied on three heaps in turn, diluted in dry weather with two parts water to one of urine. Captain Macdonald grows tomato plants up the netting sides of his cylinders and considers that he is personally supplying their potassium as well as the nitrogen activator. When he finds that a heap has stopped sinking and heating, he pulls out the anchoring pegs, moves his cylinder to another part of the garden, and starts another. The material from the top, which is not usually well decayed, is used to start off a new heap.

A doctor member of the HDRA, many years ago, used all the surplus from urine samples in the laboratory, but with caution, after stunting some of his vegetables from excess salt. His advice was to use urine purely as a compost activator. For this, it is excellent, and the cheapest of all because, in the words of Captain Macdonald, 'Everyone has a private supply, about enough to activate his own compost heaps.'

Analyses of urine vary, but the one given by West, Todd and Mason in *Text Book of Biochemistry* is an average. A normal, 24-hour sample of urine (1.25 litres from a modern, metricated adult) contains the following:

Nitrogen	13.20g
Potassium	2.5g
Phosphorus	1.0g
Calcium	0.2g
Magnesium	0.15g
Sulphur	1.0g
Phenols	0.2g
Chlorine	7.0g
Sodium	5.0g

Our bodies are taking in and giving out sodium and potassium all the time. The sodium level goes down when we are perspiring, and we can lose so much that we suffer severe cramps from salt shortage in tropical countries. Tears, too, are salty, and children can cry themselves into a shortage of available sodium that makes half a level teaspoonful of salt in a glass of water a 'magic' silence restorer. (This remedy should be treated with caution, however, since an overdose of salt can be dangerous—a sip is enough, not the glassful.)

An analysis generally measures totals, without disclosing the forms in which the substances are present: the chlorine contained in urine is not in the form of gas, but is combined with sodium, as sodium chloride, common salt. Together, these elements (7.0 and 5.0g respectively) add up to nearly as high a content as the nitrogen, which is mostly present as urea, and far more than the potassium which is mainly present as potassium sulphate. This is why urine is a compost heap activator, not a liquid fertilizer.

The 0.2% of phenols are no handicap, although they are the basis of many disinfectants, for there are soil bacteria that live, as they have always lived since kidneys evolved, by breaking them down and render liquid soil sterilizers based on phenols entirely safe. They need time for the increased bacteria to stabilize at normal levels before planting.

Household Liquid Activator has the very great advantages of costing nothing, and needing none of the layering of the Indore heap. It may be used in heaps that are likely to need layers of lime, but a chemical reaction would occur between lime and urea, which would waste most of the nitrogen. Pour HLA on any heap that has gone dry and cold, because it will correct the carbon:nitrogen ratio wherever it soaks, and provide the trace elements required by decay bacteria in the form that they are designed to take. It is the most 'Natural' of all activators and the cheapest, though not necessarily the best. Those who have lived in Hong Kong, China or Japan, or where market gardeners from these countries grow the vegetables, will be prejudiced against it, but there is a great difference between the quantities collected and used direct on the land in countries without water sanitation and our small-scale private activator.

The Bucket Fed Bin
HDRA Member, Roger Bayes, owns a caravan and uses the emptyings of its bucket sanitation to activate his compost, together with sewage sludge and Household Liquid Activator. His results are given here.

'The compost heaps are made in three bays, each approximately one metre cube. The walls are built of breeze blocks 2in (5cm) thick but having an open front provided with removable wooden boards. Covers keep rain out, and the bottom is made like a fine grate of sticks resting on bricks ventilated from the front.

'The three bays provide just about sufficient composting space for 2,000 square yards (2400m²) of garden. One more bay would be an advantage for turning the compost. Rose, fruit and other woody prunings are burnt, and ash is added to the compost.

'Hydrated lime or limestone flour is added, usually when the heap is turned after about three weeks. A dial thermometer with a probe 2ft (60cm) long is inserted in each new heap and kept in place for daily readings. The temperature settles down at 80–90°F (27–32°C) for a further three weeks or so, after which the compost is ready for use.

'I use compost on the surface, and digging is limited to lifting leeks and root crops.

'Various activators are used, but always organic in culture. It would be interesting to have a similar report using inorganic activators for comparison.

'The following significant points can be reported:

1) A temperature of over 150°F (66°C) continuously for five or six days is possible in a midsummer heap. This will rot down to usable compost in less than six weeks.

2) Spring and autumn compost heaps will not get quite so hot or for so long a period, but temperatures over 140°F (60°C) are normal.

3) Sewage sludge gives the compost heap an unpleasant smell during the 'cooking' phase. Fertosan septic tank conditioner almost eliminates this characteristic, and the remaining odour is not unpleasant.

4) The use of Fertosan compost activator improves the rotting of woody material in the heap.

5) After 10 to 14 days the whole heap shows an abundant production of greyish-white mycelia.

6) It isn't possible for me to report that the caravan Elsan produce does any good but it certainly doesn't appear to do any harm. There is no offensive smell from its inclusion in the heap.'

Fertosan septic tank conditioner, or Odorcure, is a bacterial culture normally used when disinfectants or any other accident or failure have interfered with the silent and invisible ecology of a septic tank, but Roger Bayes and other members have found that it can be used effectively as a garden 'deodorant'.

Elsan and other disinfectants and additives for bucket sanitation are based on phenols and, as the makers should state on the label (if they do not, buy another brand), are safe to use in compost heaps. Empty the bucket in the middle of the heap and have a layer of rubbish ready to cover it. A 3ft (1m) cube compost heap compartment should take four bucket emptyings. These will heat more slowly, making high temperatures all the same, but it is advisable to turn the heap to make sure of complete decay.

The problem in relying on composting to dispose of the results of bucket sanitation is the shortage of compost material in winter. One way round it is to buy straw bales and take them apart in sections roughly 6m (15cm) thick, arranging some of the pieces in a layer, with gaps between them, in the compost bin. Empty the bucket on the straw and put on another set of sections. A straw bale bin is ideal for this because it has better heat insulation, and the heap can be covered with two thicknesses of carpet for the same reason. Turn it in the spring, when there should be no smell.

Another system, used by organic smallholders who have spent their money on more milkers rather than modern sanitation, is to keep a large box of soil (ideally, dry and collected in the summer) in the 'out house', and to shovel in enough to cover every contribution generously. Ordinary garden soil will contain plenty of *Nitrosomonas*, a bacterium that can break down nitrates to gaseous nitrogen, which has no smell, and several other organisms that are natural deodorants, so that the buckets will be less unpleasant to empty than those with additives that smell strongly of disinfectant. A store of dry soil for refilling the earth bucket is desirable, and the liquid level should be kept low. Wood ashes have been used in place of soil, and the HDRA is experimenting with this method, which could produce a better-balanced fertilizer.

Empty the bucket either on straw bale sections or in a secluded corner, with more soil added, to make a stack, which should be covered with corrugated iron or plastic (not a polythene sheet) to prevent rain washing away the plant foods. In six months, this can be used as a compost heap activator. Many countrymen have lived all their lives, like their fathers and grandfathers before them, and their families, on vegetables grown without the need of a stack for the emptyings, but over trenches dug about 8in (20cm) wide and deep, and 2ft (60cm) apart, with one bucketful poured on every 3ft (1m), and filled in with soil. After about three months, in this system, cabbage-tribe crops are planted between the trenches and grow to hefty size. The problem is the risk of tapeworm eggs living on in the soil, and a strong European objection to the use of sewage on the land comes from the widespread use of this system in Germany and Austria. HLA is without this risk in temperate climates, though it could spread bilharzia in the tropics.

Experiments are under way with the use of the wastes from the Bio-loo and other humus toilets as compost heap activators. There is great scope for experiment in this field, as a method of disposal that cuts out the average of 11 gallons (50 litres) of water a day that every adult flushes down toilets, carrying away most of the plant foods our bodies concentrate to deposit them wastefully in the sea.

The Brick Built Bin

HDRA Member, Basil Clough, of Newcastle made a brick compost bin with gaps 1in (2cm) wide between the bricks of every third course for extra ventilation, with a sliding board front and two double rows of loose bricks on the earth floor. Each compartment was about a 4ft (120cm) cube to hold rather more than a tonne of compost in each. He reported in 1971.

'I have a lot of lawn, so mowings are my main ingredient—up to 50%. Excellent for generating heat, no chopping or bruising necessary, moisture content ideal. Two words of warning however—intersperse layers of mowings with coarser vegetables such as weeds, household waste, etc., and limit the depth of each layer to say 3in (7cm) to avoid the danger of producing silage. Also avoid using mowings if selective weed killers have been used recently on the lawn.

'Next constituents—Farmyard manure (FYM) preferably from a stable, and the fresher the better. I am fortunate in that there are several farms round about, and a riding school, so I can always buy a load of manure cheaply. I use up to 25% in the total make-up of the heap.

'Other materials used: Weeds—never in short supply! Household waste—a large pedal-bin holds a place of honour in our kitchen and all members of the family dutifully place therein all animal and vegetable waste all the year round. If I find a milk bottle top, toffee paper or polythene bag in it, the Spanish Inquisition comes into force!

'Occasionally I include such luxuries as seaweed (I always have half a dozen polythene fertilizer sacks in the back of the car, and our periodic family visits to the seaside always involve an enthusiastic beach-combing exercise).

'I burn only woody waste, coarse grasses and roots, carefully removing the resulting potash and placing under cover beside the heap for use as neutralizing layer.

'I use the Indore method as a basis. To start a fill, I place a mesh of expanded metal reinforcement over a few bricks, then use up any coarse stuff such as bean or potato haulms to keep the bottom ventilated. Then a barrow of lawn mowings, interlaid with weeds, and, somewhere conveniently in the vegetable sandwich, two shovelfuls of wood ashes (or lime if no ashes are available). After 6–8in (15–20cm) of vegetable matter, I apply 2in (5cm) of fresh manure, having watered, preferably with liquid manure if it is excessively dry or strawy. I aim at two further composite layers as described in the initial build, to give a total depth of not less than 2ft (60cm), the top layer always being mowings, just in case neighbours do not care for the smell of fresh manure. I then cover with a tarpaulin and leave for 2–3 days.

'Next stage is turning (I always have a horticultural thermometer on the go, reminiscent of a housewife testing her baking with a skewer) and the temperature should have risen to at least 120°F (49°C) I find that turning is essential to quick, efficient composting, the aim being to level out the fermentation process throughout the heap, and at the same time to ventilate the materials, which would otherwise become too compacted for aerobic decomposition in a heap of this type. Far from being a chore, it is a delight to fork it over and be almost overcome by the dense clouds of steam!

'Although the turning process reduces the temperature by about 40°F (22°C), it quickly reasserts itself and 24 hours later will probably be up to 160°F (71°C).

'Thereafter, further additions to the heap should take place as materials become available, with turning repeated perhaps weekly, until the heap is complete, which should be about three weeks after commencement. The heap will sink repeatedly during the rapid initial ferment, so it will take a fantastic amount of material to produce a good binful. Working on the basis of a bin per month, I start the second bin as soon as the first is full, and load out the finished compost ready for use during the making of the second binful.

'An alternative to tarpaulins for covering is sheets of corrugated iron. Some people maintain that close cover (i.e. tarpaulins) excludes vital ventilation, but I find this is not so providing the heap is regularly turned.

'The only drawback I have come across with this intensive production is that I rarely find worms in my finished compost. Worms appear only after two months. I make sure both bins are left full during the winter, however, so at the beginning of my gardening season I have the tremendously joyful task of turning out two bins alive with red, lively, virile worms.'

The brick heap, without any form of concrete floor, so the worms can move in, is permanent, and with your own labour and second-hand bricks available, is a good investment, but not a tenant's fixture, though it could be an asset in selling a house. No form of pit is advisable, because it will collect water, and the compost will go sour and water-logged in winter.

Ready Made Compost Containers

The problem of all these is the cost of carriage so that they are constantly made lighter and flimsier. There was once a container made from expanded polystyrene, that packed into four large envelopes with metal clasps and travelled at the printed paper rate, but it blew away in use unless it was at least 25% full, and was so often damaged on arrival, that it went off the market.

There are several plastic containers, but all have become a great deal more expensive as the price of oil rises and the freight costs soar. Perhaps the best value is the Rotol, which is one of the cheapest of the ready made containers. It is a cone with the top cut off and replaced by a lid 18in (45cm) in diameter, made of fluted black PVC 32in (80cm) high and 39in (1m) across the bottom. It works well because the condensed moisture trickles down the flutings and stays at the sides, which allows the centre to build up some heat.

The advantages of the Rotol are that it is neat and simple, and needs no skill in carpentry. It is ideal for small gardens, as it swallows lawn mowings, kitchen wastes and weeds, converting them to a reasonable compost, although too high a proportion of kitchen wastes in winter makes the contents too wet to heat up, and the process stops. The Rotol also attracts large quantities of vinegar flies, which are smaller and more slender than houseflies; they are harmless and stay inside the container. If rats come for the kitchen wastes, use the guard made of expanded metal described in Chapter 3 (see the section Kitchen Wastes).

Though Rotols can stand on the bare soil, it is a good idea to set them on bricks, with other bricks placed to form ventilation channels, so that there is a good airflow to help the temperature and allow for some nitrogen fixation, for if that is short you will lose nitrogen by denitrification. When your Rotol goes cold, lift the cone and see how much compost is ready. Take off the undecayed upper layer to start the next heap and use the broken-down material, which in summer can be ready in two months.

The Rotocrop is made like a barrel, with 'staves' that slide up to allow 'good compost to be shovelled out' at the sides. It is important to position this plastic container so that any shovelling out can be done evenly all round, or it will tilt sideways and jam the green plastic sliders. The whole structure travels as a bundle by rail and fits together in the garden. The slats have ventilation holes, and the container should stand over a trench which is protected from blockage by some green painted expanded metal. Though decay of the material near the ventilation holes can be reduced by the wind and draughts, this bin shares the problem, common among plastic containers, of condensation inside, and produces a wet compost, which the shape of the Rotol partly avoids. Some gardeners like these containers, of which there are now a number widely advertised, but an old carpet will make better compost more cheaply.

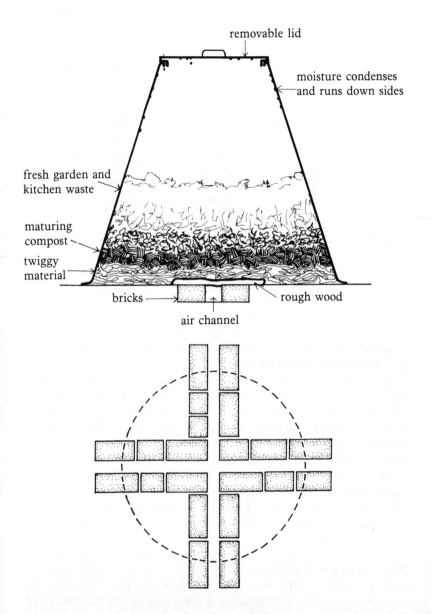

Labels on the diagram:

removable lid

moisture condenses
and runs down sides

fresh garden and
kitchen waste

maturing
compost

twiggy
material

bricks

air channel

rough wood

Rotol plastic compost bin

The only wooden compost container on sale will also travel as a bundle in the care of British Rail. This is the Huker Bin, the first compost container to be rated a Best Buy by *Which*. It is made of seasoned timber, impregnated with a wood preservative, and

47

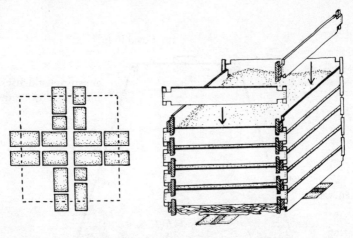

Polythene covered Huker bin compost heap with brick lined air channels covered by rough and stemmy material

consists of a series of thick, wide planks made to lock together into a bin 3ft (1m) square and 32in (80cm). It should rest on bricks arranged to form a cross of air channels, which also prevent the lower planks from rotting through contact with the ground. It is filled layer by layer like a New Zealand box, with planks being added as it builds up higher.

There are a number of containers made of stout wire welded together, which are known as 'rat trap bins', because they look like old fashioned rat traps, and are about as effective for compost making. They do not hold moisture or heat, nor do they keep out cold winds; they simply allow the material to dry out until it is fit only for a bonfire. Today there is such an interest in organic gardening that dozens of manufacturers have tried to jump on the bandwagon with something new to sell. It is now only too easy to buy enthusiasm in the gardening press by placing a large advertisement based on the advice of a writer who has never made proper compost.

The Analysis of Compost
Any analysis of compost varies according to the materials, the amount of soil that accompanies the weed roots, the activator, and the weather—for summer heaps heat best and hold less moisture. The chemical analysis, as we have seen, not only fails to reveal the forms in which elemental substances have been linked by the action of micro-organisms in the composting process, but also ignores a very important factor, the auxins, plant hormones, and enzymes that are present in the finished compost.

Compost can, however, be compared with other composts. The carbon:nitrogen ratio measures the degree of decay that has occurred, and the proportion the compost supplies of the normal plant foods present in manure. These are nitrogen, phosphorus and potassium, sometimes abbreviated to 'NPK'. (The chemical symbol K for potassium comes from its Arabic name Kali, later latinized to Kalium.) Calcium is sometimes included, but no-one can afford to spend about £9 a time on obtaining figures for each of the commoner trace elements, when they are going to vary with the material and their presence in the soil on the roots.

The figure for farmyard manure is the Rothamsted average for the 1930s, and the Indore compost is a Soil Association average from Haughley. The Indore analysis shows very clearly what the proportion of plant foods in compost should be—near a good farmyard manure but with much more potassium. The bracken heap was from cut green bracken, not red-brown fronds, dry in autumn, the tomato haulm included quite a quantity of soil from the ripped-out roots, and the only heap to contain kitchen wastes was the 'Hills Heap'. It should be said that the figures do not add up, because the materials are percentages of the dry matter. The Huker Bin Heap contained 50.6% water, with 90.6% of the remaining 49.4% as 'Ash' (the silica, alumina and other hard

	Water	Ash	Nitro-gen	Phos-phorus	Potas-sium	Calcium	C:N
	%	%	%	%	%	%	%
Farmyard Manure	76.0	—	0.64	0.23	0.32	—	14:1
Indore Compost	76.0	12.00	0.50	0.27	0.81	—	10:1
Basil Clough Compost	55.9	75.20	1.20	0.35	0.64	1.43	12:1
Hills Heap (HLA)	46.2	81.10	0.90	0.29	0.41	0.77	7:1
Huker Bin Heap	50.6	90.60	0.71	0.11	0.30	—	6:1
Rotol Heap	56.8	77.30	0.88	0.22	0.36	—	12:1
Tomato Haulm-Fertosan	29.6	66.86	1.36	0.38	0.32	2.35	9:1
Bracken-Fertosan	48.8	12.70	3.16	0.17	0.77	0.81	13:1

[— indicates analysis not available.]

Comparative Analysis of Composts and Farmyard Manure

material from the clay soil on the weed roots). Had the bin been filled with fresh bracken, the result would have been nearer the Bracken-Fertosan figure, with only 12.7% of 51.2% dry matter composed of silica in the fronds and stems.

Using Compost in the Garden

A normal dressing of compost is a barrow load to two square yards (2.4m²), but barrow loads vary according to the size of the barrow and who is wheeling it. A bucketful to the yard (or metre) of potato trench is a usual ration, for potatoes are given the lion's share of the compost. There is no need to be exact with compost dressings, for the plant foods are all in combined form, and can have none of the 'burning' effect of reverse osmosis from putting on, as an example, too much nitrate of soda.

Therefore compost can go on immediately before sowing, without fear of making root crops coarse and forky from excess nitrogen, and it can go on at the same time as lime, because it contains nothing with which the lime can react to produce free ammonia and calcium sulphate. A compost-fed crop may start more slowly in spring, because its nitrogen must be made available by the action of bacteria which 'work to rule' until the temperature of the soil as above 50°F (10°C), but they catch up later in the season.

Sandy soils use up their compost most rapidly, because the rain soaks in drawing air after it, which speeds up decay and the release of plant foods. Compost gives the best value on clays, and it is far better to put in the hard work of lightening a clay with good humus as a 'soil conditioner' than to supply chemical conditioners which can damage its fertility. Try and get the compost under when the clay is neither baked nor sticky, but see Chapter 6 for leaf-mould which is the ideal 'cure' for clay.

Some gardeners insist that compost should always go on the surface, because this is where Nature puts it, but in fact Nature uses leaf-mould under trees, and never makes compost at all. Compost is as 'unnatural' as a loaf of bread or a glass of wine, for both are inventions in applied biology made by men quite early in our history. It is not a question of principles but one of convenience.

Those who make compost well enough for it to be free from weed seeds and have enough to use it sufficiently thickly to suppress annual weeds can practice what is known as the 'no-digging system'. This involves weeding by hand, and hoeing, so that weeds in the surface layer of the soil germinate and are pulled out, while the store under the surface stays down out of harm's way. The 'digging' is done by earthworms who take down the humus and aerate the soil, which they also enrich with the minerals brought up from the subsoil in their casts.

If, however, your compost is less than perfect and you have not had time to improve its texture and breakdown by turning, then it is better dug or mechanically cultivated under. Digging puts it down where the weed seeds will be brought to the surface eventually, but can be destroyed by hoeing at seedling stage, while a motor cultivator chops it and distributes it through the top eight inches, where it will break down rapidly with the additional air supply. Both methods have their supporters and both grow good crops for good gardeners.

1. HOWARD, Albert, and WAD, K. *The Waste Products of Agriculture* Oxford University Press 1931

3 Compost Materials

An organic gardener or farmer is not trying to set up an individual, experimental closed system in attempting to run a garden or farm entirely on what grows there, what the plants absorb from the air, or what falls on it as rain. The object is simply to grow good crops according to a set of quite definite standards, and to keep on achieving a certain level of yield indefinitely. Gardens and farms live longer than their owners, who should leave their land more fertile than they found it.

The Broadbalk field at Rothamsted showed that it is possible to take more than 150 crops of wheat off the same soil without exhausting it. But no farmer can afford such a low level of production, and no gardener would be satisfied with the dwindling vegetable yield his soil would produce with nothing added and everything taken away.

An organic farm on good land can manage well by importing only lime, one on poorer land will need to bring in feeding stuffs and augment its supply of manure, while a small area of garden that is producing vegetables for a family must import either manure or compost material. Today, with ten tonnes of manure costing as much as a man's suit, imported compost material provides the better value.

Straws

The problem of all bulk imports is the cost of transport, and the more water you have to haul with it, the more expensive the load. Those who have room to stack it will find that baled straw (ideally, bales which have failed to find a buyer and started to decay by the spring) is often available for just the cost of carting, loading and transport on a trailer.

Any farmer who sells straw is very unlikely to be an organic grower, who would appreciate its value, and therefore may well have sprayed it with a selective weedkiller. The question, when you buy or are given straw, is whether you are importing trouble. Some years ago the HDRA commissioned Dr Denys Long, its scientific adviser at the time, to carry out a series of tests on barley straw from fields treated with the selective weed killers commonly used by farmers, investigating whether the effect lasted long enough after harvest to cause harm when seedlings were grown with the composted straw, or when the straw was used as a mulch. His report, now long out of print, is given as Appendix 3b because of the anxiety many organic gardeners feel about buying the only straw they can get.

Dr Long's report clearly suggests that straw so treated should be perfectly safe when composted for general garden use. The HDRA is in contact with thousands of organic gardeners, who have never reported a disaster from using composted straw. This is certainly not to recommend the use of selective weedkillers by organic farmers or gardeners, and there is always a risk that some new killer for wild oats or other weed might be introduced that could survive the composting process, but very few manufacturers are likely to release a substance that would last long enough in the straw to poison crops for the few farmers who still make manure as their fathers did.

All straws are high in cellulose, hemi-celluloses (similar carbohydrates forming part of plant cell walls, especially woody ones), and lignins (compounds which strengthen woody cells). They break down well, because their main structure is tubular and offers plenty of bacterial working surface. Therefore, they leave behind plenty of energy material in the soil, and a fairly well balanced set of plant foods. Among other woody materials dry bracken is sometimes used as packing stuff, but it is greatly inferior to fresh cut green fronds in summer. *Caution*: Woodwool, shavings and sawdust should not be added directly to a compost heap. They should only be used as deep litter poultry compost material (see Chapter 7), never in the normal garden heap.

	Moisture	Ash	Nitro-gen	P_2O_5	K_2O	Organic Matter	C:N
	%	%	%	%	%	%	Ratio
Wheat Straw	15.6	5.5	0.38	0.19	1.00	78.9	128:1
Oat Straw	16.5	5.6	0.40	0.28	0.97	77.9	48:1
Barley Straw	20.0	5.4	0.27	0.18	0.45	74.6	
Hay (average)	15.0	6.3	1.20	0.43	1.60	75.2	

The Analysis of Straws

Straws contain a low proportion of water and, if they are to be composted successfully, need ample moisture. Their main uses in the compost heap are in the disposal of wastes from bucket sanitation and, when baled, as temporary compost containers. Straw cannot be used successfully in the mixed heap because it has too wide a carbon:nitrogen ratio and always results in a lower grade of compost than a good mixed heap. However, it lasts well, dug in on a sandy soil, and is excellent mulching material under bush fruit.

Hay is far better material, ideal for use on the surface with the no-digging system, it makes good compost, but it is far too expensive today to buy for anything but stock feeding. The problem of cost also occurs with many of the industrial wastes like 'felt-hat-maker's refuse', which now goes into cattle cake. Modern industries throw away pollutants rather than contributions to garden fertility.

Weed Gathering
The best investment for anyone who lives in the country is a small trailer to go behind the car, for the passing of a luggage rack like that at the rear of an early Hillman Minx or Morris Eight, which could be extended with stout stakes to carry sacks of cut compost material, has reduced the amount our cars can bring home. A shooting brake type vehicle like a Morris Traveller can accommodate a number of fully stuffed polythene fertilizer bags, and a garden truck to collect the unwanted harvest of weeds on wasteland and roadside can go a long way towards building garden fertility.

Fortunately, a great many Councils today are giving up the spraying of selective weedkillers on the roadside verges, not to preserve wild life or wild flowers, but to avoid the cost, and local agitation could well succeed in getting rid of this expensive and unecological practice in other districts. The policy adopted by over half the English rural councils is to cut down weeds only where their height interferes with vision at road junctions and bends, which leaves the way clear for gardeners to improve their local environment by cutting weeds in convenient areas, with a scythe, a sickle, or a motor scythe such as an Allen.

Leave the cut weeds to lie for about 48 hours, so that they have time to become soft and flabby with the loss of about half their moisture, for the object is not to make hay that will keep, but mineral-rich vegetable matter that will heat in the compost heap. Always cut well before the weeds are seeding, and aim at three cuts a year if you eventually wish to kill out the perennials, or twice a year if you would like your compost material mine to last longer.

A roadside verge or a piece of waste land within reasonable distance of a garden is a real asset, especially if it is infested with nettles, thistles, rosebay willow herb, bracken or ragwort. In a neglected garden, it is better to use weeds from the land you do not have time to cultivate as compost material for heaps to improve the areas on which you have made a start, than to let the brutes seed, allow the mowings to dry and ripen seed where they lie, and then burn them in the cause of tidiness.

Your aims are to obtain as much compost material and as few weed seeds as possible, and to kill out the weeds. Therefore, allow the nettles and thistles to grow on until June or July, then mow them before they are in bud. It is not possible to give an exact height, because that varies with the quality of the soil, but if the main object is compost material aim to cut in June or early July and again around October. If you are out to kill, get in a cut in May, another at the end of July, and a final autumn cut.

Leave the weeds to wilt for about 48 hours, which will enable you to cram large quantities into plastic bags, but even if they are quite flabby you still need gloves for protection against odd stings and prickles. Two years of cutting should destroy your own nettles and thistles. However, if you are cutting verges or waste land, cut each area every other year to keep this useful supply going. Ragwort contains an alkaloid which is a danger to stock but, like the oxalic acid in rhubarb leaves, breaks down in the compost heap. It was a favourite with the late Lady Seton, once President of the National Gardens Guild, who even sowed it deliberately in her garden from carefully saved seed, and cut it twice a year for its value in compost.

In her opinion, ragwort (*Senecio squalidus*) grew more fibre to add a bulk of lasting humus than sappier weeds, which contain a higher proportion of protein and carbohydrate, and so rotted down to less bulk. On the other hand, well wilted weeds stuff more tightly into the ever useful polythene fertilizer bags than stiffer bundles. This means more plant foods and less water to carry home, as well as fast heating, but avoids importing weed seeds or soil-laden roots.

A weed that is worth cutting for compost, however small it may be, is ground elder (*Aegopodium podagraria*), a perennial with brittle white roots that break up into fragments, of which the smallest piece will grow. If it is cut every 28 days, it will die out in two years, which is far less costly in terms of money and energy than using a succession of fearful weedkillers against it.

All the ordinary garden weeds should of course be used on your own compost heap, including the ones with persistent roots. These should be spread out to dry on small-mesh wire netting before you compost them in the middle of the layers, where they will be cooked like long, narrow, potatoes if the heap heats well. Any diseased material can go on the heap, with the exception of clubrooted brassica stems, for there is never enough heat to cook the clubbing throughout in order to kill the 26% of spores, each with a potential life of nine years, that it contains. Blighted potato or tomato haulm is perfectly safe, because the disease is killed at 120°F (49°C), and the same temperature destroys rusts—even those which get right

55

inside strawberry or comfrey stems. It is a disadvantage that a tidy and well kept garden grows too few weeds to compost, but the best method of weed control is to hoe off the seedlings and leave them to dry and be taken under by earthworms, or to decay while they are at the high protein and carbohydrate stage. This builds little humus, and a very weed-free garden can be an infertile one, unless compost material, or manure, is brought in.

Bracken, Tomato Haulm and other Bulk Heaps

In terms of plant foods and humus, green bracken is the best bargain. The main question is how far it is possible to carry such a springy and awkward load, even though it averages 1.5% nitrogen, 0.2% phosphorus and 2.75% potassium when cut in June or July, and again in mid September. The object of cutting is to kill it out, and two years of this treatment will destroy it, bringing back good grass to flourish on the plant foods that are released as the roots decay.

When you have cut your bracken, leave it to wilt for 24 hours, so that it will stuff into bags, though if it lies longer the stems will dry hard and be still more awkward to load. Bring back all you can, and start by making a square layer of bracken 1ft (30cm) thick. On this, spread about 1in (2cm) of any organic manure, ideally from pigeons or poultry, then add the same amount again of bracken, and about ½in (1cm) of old compost or good garden soil, with enough lime scattered on it to whiten the surface. Follow this with more bracken, and more manure, repeating the process until you have used up all the material, or reached a height of 6ft (180cm), when the difficulty of forking the material up will make it easier to extend the heap lengthways or start another one.

The soil layer will provide bacteria that would otherwise be missing from cut bracken without soil on the roots. If assorted weeds can be added to an equal quantity of bracken, additional soil will be unnecessary, but it is as well not to miss the scattering of lime, because bracken heaps are always on the acid side. If the heap is to supply humus for a forest nursery, leave out the lime anyway, because you need an acid soil for conifer seedlings. Build the heap up tall and squared off, like a haystack, but sloping in a little so that if it is 6ft (180cm) wide at the bottom and 6ft (180cm) high, the top will be about 4ft (120cm) square.

As bracken heaps can be expected to have to withstand high rainfall and strong winds, the best covering is polythene. Modern nurseries no longer cover the soil in their tomato house with old sacks to hold in the smell when they have used a liquid soil sterilizer, or steam sterilized – they use large sheets of clear polythene for covering down and dump them as soon as they get a bit battered, giving away something that could cost at least £5 if bought new. Use one of these polythene sheets to cover the heap, with stakes, lumps of concrete, or anything long and heavy, to hold the edges down against the wind and the rain, especially for the September-made heap.

The heap will steam as it heats, so that moisture condenses on the polythene at night, trickling back down to wash the layers of soil and activator through the heap. With large heaps made in this way, there is usually enough air trapped among the material to provide the oxygen for decay. The polythene conserves the moisture, which is important when the heap is built out of reach of a hose.

Tomato haulm (and aubergine and sweet pepper plants) ripped out by commercial growers and given away to save the labour of burning are often available free for cartage. As the plants are usually accompanied by some soil still caked in the paper pots in which they grew before being planted out in the houses, they should be heaped in the same way as bracken, but without the layers of soil. Chrysanthemum plants, far woodier, can take about two years to decay on this system, and so can capsicums, though both are usually ready by autumn in the year after the making of the heap.

Tomato haulm in bulk is difficult to heap, because its tough stems tend to remain apart; the heaps should be trodden down well during the building, unlike compost in normal small bins. The other drawback is that nylon strings of great length are used to support the mighty modern plants that coil along the ground as yields of at least a hundred tonnes an acre are picked, and that nylon or plastic ties have replaced the older materials. Instead of decaying, nylon will lie in the soil like the broken stems of 'church warden' pipes, which were the non-biodegradable by-product of gardeners and farm workers a hundred years ago.

The question of whether or not to import compost material grown with chemical fertilizers is one for every gardener and market gardener to decide. The best rule when you are growing crops for sale is to confirm that the treatment is within the standards you are observing. In Great Britain, these should be the ones adopted by The Soil Association. The real point is whether or not persistent pesticides have been used, so ask what the grower has been using and look it up among the standards at the end of this book (Appendix I).

Lawn Mowings as Compost Material

Grass mowings are perhaps the ideal material to bring in. They are often available in bulk from tennis clubs, sports grounds, parks and, above all, along access ways and footpaths in every suburb and country town. It is a constant complaint among those responsible for collecting our refuse that modern gardeners fill their dustbins with garden rubbish, most of which make good compost. Perhaps 80% of our grass mowings are squandered every year by gardeners who buy expensive peat and still more costly manure.

Parks, tennis clubs and sports clubs are likely to have used selective weedkillers. The best policy is to ask if they have used a chlordane wormkiller, for this is a highly persistent organochlorine compound which lasts 15 years in the soil. No organic gardener would be fool enough to kill the earthworms, which are among his many friends, and as chlordane is absorbed through the skin (see Rachel Carson's *Silent Spring*), no-one with children should let them tumble about on the lawn in summer when there is a risk of accumulating what has been described as 'one of the most toxic of insecticides' in their bodies. The keepers of greens for bowling or golf, and any other lawns where worms *must* be killed, should dissolve ½oz potassium permanganate crystals in a gallon of water and apply it to a square yard (or 10gm in 44 spread over 1m^2) with a rosed can. Sprinkled in the day time, this quickly brings the worms to the surface, where they can be swept up. Those who do not have chickens to whom to throw the swept worms can scatter bread crusts to attract the local sparrows, who will also appreciate the extra protein.

Ask, too, if a selective weedkiller has been used soon before the cut you are going to take. Though, like MCPA, 2–4–D is not very persistent, all weedkillers are at their most efficient where their effects are unwanted, and it is as well to make sure that you do not get the next mowing after a dressing with weedkiller. The one after that will be safe.

Lawn mowings, with a carbon:nitrogen ratio between 12:1 and 14:1, are not only compost material which is low in lasting, humus-making fibre, but can also be dug direct into the soil as a 'green manure', and are also an ideal cheap mulching material under bush fruit or for 'no-digging' gardeners. Accounts of these uses will be found in later chapters. Organic gardeners will find that a lawn is one of the best sources of organic material, since they cannot normally grow a farmer's ley full of chicory. To keep a garden as tidy as your inorganic neighbour's, replace selective weedkillers with an old-fashioned lawn sand.

Mix 7oz (200g) of ammonium sulphate, 3oz (85g) of iron sulphate and 10oz (280g) of dry sand and broadcast at the rate of 3–4oz a square yard (100–140g/m²), where clover, daisies, dandelions and plantains are plentiful. This is a good remedy for clover where one is needed, because if ample nitrogen from a chemical fertilizer is available, the nitrogen fixing root bacteria not only stop working—they 'demand' more carbohydrate for doing nothing until its loss kills the clover. Dried sewage sludge may be used in place of the sand, for the heat drying process will have slowed the availability of nitrogen; it has a long term tonic effect on the lawn. If sludge is available, give a spring dressing of 8oz a square yard (270g/m²), anyway, without the chemicals if the weed problem is not extreme, and regular treatment with dried sludge is the best way of keeping up the mowing production in a hard-working lawn.

If you can obtain tea leaves (not tea bags) from a cafe, they are an excellent lawn dressing brushed in, as available, for the worms to take under. Tea leaves have about the same analysis as poultry manure (see the table later in this chapter for an analysis of kitchen wastes), but the nitrogen is locked up by the tannins. It will become slowly available, by the action of the earthworms and soil bacteria, giving tea leaves lasting value as a humus dressing, especially on sandy soils. It is not possible to prescribe exact amounts because the weight varies with the moisture, but you should apply enough to show brown all over the lawn.

On estates where gardeners have been employed until recently, there may well be stacks of fallen leaves up to ten years old, never used because it was considered more convenient buy peat. If you are lucky enough to get hold of a mature heap of leaves, chop them small and apply a generous scattering on your lawn in the spring or autumn to provide a feast for the worms and a store of fertility that will be returned in more home grown compost material.

As everyone who has mown a lawn knows, the heap of cut grass will become too hot for a hand to bear in a few hours. This results from the action of a number of fungi with microscopic spores that are always floating in the air. Soon, however, the temperature falls through lack of air and increasing acidity to leave a slippery mess, harbouring white mycelia of the fungus known to gardeners of the horse manure age as 'fire fang', which turns fixed nitrogen back to the gas and breaks down humus.

Grass mowings used alone need special composting, with a layer of rough stuff, and a row of stakes, even bamboo canes or hoe handles thrust in upright along the ventilation channels and withdrawn when the heap is complete, to leave behind extra air inlets. As mowings are rich in protein, they contain plenty of nitrogen, and therefore herbal or bacterial activators such as QR or Fertosan will do. Every alternate layer of mowings should be well whitened with slaked lime.

The best container to use is one of the New Zealand Box type, for carpet or polythene covered heaps get too wet and take in too little air to make good compost from mowings. The material will sink rapidly and the stakes must be replaced to keep the channels open for the new load piled on top. There is so much water, protein and carbohydrate present that a box need topping up five times to produce a cube of compost.

An all-grass heap will always be inferior to a mixed one, and it is better not to let mowings make up more than half. Mowings, with additions, always improve the heating and leave behind better value in humus than grass alone. Try and avoid stacking the grass beside the heap while other material accumulates, as it will waste much of its value in making the inferior silage-type compost.

Home-Grown Compost Material

The best material to have ready for the harvest of summer lawn mowings is sunflowers, which are the finest crop to sow for grow-your-own compost. Some years ago, the HDRA tried out all the tall, strong-growing, hardy annuals to see which would grow the most lasting humus from a small area in the shortest time. The ordinary striped sunflower seeds sold in pet shops for parrot food were a clear winner.

Sow the large seeds 1ft (30cm) apart each way in staggered rows, on ground that has been rough dug and levelled, at any time from March to early August. When they reach 4ft (120cm) high, or as soon as they show a bud, pull them up, knock as much soil as possible off the roots and stack them in your compost heap with lawn mowings and other material. Do not leave them to flower, because the stems which can grow to 3in (7cm) thick, will not decay unless hammered laboriously with an axe-back on concrete, for they are as tough as cabbage stumps. You need them at the first stage of maturity, before they start to build the hemi-cellulose 'girders' that will support flower heads as big as dustbin lids.

It is not worth cutting sunflowers down to sprout from the base, because the seed is so cheap that it pays, in terms of good, readily composted material, to rake over the bed and sow another batch. On very weedy areas, sow 8in (20cm) apart each way for a quicker complete cover as there is time, before the leaves and stems meet in a solid mass, for weedseeds to germinate and be killed out; spacing the seeds 1ft (30cm) apart gives rather more time for weeds to sprout and die if there are not all that many.

Because sunflowers are a tall and greedy crop, they cannot grow as compost material between vegetable rows, where they shade everything and take up so much water that surrounding crops are stunted. The ideal place for them is an area that has been overmanured with sewage sludge, poultry droppings or the emptying of bucket sanitation. This kind of site will grow far more than the 20lbs a square yard (10kg/m²) of a normally composted vegetable garden, where the normal four squares for crop rotation could well be augmented by a fifth, resting under a compost crop of sunflowers, which are composites and are therefore not subject to any of the usual pests or diseases. You cannot, however, expect to keep on taking two or three crops of this bulk in a season without exhausting the soil, so the compost plant section should be well manured through the winter before sowing.

The runners up among the annuals were two members of the mallow family, *Malope grandiflora* and *Lavatera trimestris*, but though both were attractive and provided good cut flowers, they were capable of growing only 3–4lb of compost material a square yard (1.7–2.2kg/m²), though they were not greedy for plant foods or moisture and could be included in the vegetable garden. However, their yield is considerably less than that of sweet corn, which produces compost material as a by-product of cobs. Suttons Earliest of All seems to be the fastest ripening variety.

Plant Material	Moisture %	Potash %	Fibre %	C:N Ratio
Sunflower, Striped 4–5ft	90.0	2.51	25.2	14:1
Sunflower, 6–8ft	83.0	5.78	29.5	30:1
Malope grandiflora	81.0	2.12	38.6	17:1
Lavatera trimestris	81.0	1.59	40.6	30:1
Lawn mowings	80.0	0.60	4.4	12:1
Sweet Corn	80.0	0.33	20.0	19:1

Analysis of annuals for compost material

Kitchen Wastes
If all families in Britain were to compost all their kitchen wastes, it would be possible for Councils to collect refuse only once a fortnight, because it is the compostable portion of waste food that attracts the flies and produces the smell. The food consumed by the

average household comes from perhaps ten different countries and though ready prepared 'convenience foods' leave behind nothing for the compost bucket, the peel from fruit and vegetables adds up to a useful supply of trace elements. As a rule, kitchen wastes are low in fibre and leave little lasting humus, but they are worth adding to the compost heap and the kitchen compost trench. Those who have pigs or chickens need two buckets and will get a better saving out of using the waste as food for either, as they will supply manure, than by composting. The following table shows some of the principal ingredients of kitchen wastes, all on a fresh weight basis.

	Nitrogen	Phosphorus	Potash
Apple cores	0.05	0.02	0.10
Coffee grounds (dried)	1.99	0.38	0.67
Egg shells	1.19	0.38	0.14
Orange peel	0.20	0.13	0.21
Peanut shells	0.80	0.15	0.50
Tea leaves	4.15	0.62	0.40

Analysis of kitchen wastes[2]

Fruit peel is always relatively high in potassium, which is readily available; nutshells also provide plenty, but more slowly. The most attractive of all these substances is tea leaves. Potato peel, carrot peelings, cabbage and celery leaves are all recyclable wastes from one's own garden, and for about six months of the year there is usually sufficient garden rubbish to make it possible to empty the daily bucketfuls on the heap and cover down with green weeds and other refuse, so that both compost together.

The following materials are all worth including: shrimp heads, banana peel, nutshells of all types, food scraps if you do not wrap them in a great deal of newspaper. You can add the sheet of paper lining the compost bucket, and up to about 5% of such materials as orange wrappers, but not colour-printed glossy magazines. Newspaper ink, consisting mainly of carbon black, linseed oil and paraffin, is safe, but coloured inks can contain up to 600 parts per million cadmium in the yellows and 400 p.p.m. lead in the reds. Vacuum cleaner emptyings used to be recommended, but today nearly all the fluff comes from man-made fibres, which will not decay, and can contain up to 500 p.p.m. of lead blown in through your windows and brought in on your shoe soles from the tetra-ethyl lead in petrol. Now that dust is no longer safe, you do not have to pollute your own compost heap.[3]

Exclude milk bottle tops, which are aluminium and lead, and take them instead to the local OXFAM shop for recycling; as much paper as possible should also be recycled if there is a local scheme. All plastics, bones and meat scraps (fish can be included), man-made fibres (real wool or cotton garments can be cut up and added to the heap), broken china, tins and metal of all kinds are undesirable. Also avoid winter tree prunings (summer prunings rot down well), rose prunings (because the thorns stay sharp for a long time in compost), shavings, sawdust and thick branches of any kind. Ordinary hedge clippings will decay in time, but yew or other conifer cuttings, which contain turpentines that retard decay, should be burnt in one of the rare bonfires lit by organic gardeners.

As there is always a risk of rats when food scraps are used, it is worth fitting rat excluders to your heap. Buy a sheet of expanded metal (which is used by builders for nailing on beams to hold plaster) rather larger than your bin, paint it with black bitumen paint to prevent rust, and leave it to dry thoroughly. Then fit it to the bottom of your New Zealand box, bending it up at the back and ends, securing it with large headed nails, and in front round the ends of your air channels, nailed to the removable boards. Get someone to hold a brick with the end against where you are going to hammer to take the shock. A Rotol bin needs a square of expanded metal about 1ft (30cm) larger each way than the diameter at the bottom. Bend up the edges, cutting them with strong shears so that they grip round the bin, and secure them with a stout wire threaded through them like a drawstring. Then sit your bin on the air channels.

The expanded metal is fairly expensive, but it is too strong for rats to gnaw through, and will also exclude mice. Any spare pieces or short ends that you can obtain are excellent painted and placed across the bricks to prevent blocking of the air channels.

Compost Trenches
The compost trench is a way round the problems of both kitchen wastes and brussels sprout stems or cabbage stumps. Dig trenches about 8in (20cm) wide and 1ft (30cm) deep, one at a time, where you are going to sow or plant next year's runner beans, empty your compost bucket in the trench and shovel the soil back over it. As they became available, dig up your cabbage stumps and lay them in the bottom of the trench, pouring the bucket contents on them, and working the soil between them, treading firm as you go. If you dig several trenches at once, the sides crumble in, making it awkward to reach them with a full bucket.

Sow your beans at the normal time in the trenches, which will have sunk with decay and left a depression, which is good for trapping water hosed on the roots—never the leaves or the blossoms, or these will drop from the shock of cold water straight from the mains. If you leave a row without filling the trench with stumps and kitchen wastes, you will notice that it has a far smaller crop, and when you take up the rest of the beans with the trench at the end of the season you will find that the sprout stems have broken down completely into dark humus, with very little of the kitchen wastes remaining.

What you have made is a series of long, narrow, compost heaps activated by nitrogen released by the bacteria in the bean roots. In addition to gaining the value in humus and plant foods from two materials often dumped in the dustbin or burnt, you will also have destroyed two awkward pests. One is the mealy cabbage aphis, *Brevicoryne brassicae*, which has a population explosion every time there is insufficient rain to beat down the winged stage before it migrates from cabbage fields to gardens, to over-winter on brussels sprouts left in to grow the last 'spring greens'. The other is the cabbage white fly, *Aleurodes brassicae*, like a tiny white moth, which soots the leaves and rises in clouds from the cabbage bed after mild winters. If everyone trench-composted their brassica stumps we should, as a by-product of increasing fertility, go a long way towards exterminating this pair of pests without harming the environment.

Many gardeners have used kitchen wastes alone for peas, which have less powerful root bacteria and cannot cope with cabbage stumps. Starting in about November after sowing their broad beans, they trench their way across the pea tribe section of their rotation, getting ready, first for the peas, and then the french beans, on the kitchen waste alone. After this, they make rather wider and deeper tranches, adding cabbage stumps as well, for the runner beans, including the white-seeded runners to dry for butter beans, and the climbing french beans, such as White Achievement, to dry as haricots.

There are two problems with this system, which is increasingly popular among organic gardeners who grow more legumes than their inorganic neighbours because they want to gather nitrogen from the air rather than buy a bag from the garden centre. First, it cannot be used to dispose of cabbage-tribe stalks when there is a danger of clubroot, so though it is easy to get your neighbours or fellow allotment holders to give you all their sprout stems, it can mean importing spores. A way round is to cut the stumps off an inch above ground level with pruning shears, leaving the clubroot spores in the soil, but those who are nervous should stick to kitchen wastes. Fortunate gardeners with clubroot-free soil can use the system as much as they like, as long as they never buy any cabbage plants. Manure also carries clubroot spores when infected kale or turnips are fed to stock.

The other problem is that potato peelings can include the eyes, for, incredible though it may seem, these can grow like tiny seed potatoes, using the food supply in the fragment of peel as a substitute for the tuber, and a potato in the wrong place is an awkward weed. It is best therefore to sow peas in the late autumn-made heaps which have time to get the frost into the soil to kill the eyes. It is easier to dig 'peel potatoes' out of the later made trenches before the runner beans are sown.

Those who wish to sow radishes or plant out early lettuce between the runner bean rows can do so in the soil between the trenches, and there is no need to dig after the beans are cleared. The surface can be hoed off and the cabbage tribe can be planted straight into the trenches. If spacing is such that some plants come in the rows, and some between, it is easy to see how much fertility this method has added from the compost trenches.

Compost Material Shredders
These are used extensively in the USA, and the first British model was tested on the HDRA Trial Ground in 1972. Members were asked to bring rose prunings and hedge clippings, mainly privet and lonicera, to open days. These went through the machine driven by a 3½ h.p. petrol engine at noisy speed. The shredded material was composted and the result was tested on one of the standard nine plot Latin squares, to allow for the original soil fertility differences and any variations arising from position (Appendix 3 c).

The action of the chopper was to cut the woody material into short lengths which gave too little working surface for the bacteria to complete their decay in the time available, and the result was nitrogen robbery. The large machines used in the USA and on British nurseries have a shredding action like a municipal compost pulverizer, with teeth rather than knives; they cost at least £500 and are far more effective.

One of these machines, the 'Mighty Mac' has been imported into Britain and was tested on the HDRA Trial Ground at Bocking (Appendix 3d). This has a 5 h.p. engine and a rather different action, as it pulverizes rather than chops. Though it is capable of chewing up a pole 3in (7cm) thick, this is a waste of wear and petrol.

The value of this type of shredder lies in chewing up sprout stems, sweet corn plants, and sunflowers that have been allowed to go to 8–10ft (2.5–3m) for maximum potash and fibre, as well as taking all the rose prunings and hedge clippings and chewing them into compostable material.

It is one of the principles of municipal compost-making that almost anything can be composted if it is organic, wet enough and sufficiently pulverized, but it is important not to push your luck too hard. A shredder will still not make it possible to compost quantities of paper or cardboard, or thick branches. These, including newspapers, are best composted in deep litter.

At the moment, the Mighty Mac machine costs about £450, which is expensive for the amount of work there would be for it in an average garden. It is on wheels and could be moved from garden to garden or allotment to allotment if it were bought by a society or group, or it might be suitable for a garden contractor who could reduce a pile of woody rubbish to good compost material, or even put rough compost through the machine to turn it into super fine broken down perfection, but the charge would have to allow for time and depreciation as well as petrol and oil.

Every now and again, a new hand operated shredder comes on the market and then goes off again, because anything like a mincing machine, where you turn a handle with one hand and feed in fruited raspberry canes with the other, is too slow to be worth using. Even an old mangle with a good crushing action would be better than the hand chaff cutters often sought second hand, which merely chop into short sections, but neither is worth using compared with the simplicity of Sir Albert Howard's first compost crusher at Indore.

He used to spread all his woody material in the road outside the Research Station, and the bullock carts creaking slowly by crushed it with their massive wheels.[4] An HDRA member living in a private road in a suburb of Cape Town used to repeat this method, by spreading roots of Kikuyu grass, like tough, over-sized couch grass roots, in the road where it would be crushed by passing cars. Anyone who tried this in modern Britain would probably be fined for depositing rubbish on the highway, but there is no reason why those who live in private roads, or have long drives to their garages, should not experiment.

References on p. 100.

4 Comfrey for Gardeners

Comfrey is a perennial that looks like something between a horseradish and a foxglove, but is very much stronger than either. Used as a medicinal herb for the past 1,500 years, it also serves as a stock feed, a very minor vegetable and, above all, the best source of non-chemical potassium so far known to organic gardeners. With forceful roots that can push as deep as 6ft (2m) in Britain, the plants are highly efficient mineral gatherers.

The main roots of a comfrey plant can reach a diameter of 3in (7cm) at their base. They die off after about four years, but are continuously replaced during the plant's forty-year life-span; they produce powerful secretions, and have root hairs that appear to make available large quantities of plant foods and trace elements. A tree with the same type and depth of root system would lock up nearly all its mineral gatherings in wood, but comfrey keeps its minerals in sappy leaves and thick stems that are so high in protein that they have a carbon:nitrogen ratio of 9.8:1 and can be used as a kind of 'instant compost'.

Cultivated comfrey is a mixture of several variations on the cross between *Symphytum officinale*, common or herbalists' comfrey, which grows wild all over Europe including Russia and Britain, and *S. asperum*, the prickly comfrey, found wild only in Russia, but introduced to Britain as a border plant in about 1790, because of its pure blue flowers. Henry Doubleday introduced the hybrid, which he called 'Russian Comfrey', in the 1870s. It was described in 1879 as *Symphytum peregrinum*, but is more correctly named *S.* × *uplandicum*, after the district in Sweden where the natural hybridization was first observed. It will grow up to 6ft (2m) high in flower, but it is rarely allowed to reach this height, for it is regularly cut as fodder for pigs, horses and goats, or as a means of increasing fertility in the garden.

The hybrids that have intermingled with the wild *S. officinale* since the 1870s vary widely in flower colour, and the leading variety is known as Bocking No. 14 from the HDRA Trial Ground where the sorting was carried out. This has thin stems, like those of *S. asperum*, and magenta flowers. It is the variety that starts earliest in the year, is richest in potassium (which makes it bitter eating and unpalatable to rabbits—an advantage in some gardens), and is also partly resistant to comfrey's only disease, the rust *Melampsorella symphyti*, which frequently attacks the wild species. The other branch of the family has large leaves and thick solid stems, much nearer to *S. officinale*, and the leader in this class is Bocking No. 4, which produces a higher yield, makes a tastier vegetable, and is more palatable to stock (including rabbits and poultry), being lower in potassium. It is also more subject to rust.[1]

Though the RHS *Dictionary of Gardening* still describes *S. peregrinum* as a border plant, it is far too powerful for anything other than a bed on its own, and grows fertility rather than flowers. The only really good flowering species among the sixteen in this genus of the borage and anchusa family, the Boraginaceae is *S. grandiflorum*, which is a ground cover plant, tolerant of shade, with stems that hug the soil. From March to June, it carries pale yellow, bell-like flowers ½–¾in (10–15mm) long on branched stalks rising about 7in (17cm) above the mat of small, deeply veined leaves.

The Analysis of Comfrey

The value of comfrey for gardeners lies in its remarkable analysis. It is so low in fibre that it leaves little humus in the soil and should be used as a compost activator or 'vegetable manure' rather than compost material. It is not a green manure plant, for these are annuals to grow in winter, or between other crops in summer, for digging in. You cannot dig in a comfrey plant. You cut its foliage for many uses in the garden, and it grows on year after year as a kind of fertility mine, bringing up minerals from the subsoil.

During the early years of the Bocking Trial Ground, which began in 1955, a set of the hybrid variations was presented to the National Institute of Agricultural Botany at Cambridge, where ash analysis tests produced the following results:

Composition	7th April %	15th May %	26th June %	7th July %	6th Sept. %
Potash as K_2O	7.95	5.94	7.44	8.25	7.83
Phosphorus as P_2O_5	1.25	0.72	1.15	1.01	1.05
Calcium as CaO	1.86	2.70	1.81	2.65	3.10

Ash Analysis of Comfrey

Comfrey foliage is always used wilted, after losing the first 10–15% moisture, and the next table shows how this 'compost' compares on a fresh-weight basis with ordinary compost and farmyard manure.

Material	Water	Nitrogen (N)	Phosphorus P_2O_5	Potash K_2O	
	%	%	%	%	C:N
Farmyard Manure	76.0	0.64	0.23	0.32	14:1
Russian Comfrey (wilted)	75.0	0.74	0.24	1.19	9.8:1
Indore Compost	76.0	0.50	0.27	0.81	10:1

Comparative analysis of comfrey, compost and farmyard manure

The mineral content is fairly constant through the year, though there is some variation between the hybrids. The following figures are from comfrey dried as hay for stockfeed or for the tea that is widely used medicinally:

	Bocking No. 4	Bocking No. 14	*S. officinale*
	%	%	%
Calcium	2.35	2.77	1.31
Phosphoric Acid	1.25	0.75	0.72
Potassium	5.04	7.09	3.09
Iron	0.253	0.144	0.098
Manganese p.p.m.	137	133	85
Cobalt	Trace	Trace	—

Comparative mineral analysis of comfreys

Comfrey contains the same group of alkaloids as ragwort, and research in Japan and Australia has shown that, if 16% of the diet consists of young comfrey leaves, this can cause liver tumours in rats. Experiments by the HDRA in co-operation with the Liverpool Polytechnic School of Pharmacy and the Medical Research Council have shown that there is one quarter as much alkaloid in mature leaves as in young, and other work indicates that dried comfrey tea contains one fifteenth the alkaloid in these mature leaves.

This does not affect the fertility uses of comfrey, any more than outbreaks of cattle poisoning after the animals have eaten ragwort are any reason why that should not be composted as safely as, say, deadly nightshade (*Atropa belladonna*) or tomato and potato haulm. As far as eating comfrey as a vegetable, cooked like spinach, or as young leaves raw in salads is concerned, there is some risk. But we have so many other good green vegetables that there is no need to use it for this purpose in such large quantities.

The Cultivation of Comfrey

Russian comfrey is a semi-sterile hybrid that rarely sets seed. There are strains that set seed freely, but they are undesirable since they could become a pest. Because every fragment of comfrey root will grow, it cannot be destroyed by hoeing, and if it is merely dug up, root fragments left in the ground will grow again and again. Comfrey should be planted from offsets in a bed where it can stay without disturbance—if it were to seed freely it would be a ferocious weed.

Choose your site in full sun, away from trees or hedges, whose roots would crowd in after the nutrients and moisture that comfrey plants require to produce plenty of foliage for cutting. Five cuts of foliage a year from a dozen will give the equivalent of 3½cwt (180kg) of wilted materials ready for use. Any type of soil is suitable, but the plants will not do well on thin soils over chalk, or those that are peaty, with rock below, as they need a good search area for their mineral-gathering roots.

A comfrey bed—like the ground for asparagus or rhubarb—should be thoroughly dug to remove the roots of perennial weeds, especially convolvulus, couch grass and docks. It then needs some lasting sources of nitrogen and potassium dug in, starting with 1lb a square yard (540g/m²) of coarse bone meal. Feathers, wool shoddy from the stuffing of old mattresses, and human hair, if you can get it from a barber, are far more lasting than manure, especially on sandy soil. (Chapter 9 provides details of application.) Failing these, use manure. It is a good idea to prepare your bed in the late autumn for planting in the spring.

However, comfrey can be planted at any time of the year except December and January, when the roots are fully dormant and planting can mean heavy losses in hard weather. A start in early September gives the plants time to establish growth before winter, and March and April are also good, but they can go out even in the height of summer, if they can be watered for the first few days to start them growing. Plant them out with a trowel, 2ft (60cm) apart in staggered rows, with the growing points of the offsets just below the surface. Hoe between them as weed seedlings appear.

Leave the new plants till the following July or August before cutting them with shears 2in (5cm) above the ground, which will prevent their flowering in the first year and provide enough wilted foliage for a trial batch of liquid manure or foliar feed. It is best to let what would be the second cut die down on the plants during their first season, to build up strength for the next, as with newly planted rhubarb.

The next year there should be four or five cuts spaced out to suit the needs of the garden, with the first in April and the last at the end of September or early October, which will leave time for some growth to die down on the plants. In the late autumn, dig between them and fork in 8oz of slaked lime a square yard (250g/m²) every other autumn. Comfrey will suppress all annual weeds once it is growing fast, but the autumn digging is important, to extract perennials and to keep down grass. Apply manure regularly every spring, always on the surface or lightly forked in; you can use fresh poultry or pigeon manure, sewage sludge, even cesspool pumpings, for comfrey can take its nitrogen crude, but never cover the crowns with pigeon manure. If you can obtain a straw or peat based deep litter compost to spread on the surface, this is ideal.

Comfrey grows faster than any other plant in your garden and needs a good supply of nitrogen to keep it gathering the other plant foods and trace elements, since it is not a legume and therefore cannot fix its own supply. Compost contains too little nitrogen to keep pace with its greed, though vegan gardeners can use their animal-manureless compost on it, making do with a lower yield. If dried blood or fishmeal are used on the comfrey bed, they should be applied between May and July, when the soil is warm enough for them to break down fast instead of going mouldy and being wasted, as they would in winter. Household liquid activator can be used, though not on clay soils, because the accumulation of salt can produce a sodium clay which is permanently sticky. Remember, a comfrey bed is going to live about as long as an apple tree.

The best way of increasing comfrey is to cut through well established plants about 3in (7cm) below ground level, with a sharp spade, in March or early April, then lift off the top of the crown. Slice it up to make offsets, each with a growing point and a section of brown-barked root, like those you bought to start your bed. The portions left in the ground will grow enough foliage for another cut by July. With this method, you increase your comfrey and have it too, whereas if you had dug up the clumps, cut the roots into sections 1in (2.5cm) long and set the pieces out at intervals of 1 in (2.5cm) along furrows 2in (5cm) deep, you would have several hundred plants from your original dozen by the following year, but you would also have left in and dropped fragments to grow everywhere unwanted.

If you wish to move your dozen plants to make way for something else, take off the tops in the same way, then cover the cut surfaces left in the ground with about a ¼in (6mm) layer of ammonium sulphamate, which is the safest known weedkiller. In about three weeks it becomes ordinary ammonium sulphate, a chemical nitrogen fertilizer which will wash harmlessly from the soil. Use it only in spring and summer, when weeds are growing well; four weeks later there will be no danger in sowing or planting where it was used. Unlike sodium chlorate (hard to buy today because it is used by terrorists to make home-made explosives), or more deadly chemicals, ammonium sulphamate is a synthetic plant food rather than a poison, and its effect is malnutrition, on weeds, which take it up greedily, as if one killed rats by feeding them only white sugar and white bread, with bad food rather than poison.

Do not get it in your eyes, for like common salt or washing soda it will do them no good; remember, too, that it is not selective and cannot be used to clear convolvulus out of gooseberry bushes or ground elder from a border of tree peonies. If you are left with an area in which comfrey plants persist because you filled it up with broken roots in an attempt to clear it with a hoe or rotary cultivator, wait till the comfrey is growing well in June. Then cut back the plants and wait three days for them to start growing again, when you can mix 1lb of ammonium sulphamate with a gallon of cold water (100g per lt) and water it on over 100 square feet (9m²).

Old comfrey plants gradually come to resemble moon craters or coral atolls in shape as the main roots die out from the middle and replacements grow outwards. How long this takes depends on the quality of the soil, but if the result is merely a fall in yield, take up some plants in March, as directed, and transplant the offsets in the hollow centres. Otherwise, use the crown removal and ammonium sulphamate method, selecting plants that have grown best over the years for the new bed, cutting off the ones that have made worn-out rings at only 1in (2cm) or so below the surface, and sprinkling on the ammonium sulphamate with care. The idea of using dry crystals is to make sure that they are carried down in the reverse stream of sap that delivers energy as sugars, and any minerals gathered through the leaves, even as far as the root tips.

Comfrey has no pests—though some caterpillars will eat it occasionally—and only one serious disease—comfrey rust. The uredospore stage of *Melampsorella symphyti* becomes visible as an orange powder on the undersides of the leaves, usually in May and June; in July the spores blow like orange smoke, which is how the disease spreads from the wild comfrey that 'joyeth in watery ditches' as John Gerard said in 1633, to those we cultivate in modern gardens.

If you notice the bright orange powder, pick off affected leaves and dump them in your dustbin—though they are safe in a compost heap or a liquid manure butt. This is the policy most comfrey growers adopt, and if they observe more than the odd rusty leaf, they mark the plant, cut it every four weeks instead of every six, and give it extra feeding. This rust is one of the awkward type, like the Mint rust (*Puccinia menthae*), that gets right inside the roots and stems, and though the hot water treatment used for strawberry virus has also been lined with mint rust, you cannot get all the comfrey roots in a bed into water at 110°F (43°C). If there are too many rusted comfreys in a bed, it pays to kill them out and start again with fresh stock.

Comfrey as 'Instant Compost'

The first cut from a comfrey bed is usually in April, which makes it just right for planting maincrop potatoes, though rather late for the earlies. The best policy is to set out even the earlies in chitting trays, leaving them till at least mid-April, because they lose nothing by growing firm shoots in the warm, when the soil may be too cold for quick growth—especially if many have been halved to make expensive seed go further. This gives plenty of time to have enough comfrey ready for them.

Spread the cut comfrey out to wilt in the sun for twenty-four hours, ideally turning and leaving it for another twenty-four, if you are using a thick stemmed variety other than Bocking No. 14, to make sure the stems are really well wilted, to prevent them growing. Take out potato trenches and lay the wilted comfrey along them at the rate of 1–1½lb to the foot of row (1.5–2kg/m); set the seed along them, 1ft (30cm) between tubers for earlies, 15in (40cm) for maincrops, and spade the soil back. This is a version of the old trick of filling the trenches with lawn mowings so that the acidity of these long 'compost heaps' reduces damage by the potato scab fungus (*Actinomyces scabies*). Comfrey has the same effect, but supplies more nitrogen and twice as much potassium. A test of this system was laid out on the Bocking Trial Ground in 1970 (Appendix 3e).

HDRA member Mr Allan Thompson of Stinsford has found the most popular method of ensuring that there is enough comfrey for early potatoes. He planted his unsprouted Arran Banner on 2nd April in furrows 4in (10cm) deep, 30in (75cm) apart and 12in (30cm) between tubers. The whole plot had an unmeasured quantity of 12% potash fishmeal (fishmeal with potassium chloride added) applied evenly when the ground was dug. All the rows were covered with fresh compost to keep the frost off the seed at planting time. When there was enough comfrey available, some rows were

73

mulched with leaves left in the sun a few hours to wilt, and spread over and between the rows just before earthing up to 8in (20cm) high. The compost rows had exactly the same treatment, but with no comfrey.

The crop was lifted as most people lift earlies, when they were wanted for eating; and the results for 96 plants were that compost plus comfrey produced a yield of 158lb 15oz (72kg) against 82lb 3oz (37.2kg) for compost alone (see Appendix 3f).

The special value of comfrey plant foods is for potash-hungry crops, which explains the frequent use of the instant compost system for potatoes—not as a replacement for ordinary compost, but to make it go further, while also providing the extra flavour that gardeners who grow their own expect from compost. A 'blindfold test', no less accurate than the ones comparing brands of whisky, was carried out in 1960, with 28 members eating Majestic potatoes labelled only with letters. Of these, 16 put comfrey grown first for flavour, compared with 7 firsts for manure, 4 for compost and 1 for chemical fertilizers.

The other crop for which this method is useful is onions, which also require potash in quantity. The problem is that onion sets go out in March before comfrey is ready, and, if the onions are put out late, the sinking of the comfrey which has been dug in before planting loses more on root disturbance than is gained on potassium. This also applies with runner beans and tomatoes, which have been tried in square holes filled with trodden comfrey. The only way to use wilted comfrey for onions is to dig in the last autumn cut and leave the ground to settle through the winter before spring planting (see Appendix 3g for a trial of this method).

Comfrey as Liquid Manure and Foliar Feed
The most popular use of comfrey is as a source of an all-organic liquid manure made very simply by a process discovered in 1955 by HDRA member George Gibson of Guernsey, who grew the crop solely to provide a high potash food for his tomatoes. The procedure is to place about 14lb (6.3kg) of cut comfrey, in a 20 gallon (90lt) water butt, and then fill up from the tap or with rainwater, replace the lid and block the hole in it with wood or a large tin lid.

The comfrey goes black rapidly and ferments until, in about four weeks, a clear liquid can be drawn off from the tap at the bottom. This is an excellent feed for tomato plants setting their first truss, as the following analysis shows:

Composition	Tomorite %	Marinure %	Comfrey %
Dry Matter	0.1410	0.0480	0.4090
Nitrogen	0.0130	0.0070	0.0140
Potash	0.0139	0.0019	0.0340
Phosphorus	0.0093	0.0001	0.0059

Analysis of Comfrey Liquid Manure and other Tomato Feeds

Tomorite is the usual inorganic liquid feed, while Marinure seaweed extract is a popular organic one. All were made up for the trial according to the makers' directions for tomatoes. The comfrey liquid was far higher in dry matter and had three times as much potassium as the chemical, a third less phosphorus and rather more nitrogen, which makes it a good balanced liquid feed for anything potash demanding.

The object of covering the butt and blocking the pipe hole in the lid is to keep out drone flies, which will lay eggs that develop into very unpleasant looking larvae known as 'rat-tailed maggots', and also mosquitoes, for this kind of protein rich brew is highly attractive to a number of creatures out to break it down at a profit for themselves.

Sealing the cover also reduces the smell to some extent, but unfortunately the worst stinks of all come from the breakdown of proteins, of which comfrey averages 3.4% on a fresh weight basis, even more if it is wilted (and those who aim at an extra strong brew can wilt the foliage before it goes in). The smell from a sceptic tank that is having bacterial labour problems also results from the breakdown of proteins, and the best remedy for that is to mix a teaspoonful of Odorcure, as recommended for bucket sanitation, in a teacupful of tepid water, leave it for about an hour (like waiting for yeast to rise), then tip it in the tub. After four days, the smell has gone, and the treatment lasts until the tub is finished and the spent foliage dumped on the compost heap.

The clear liquid manure can be used as a feed for runner beans and anything that needs a tonic, including house plants. Because the leaf and foliage should float, leaving the liquid without suspended solids, it can be used through a Keyluter or other commercial liquid feeder, though this needs care in case it does block.

Another use is as a foliar feed. As far as we know, seaweed has a full house of trace elements and comfrey a less generous one, but as far as potassium is concerned all its cards are aces. The value of the liquid comfrey idea is that anyone can make it easily and in quantity.

There are a number of variations on the Gibson recipe, which was invented by a commercial tomato grower trying to save money. The easiest method is to cram fresh comfrey foliage into a large container that has a hole near the bottom. Not a metal drum, unless it is well coated with bitumen paint inside and out, because it will rust and cause complications with the fermentation process. If it is a barrel with a tap, fill it with sand to tap level and pack the sand down before stuffing the container solid with cut comfrey. Then inset a large piece of concrete, or anything really heavy, to press out the concentrate as the comfrey 'stews in its own juice'. Place a can underneath the tap or hole to catch the drips which will start in about two weeks. When it stops dripping, add some water for a second, rather weaker brew, and finally remove the residue to the compost heap.

Analysis of the concentrate has shown the following plant foods:

Nitrogen (N)	0.11%
Phosphorus (P)	0.06%
Potassium (K)	0.55%

To produce the equivalent of a chemical tomato feed, add 4fl oz of concentrate to a gallon of cold water (25ml per lt); a less powerful brew can be half that strength. If you do not wish to use all the drippings at once, store the remainder in a screw top bottle. The advantages over the standard method are that there is far less smell, you do not need a watertight barrel, and there is less liquid to filter through an old pair of tights for use in pressure sprays or a syringe for foliar feeding.

Comfrey liquid manure is ideal for tomatoes, capsicums, aubergines, cucumbers, squashes and marrows, and also peas and beans. If soft fruit bushes show symptoms of potassium shortage—scorching or turning dull purple at the edges of the lower leaves before you have begun to pick the fruit—water on a gallon (4.5lt) of liquid per bush every week until picking finishes or the symptoms disappear.

A third method has been found effective by Mr F. I. T. Daniel of Highcliffe, Dorset:

'I put 1lb (450g) of cut comfrey in a 2 gallon (9lt) bucket, plus about two pints (2lt) of urine. When the fermentation stops, as it does after 10–14 days, I use the liquid diluted with 10 parts of rain or tap water to one. There is some smell, but not as much as with fresh manure, and the method is much faster'.

This is a way of producing a very high potassium feed, with rather more nitrogen. It is 'all organic', in fact comfrey is the best organic source or potassium there is. Nettles and other sappy material will make the same kind of liquid but, because they are higher in nitrogen, there is more wastage.

The last method cannot be used for foliar feeds, but all result in costless versions of the fluids advertised expensively in organic periodicals as being rich in vibrations and filled with cosmic forces. The question is, always, just how much trouble these ideas entail, and it will be found that they have little effect on well composted gardens while in those that are poor or inorganic, foliar feeding produces good results, because the crop is short of what the foliar feed supplies.

Comfrey Mulching

Summer cuts of comfrey are often spread between tomato rows to suppress annual weeds and release some potash as they decay, or are crushed by treading as you trim and pick. A leading exponent of this system is Mr Jack Temple of *Here's Health*, who has grown tomatoes in the same greenhouse for twenty years, using compost and comfrey alone, without steam sterilizing his soil. Part of his freedom from disease may be due to his isolation and the fact that he grows his own plants, but ample humus and balanced minerals deserve their share of the credit. Outdoor tomatoes are usually followed by November-sown broad beans, the remains of the comfrey foliage providing the potassium they need.

Comfrey is also an excellent mulch under bush fruit, especially gooseberries, and here the best value is achieved by covering the comfrey with lawn mowings after it has wilted flat to a coat of foliage 1–2in (2–5cm) thick. The mowings should be kept away from the stems of the bushes, as they can heat up to cause damage—they should make a thin coat of 'compost' which prevents the comfrey from drying out and allows it to decay as an organic potash source of special value on sandy soils.

Blackcurrants are always said to 'demand' nitrogen, just as some people demand biscuits, cakes and sweets that put up their weight, and the results are the same. It is very easy for any gardener to pile on manure and grow bushes too big for his garden. Comfrey instead of manure between the rows, with either grass mowings or straw on top is closer to a sound diet. This applies also to raspberries and red or white currants. Raspberries are very liable to mineral deficiencies caused by cutting out and taking away the fruited canes each year, which removes a far greater proportion of minerals than the pruning of any other fruit. The assorted minerals provided by comfrey are therefore as welcome as the surface coat of lawn mowings which keeps the roots cool.

Comfrey mulches should not go on before mid-April because the soil must have time to warm up first, and they should always consist of non-flowering foliage. It is a mistake to let comfrey plants run up to four or five feet high with flowers and thick, heavy stems, because they can then produce the occasional seed, and the stout stems can hold on to their moisture long enough for stray leaf buds to take root and grow. In the wrong place, comfrey is a weed. The right place for mature plants is on the compost heap, providing you have let them grow so as to give plenty of leaf rather than bulk.

Comfrey for Compost

It is often said that comfrey 'provides bulk for the compost heap', but this is exactly what it will not do, since it consists very largely of protein, carbohydrate and water. To produce one barrowload of pure comfrey compost would mean wheeling eight barrowloads of cut comfrey. The first standard 3ft (1m) heap built on the HDRA Trial Ground in 1956 was made entirely with comfrey, and it shrank to about three inches of black mess with stems in it. This was so close an imitation of cow dung that it attracted a number of the light brown flies that lay eggs in cow pats and keep the plant foods dispersed and recycled.

Comfrey should always be mixed with other materials in the compost heap, because it has such a close carbon:nitrogen ratio that the proteins break down to waste. If it is used merely as the sticks and paper for lighting bacterial bonfires, it is far more effective. Many vegan gardeners use comfrey as a compost activator because they will reject all animal matter, even household liquid activator. In fact, it possesses all the qualities of seaweed, but with less salt and a narrower range of trace elements. (Test Appendix 3h). The usual procedure is to add 3–4in (7–10cm) layers just as though the comfrey were manure, adding a scattering of old compost to provide bacteria, if the material does not include weeds with soil on their roots.

The content of dry matter was high, even though the plant foods at 31.55% were rather lower in nitrogen and potash, because the ash level was very high. Comfrey and wheat straw are both high in silica, which bulked larger and larger in the ash as the cellulose in the straw and the protein and carbohydrate in the comfrey broke down. It made a good compost, but in terms of plant foods and humus it would have been better as a surface mulch.

Comfrey in no way replaces compost, but it uses as a fertility mine and a means of exchanging crude nitrogen manure for a useful liquid feed, as well as sheet composting material and almost a vegetable manure, help gardeners to make compost go further.

5 Green Manuring, Mulching and Mounding

Weeds have been defined as 'plants in the wrong place', but there is an important difference that those who 'make friends with their weeds' rarely understand. Weeds like chickweed and groundsel are adapted to race over the bare ground, snatching the surface nitrogen before it can get away, and vast numbers of their seeds are present in every fertile soil. Both of these examples can seed when only 1in (2.5cm) high on poor soils and 'One year's weed' is quite literally the 'seven year's seed' of the old gardener's proverb.

However thick the carpet of seedlings between your unhoed rows may be, there will be still more ungerminated in the soil. The classic case is charlock, with seeds that can last a hundred years—as they demonstrated in 1941 by germinating on London bombed sites that had been farm land ninety years earlier. Organic farmers control this weed by giving up ploughing, because it brings more seeds to the surface, and arranging their cropping so that any infested field needs only surface cultivation.

Green manuring enables you to use your choice of 'weed' to grow as fast, though without storing trouble for the future, so that it can hold on to the nitrogen (fixing extra, in the case of leguminous crops), prevent other plant foods from washing out of the soil, and add energy material, both for immediate use and to be retained in the greatest quantities possible in the soil.

Mustard for Green Manure and Wireworm-Control

The green manure crop everyone knows is mustard, and seed is available relatively cheaply at any garden shop. Though it is a relation of charlock, all the seeds germinate at the same time, if they are sown on a raked level surface so that none are buried between clods to come up as 'weeds' among later seedlings. Sow thinly, aiming at 2in (5cm) between seeds, which spreads an ounce over 3–4 square yards (35g over 3–4m²); cover it with a scattering of soil, and dig it in when it looks like a thicket of slender tomato plants about 1ft (30cm) high, but always before the flowers open.

Between April and July, it is possible to snatch a green manure crop like this in four to five weeks, but mustard has the very great disadvantage of belonging to the cabbage tribe and therefore increasing clubroot. Its main garden use is in allotments and gardens newly cleared from pasture, which can be full of wireworms, the ¼–¾in (6–19mm) long, light brown, thin and leathery larvae of the click beetle (*Agriotes lineatus*), which attack many roots, but especially carrots and potatoes.

Sow thinly in July or August, ideally after turning the ground several times with a rotavator to kill out couch grass and other perennial weeds. Let the mustard grow up to even 2ft (60cm) in height, then tread down and dig it under with a sharp spade, tucking it well into the trench bottoms. Farmers who use mustard to minimize wireworm damage when potatoes must follow pasture will plough it in with headlights on their tractors if frost threatens, because frost spoils it as wireworm food.

The click beetle lays its eggs on grassland, and the larvae live between three and five years according to how well they are fed. They are small and white in their first year, when they live on decaying grass roots, but in the spring they will feed on the rotting mustard (instead of your potatoes and carrots) so greedily that they will become beetles in record time and fly away to lay eggs in other grassland. Mustard green manure can double the yield of undamaged potatoes, and as wireworm is always a pest of cleared grassland, there is no clubroot present to be increased.

Hungarian Grazing Rye

All-summer green manure crops reduce the land available for summer crops, and it is only in winter that small gardens have space to spare. Here, the best green manure is Hungarian grazing rye (the variety known to farmers as Lovazpatoni), bred to grow winter grazing in a climate colder than that of Britain.

Sow it between early August and the end of October, at the rate of 1oz a square yard (35g/m²), on ground which has been raked level, just as if you were sowing a thin lawn. Those who have difficulty in sowing as thinly as this can take out furrows 4in (10cm) apart and space the seed, like larger grass seeds, at 2in (5cm) intervals along them, which will make it go even further. By April it will be 12–18in (30–45cm) high and ready to dig or rotavate under.

Its value is greatest on sandy soils, where winter rain on ground 'left rough for the frost' can wash out plant foods faster than you can supply them. The foot (30cm) deep web of roots from each rye plant holds on to the minerals and nitrogen, and decays to leave humus in the soil, in addition to the value of the foliage. The rye will be at the high protein stage and can be followed after digging in by potatoes, or cabbage-tribe crops, without risk of nitrogen robbery.

A second crop of rye with ears like slender barley can follow the first to grow on for seed. When the ears are yellow and the lowest seeds have fallen, the crop can be harvested with shears and the seed rubbed out and stored for autumn sowing. The straw should be used for chickens or composting and only the roots dug in, if the rye is allowed to ripen.

An HDRA member, Mr H. Coaker of Torquay, used grazing rye for five years with average results. Then he tried a variation:

'This spring I used the following methods. I pulled the first 4ft (120cm) of rye up by the roots and put it at the far end of my plot. I then turned some ground rough to make a trench, and pulled up the next foot (30cm) of rye and laid it in the trench, giving it a light dusting with seaweed meal. I turned two spits along to cover the rye and make another trench and repeated the process and when I got to the end I used the rye I had taken from the front.

'I mention this as I have had amazing results this year. My sprouts are half as high again as usual and Pentland Crown potatoes yielded 2½cwt (127kg) from 64 tubers on the rye. Maris Peer gave me just over 1cwt (51kg) from 90 tubers without rye.'

The seaweed meal acted as an activator for the thin underground compost heap, and the potatoes were in a position to grab everything in the way of nitrogen and plant foods before it washed away. In Torquay, with its mild climate, the rye grew maximum bulk and Mr Coaker got his good result by using growing time and space wasted by his fellow allotment holders.

Winter Tares
The modern strain of winter tares does just as well from spring sowing, and is perhaps the best leguminous green manure crop, both fixing nitrogen and suppressing weeds, as well as holding plant foods and growing humus. Sow seeds from August until the second week in October to turn under in March or April, and between March and May to dig in during July, or whenever the buds are just showing. Those whose gardens are large enough to afford a resting plot every fifth year could sow three times, with a third sowing of tares in July to be dug under in October, in time for a fourth. A sowing of mustard against wireworm, followed by tares, is also a good policy for new gardens.

An ounce of the large seeds sows about 80ft (25g for 21m) of rows 6in (15cm) apart and 3in (7cm) between seeds, either along a furrow taken out ½in (1cm) deep with the corner of a hoe, or down holes of the same depth made along a line with the point of a dibber. Broadcasting does not pay because it is hard to hide the seeds from birds. Leave a row to seed, and cut it down when the pods are black and some are splitting. Tie the stems in bunches and hang them in a dry shed over newspaper to catch the seeds. These tares are a strain of the species *Vicia sativa* and therefore stay true, however long you keep saving your own.

Grazing rye does not appear to be attractive to rabbits and chickens dislike it, but winter tares are a rabbit's delight, so fence them in well. Some gardeners with a portable poultry fold use a sowing of tares to provide their chickens with welcome green food in the early spring when the brassicas run low.

The Tares Lawn
Where birds are a major pest and the soil is poor, winter tares can be used as a nurse crop for a lawn, just as they have been used by organic farmers to establish leys. Rake your ground level in September or early October, then sow the tares. Leave them until May or early June, when they will have grown about 18–24in (45–60cm) high, then broadcast the lawn seed over them at the standard rate, shaking the plants a bit to make sure it all falls to the ground. As soon as the seed is well up, run a rotary mower, set as high as it will go, over the tares and leave the tops where they lie, if the weather is hot and dry, as a sun shield, later taking them off for compost material. In wet summers, remove the tops immediately after cutting. With two more mowings, the grass will thicken up as the tares die out.

When any leguminous plants are mown, this reduces the carbo-hydrate building power of the leaves, so that the plant has less to 'pay' the root bacteria with, which means 'redundancies' and the release of nitrogen into the soil, giving the grass roots a tonic just when they need it. If you hoe between the rows of tares during the autumn to clear seedling weeds when they are well up, no more will be brought to the surface, and the grass will have a clear start away from weed competition and bird damage, while the tares will have helped it away by providing both shelter and free nitrogen.

The Easiest Green Manure
Those whose gardens have started with bulldozers scraping away the top soil and smearing back raw clay need humus fast, without any delay while compost matures, and (with modern house prices and moving costs) will not want the expense of buying bale after bale of peat. Their best answer is lawn mowings used as a green manure.

If the owners of new gardens can obtain a large supply of mowings from a tennis club, park or sportsground, they should spread them in a layer 3–6in (7–15cm) thick on the surface, and have it mixed into the soil 8in (20cm) deep with a rotavator. Most local papers carry advertisements from men who earn their livings with large rotavators, and they provide far better value for a new garden than having a pensioner dig slowly and expensively across it, since rotavator action mixes the mowings thoroughly into the top spit. Before having a second run-over, spread 8oz a square yard (280g/m²) of slaked lime to correct any acidity.

Mowings can be just as easily dug in by fork or spade—with a generous liming at the same time, unless they are to be followed by potatoes. It is important to dig them in fresh and not wait until they have become slippery 'silage', because the micro-organisms that heat lawn mowings are fungi which specialize in quick breakdown, with gaseous nitrogen and carbon dioxide the main end-products, so that little of lasting value is left. The advantage of mowings over green manure is that neither space nor time is spent on growing the crop, and those who have nothing to add to a poor soil can use lawn mowings as a second-best expedient.

Annual Lupin
Another good legume for green manure (though it is unfortunately hard to obtain at present) is the annual lupin (*Lupinus angustifolius*), which is very popular in South Africa and New Zealand. It carries extra-powerful symbiotic fungi in the roots which make phosphorus available from insoluble compounds, and is therefore cherished in these phosphorus-poor countries.

If you can get any, sow it between April and July, 6in (15cm) apart and 1in (2.5cm) deep. On good soil, the plants grow to a forest 3–4ft (90–120cm) high, which can kill annual weeds by light starvation, but they reach only 12in (30cm) on poor land. For maximum effect, wait till the first buds show and then dig the plants in before they flower, running the roller over them if they are too tall to tread down like mustard.

As their attractive blue flowers are followed by large, chunky pods, their seeds is easily saved from the first sowing, while stems too tough to dig in make very good compost material. Like the perennial garden lupin (*L. polyphyllus*), they contain an alkaloid that is poisonous to stock and gives them immunity from rabbits. There is a white flowered variety (*L. albus*), as well as a blue and white species (*L. hartwegii*) grown as a hardy annual, but neither produces as much bulk as the green manure kind. There are sweet lupins grown for stock feed that have no alkaloid, but these usually need a different root bacterium from the one, found everywhere, that serves our clovers. There is unfortunately no crop that is poisonous to rabbits—if it is bad for them they ignore it.

Buckwheat

Buckwheat (*Fagopyrum esculentum*), a member of the Polygonum family, does not fix nitrogen, but nor does it encourage clubroot. It is one of the best of all weed suppressors and thrives on a heavy clay soil. Sow the large seeds, which look like tiny road flints, at 3in (7cm) intervals in furrows 8in (20cm) apart, so that one ounce is enough for one hundred feet (25g for 27m) of row. Sow them too thickly, and they cramp each other. Buckwheat can be sown any time between April and July. It flowers over a long period, with feathery white blooms attractive to both bees and hoverflies.

Of the 250 species of hoverfly in the British Isles, 38 have larvae which eat aphids, though the adults feed on nectar and pollen. Their short tongues restrict them to flowers with easy access, and buckwheat comes second in popularity to *Convolvulus tricolor*, the easy annual bush species. Fruit growers could well sow a strip of buckwheat in an orchard to attract *Syrphus balteatus*, whose slug-like larvae will root out the larvae of American blight (*Eriosoma lanigerum*). The seeds, which ripen over a long period, are also attractive to pheasants.

Crush your buckwheat with a roller, or tread it down, while the leaves are green and flourishing—yellowing leaves are a sign that it is getting on the stemmy side. Some gardeners solve the problem by sowing lupins for nitrogen and buckwheat for bulk in alternate rows, and others follow Mr Coaker's trick with rye, trenching them in with seaweed meal or dried sludge, which is harder work but rewarding. But, like other weed suppressors, buckwheat and lupins fail to crowd out such perennial weeds as creeping buttercup, spear thistle or docks.

Tagetes for Weed and Nematode Control

However, there is a plant that can be effective against some perennial weeds (though it is a producer of compost material rather than green manure). This is *Tagetes minuta*, named by Linnaeus from the small size of its star-shaped flowers, not entirely appropriately, for it grows 4–10ft (1.2–3m) high. The full story of the development of this crop, whose root secretions appear to kill potato and other eelworms, will be found in *The Tagetes Effect*, a translation of the original work at Wageningen Research Station in Holland, and *The 1961 Tagetes Experiment* (both available from HDRA).

This plant is one of the 32 species of *Tagetes* of which only three are in cultivation, *T. erecta* (the African marigold), *T. patula* (the French marigold), and the edging species *T. tenuifolia*. Though it is also a composite (like 13,000 other species), it is not a close relative of *Calendula officinalis*, the Pot marigold, and confusion has been caused by writers who are concerned with herbs and 'plant affinities' and use popular names without botanical knowledge.

The root secretions of *Tagetes* are still under investigation, but it produces five, and though all of them have been given highly complex names, it is not yet certain which of them perform which functions. They are thiophenes, substances containing sulphur, also found in crude oil wastes from the plants of the past. It has long been known that plants have 'affinities', that is, some grow well after other kinds, or in the same bed with them. We now know that they also have antagonisms, and that some can defend themselves against underground enemies. For example, a weed with the charming name of Gold of Pleasure (*Camelina sativa*), a relation of charlock, has an antagonism to flax and can destroy quite a patch of the crop round itself.

Tagetes has some very powerful antagonisms, first, to ground elder or gout weed (so called because the Romans introduced it as a cure for gout), second, to convolvulus (both *C. sepium* and *C. minor*) and, third, to couch grass, also known as twitch (*Agropyrum repens*).

Clear the weeds as you always do, removing as much as possible of the foliage and roots, and rake down for a seed bed in April, then sow *Tagetes* in furrows ½in (10mm) deep and 1ft (30cm) apart, thinly like carrot seed, which it much resembles. It can also be broadcast like seed for a thin lawn and, on poor soil, can be covered down with dried sludge. The most certain method is to sow in a frame or greenhouse in early March (or February, with heat) and prick the seedlings out into boxes, as with its relation, the French marigold, to plant 1ft (30cm) apart in early May.

The plants will grow fast as the weather warms, swamping the weeds with the stealthy, silent speed of milk boiling over. From the experiences of some 700 experimenters, it should be said that when *Tagetes* grows to 6ft (2m) or more high it produces a complete kill of ground elder, convolvulus and couch grass, and also has a certain soil-conditioning effect on heavy clay, which it reduces to a powdery structure around the roots. It has been grown as a hedge to keep weeds from encroaching from a derelict garden next door, and is safe between trees and shrubs, provided these leave moisture enough for it to grow. Because of its size, any plants, especially bush fruit, will suffer from the smothering if it is sown or transplanted between them. Trees and shrubs will not be harmed by its secretions, but bushes such as blackcurrants will never gather enough speed to overcome an interplanting of *Tagetes* seedlings.

In late October, or even November, cut down the giant stems with secateurs and hammer them on a hard surface, like brussels sprout stalks, for compost. They can also be cut 6in (15cm) above ground level, when they are 4ft (120cm) high, to branch and produce more, but slimmer, compost material. If the bed is required, dig out the roots, shaking off most of the soil before composting. It is easier to leave them until the spring, when they will break up easily. *T. minuta* is a half hardy annual, and does not flower until October, which is too late to set seed in the British climate, though in Australia, South Africa and Rhodesia it is a serious problem, because its small, light seed spreads fast.

The procedure is exactly the same when *Tagetes* is grown against nematodes and, many years of experiments have shown that if you plant *T. minuta* your count of viable potato eelworm cysts goes down. The number also decreases if you plant ordinary French marigolds, and if you rest the ground under another crop there is a smaller fall. Plant potatoes, of course, and it goes shooting up. The natural wastage of potato eelworm cysts in the absence of a crop they can attack is about 17%, while after Tagetes the average fall is 55%.[1]

Potato eelworms, *Heterodera rostochiensis* and *H. pallida*, are more common in gardens than gardeners realize, and the symptoms of small, pale leaves, stunted growth and tiny tubers are often put down to other causes. As a further complication, each species contains a number of sub-types, each given an identifying letter. The female eelworms, swollen into cysts, are small, dull white spheres, about the size of pinheads, on roots and tubers. The first answer should always be to try the resistant cultivars Maris Piper (maincrop) and Pentland Meteor or Pentland Lustre (earlies). These resist *H. rostochiensis* pathotype A, but succumb to *H. pallida* pathotype E, so that it is worth trying to establish your eelworm type. Then grow *Tagetes minuta*, and if your plants grow over 7ft (2m) high there will be a useful kill, even if it takes several years to clear the bed.

'Rose sickness', where roses have been grown for many years in the same soil, is caused by several non-cyst-forming or migratory eelworms, of which *Pratylenchus pratensis*[2] is the most common.

Because they do not have the protection of a chemical-proof coat, they are more easily destroyed, and ordinary French marigolds bedded out between the roses, or planted after their removal, are effective. The best varieties appear to be Harmony and Golden Ball.

The main problem of *Tagetes minuta* is that no seedsman can grow a really reliable stock, for it is illegal to cultivate the species in countries where it thrives. The Henry Doubleday Research Association relies for seeds on members in Australia and South Africa, who collect it as English members might go out and gather thistledown. In many parts of Africa it is used to repel fleas, and the foliage contains an essential oil smelling rather like antiseptic. It also contains an alkaloid similar to that in the safe pesticide, pyrethrum, but one that is less stable and in far greater quantity, for it is only necessary to compare the small flowers of *Chrysanthemum cinerariaefolium*, which grows mostly in Kenya, with a bed of *T. minuta* taller than a man, to see how much could be extracted once we found the way.

Most of the green manure seeds and those of *T. minuta* are available from the Association.

Mulching

A mulch is a material spread on the surface to suppress weeds, retain moisture and provide humus and plant foods as it decays on the surface and is taken under by earthworms. The school of organic gardeners known as 'no diggers' contend that Nature does not dig, but spreads all organic material on the surface for recycling. These who do not belong to this group argue that Nature does not make compost either—like cheese, beer and wholemeal bread, it is a relatively recent invention in the field of applied biology, and no less 'natural' than making fire or flint axes.

Like the argument about the different merits of veganic compost, made purely of plant-derived materials, and the standard kind, this does not matter. There is no such real division between the various schools of organic gardening as there is between the organic and the inorganic. They are merely different ways of doing the same thing, and there are many knowledgeable and successful gardeners who never dig, just as there are others who take an aesthetic pleasure in wielding their shining spades with virtuosity.

If your compost is never very good, and you always have a crop of seedling weeds after putting it on, then you cannot use it as a weed supressing mulch and you would do better to dig it in. If your garden is infested with perennial weeds, especially convolvulus, docks and horse-tail (*Equisetum arvense*) do not become a no-digger until you have dug every fragment of root from your garden because, however thick your mulch, the weeds will come through it.

The essential is a good supply of a mulching material, either compost, peat or some other source, to build up a capital of humus on the surface. Though you will cut out digging, gardeners spend a relatively short time on this job, and you may well spend more on gathering compost material and turning the heap, so that there is no large saving in time, but you will gain by cutting out a heavy job, especially on clay. Hoeing, efficiently and in good time, is always the best weedkiller, and as you kill out crop after crop of seedlings you gradually get rid of all the seeds in the top inch (2.5cm) of soil. Without any digging, you bring no more seeds to the surface, and in theory, your garden should be free of weeds, apart from those blowing in from your neighbour's.

Green Manuring without Digging
Just before you are ready to plant potatoes, mow your winter tares and either rake the mowings up for compost or leave them on the surface. Set the seed tubers at standard spacing and place a good forkful of manure or compost over each. Then cover them 6in (15cm) deep with partly decayed straw, which you can prepare by stacking the bales in the open with 2in (5cm) gaps between each, hosing them well, and leaving them until they are rotting and brown in the centre. Straw stacked soon after the harvest will be usefully rotted by spring. The best bales for mulching are the ones that have already spent a year as the sides and ends of a compost heap, and therefore need no stacking.

On top of the straw, pile at least 3in (7cm) of grass mowings, adding a second layer if enough are available. If ordinary fresh baled straw were used, the potatoes would grow through it, expanding against the area of least resistance, rather than push down into the firm soil below, and over half the crop would be green from exposure to light (and therefore poisonous to many people because of the presence of the alkaloid solanine). Partly rotted straw binds together, and with the mowings on top, forms a light-excluding coat that decays slowly.

At lifting time, the layers of straw, grass and manure can be turned back and the potatoes removed, clean, white and with very little scab, because the spores will be under the soil surface, and the 'flat compost heap' you have made is entirely acid. Take care to extract all the potatoes, so that the bed will be ready for the cabbage tribe to follow first the earlies, then the second earlies, and finally the maincrops, planted straight through the remains of the mulch with a dibber.

This system has also been used as a method of eelworm control, with three or four thicknesses of newspaper on the soil surface to keep the roots out of danger. In theory, the eelworms stay in their cysts and die out year by year, while the gardener plants potatoes in rotation round the allotment or garden, taking a heavy dressing of compost as a bonus. In some seasons, the straw decays poorly, and then it is best to chop it up with a rotary lawnmower. Mice can give trouble by sheltering in the straw and eating both seed and crop, while birds may scratch the straw until it blows round the garden. A narrow strip of small-mesh wire netting staked around the bed is the best answer, but ample mowings also defeat birds.

Both brussels sprouts and broccoli, which need firm soil, do very well on this system; so do leeks and broad beans, simply pushed down into the decayed mulch in November. Digging up leeks is not easy for those who wish to keep all weed seeds under the surface, but if the plants are dropped down dibber holes a mere 3in (7cm) deep and watered in, they will grow just as well as any others and can be extracted with very minor fork disturbance. They will of course have only a small portion of blanched white stem, but the grey-green leaves are the best part, and contain far more vitamins A and C than the stem, which is all that greengrocers usually sell. In parts of Belgium, where the water table is so high that most vegetables are grown in raised beds, leeks are always grown this way and sold with the leaves shortened to about 8in (20cm) long, for eating as an onion flavoured leaf vegetable.

Mulching Materials

Straw is used only because it is available. Hay is far better, but so little is made today in this country that the 'spoilt hay' advocated by Ruth Stout, the pioneer 'No-Work' gardener in America, is not obtainable. Or rather, even if it has become 'spoilt', British farmers ask the same high price for it. In analysis it is far richer than wheat straw, and it binds down well on the soil, so that there is no risk of its being spread all round the garden by wind and birds, or drying out and excluding the moisture. It decays readily and, while it is attractive to slugs, does not delight them like slippery lawn mowings. California has more organic gardeners and fewer slugs than any part of the USA, and even Oregon and Pennsylvania, whose climate most resembles that of Britain, rank far below British gardens for slug levels. In the USA, snails are reputed to take fifteen days to crawl a mile, while slugs can whizz down the course in three, with those from Texas faster still.

It would be possible for any gardener to make hay good enough for mulching by mowing an area of rough grass when it had reached 10–12in (25–30cm) high, leaving it for a day, then raking to turn it and raking it all up about 48 hours later (or when it was dry). Anyone who could stage a hay-making party for fun might well profit with a useful stack. The 'Salt hay' referred to in American organic gardening books is simply hay cut on salt marshes, which used to be sold under that name in New York and other east coast cities to 'power' the horses, as Essex hay fed horses in the London of Sherlock Holmes.

The problem of all mulching materials is that the cost of transporting them remains just as high, however poor they may be in added fertility. Hay and straw bales are valuable in terms of fertility, but unless you are very near the source of something a manufacturer really wants to get rid of you are not likely to find bargains today, and your cheapest mulches will always be home made.

Close-Ratio Mulches
There are three types of mulching material, close-ratio, weed killing, and wide-ratio. Close-ratio materials either have proportions of carbon and nitrogen that are near enough to the 10:1 of a fertile soil to cause no nitrogen robbery if they are accidentally dug in, and decay easily on the surface to provide humus and release plant foods, or have their carbon compounds locked up so they are still entirely safe; lawnmowings are an example of the first type, peat and leaf-mould of the second.

Weedkilling mulches such as newspaper and black plastic, which are merely used to exclude light and kill weeds, make no contribution to soil fertility, though they do conserve moisture and destroy a number of awkward weeds without the use of chemical killers or hours of digging and picking out hated root fragments by hand.

Among the wide-ratio mulches, sawdust will reduce a garden to a disaster area if it is dug in. But if they are employed with care, wide-ratio mulches can provide a use for quantities of by-products that could not otherwise be composted for humus and plant foods. They compost themselves slowly on the surface, where they have access to unlimited oxygen in the air for 'burning' their surplus carbon, and return the minerals their deep roots once gathered to circulation in the soil.

This system is popular in warm climates, where the breakdown becomes quicker as the conditions more nearly resemble those of the Amazon. Unfortunately, it is written about more often than it is successfully practised, because so many organic books are written in America and then copied without editing to suit a temperate climate. Conditions in the Southern States approach those in South Africa, where compost heaps as we know them often fail because they break down too fast and too far.

The other problem, in Britain, is that gardeners have to compete with industry for raw materials. Sawdust is used in making up hardboard for building, on butcher's shop floors and, even if it comes from small woodworking factories, goes for stable litter, or for burning. Materials like coffee grounds from instant coffee factories go into cattle cake instead of the oil seed residues that once made good organic fertilizers, while municipal compost (made from dustbin refuse and sewage sludge) is being phased out all over Britain, because of well exploited fears of toxic metal contamination and pathogenic nematode eggs, as well as the very real problem of tattered fragments of plastic bags and nylon tights which would blow round the garden. The cost of loading and hauling a ten-ton lorry of something doubtful is very little less than that of carting a full load of farmyard manure. Baled peat, dry, weedfree, and delivered, may be more expensive, but you do not have to take a full load to bring the cost down and wheel it in from the road.

The easiest mulch of all is lawn mowings, but the average garden, with a small lawn in front and one at the back to take dripping water from the clothes-line, tumbling toddlers, and deck chairs on summer evenings, will only have enough to go between the raspberry canes, with perhaps a little to spare for the compost heap. The organic gardener needs more, and should therefore encourage neighbours to keep up their lawns, and collect their surplus mowings, as well as chasing up parks, schools, tennis clubs and sports grounds.

Early mowings go in potato trenches, a regular supply adds quick heating material to a mixed compost heap—with up to 25% mowings an ideal proportion—and they can also be used to speed up the decay of dead leaves into leaf-mould, as described in Chapter 6. With or without comfrey underneath, lawn mowings are the perfect mulch for bush fruit. If the lawn is mowed every two or three weeks, there is only a small risk that grass seeds carried across in the mowings will germinate and cover the ground between the raspberries. If seed does germinate, it is easy to dig out the tufts, once the humus from the sowings has built up after a few seasons.

All bush fruits are shallow rooters, and therefore gain from a mulch of mowings put on at least every three years, in April when the soil has warmed. Fork the mulch under in October after pruning, but shallowly, make the most of another special advantage. The grubs of the raspberry beetle (*Byturus norvicus*) drop from the fruit and pupate in the soil round the canes, but they tend to penetrate only just below the real soil surface, having burrowed through the soft mowings first. This keeps most of them in the shallow forked soil, where the robins which are always on the watch when digging is in progress can peck them up. Robins are specialized to eat small soil life, and their black, beady, experienced eyes recognize what we would take for small stones as the pupae of many pests. Missing the value of the robin as a pest controller is one of the disadvantages of the no-digging system.

Do not pile the grass cuttings so that they touch the stems of any bush fruit, and do not use them between such seedlings as lettuces, carrots or beetroot, because decaying mowings harbour slugs. Mowings can be spread thinly between carrots at fortnightly intervals in summer to provide a hay smell as a repellent for carrot fly. This, like all scent repellents, baffles distant pests but is ineffective against the brutes that hatch next door and use their marvellously well-adapted compound eyes to home in on your carrots. Still, this trick is better than nothing, and is cheaper and easier than most carrot fly controls, whether organic or inorganic.

Mowings are not a no-digger's mulch. They go well on top of a really thick coat of manure and straw over the potatoes, but in the later stages of rotation, cabbages and their kindred do better with leaf-mould, followed by peat for the legumes and compost for root crops. As the soil builds up humus, it will be possible, even on sands, to skip a surface coat at intervals, cutting out the peat, for choice, as it has to be bought.

Leaf-mould is an excellent surface mulch, but must be well broken down, for if it is only the harvest of the previous autumn, the leaves, still almost intact, will dry, disengage themselves from the sticky pile, and scamper round the garden in every breeze. Leaf-mould that has rotted down small can be taken under by worms and presents less sail area to the wind. It is also excellent as a weed suppressor between herbaceous plants, as it is less attractive to slugs than either compost or mowings.

Peat is best value when bought in bales, which should be chopped fine with a spade, hosed well, shovelled about, then hosed again, and left for the water to soak in, before it is spread in a layer about

2in (5cm) thick. The difficulty with peat is that the surface layers dry out in summer winds and take up air. When it does rains in a dry season, the moisture stays on the outside and dries off again without ever reaching the soil. There is a grade of moist, black peat that is sold in polythene bags and does not have this disadvantage, but when you buy it you are paying for the additional water.

Since both peat and leaf-mould have their plant foods locked up by tannins, it is important, if either is used exclusively, to scatter at least 2oz a square yard ($35g/m^2$) of fish meal, or blood, fish and bone meal—which has the advantage of not containing a potassium chemical fertilizer. In some areas, only '10% potash fishmeal' can be obtained. However, no fish that swims contains as much potassium: obviously added chemical fertilizer has pushed it up to this level.

Coffee Grounds and Spent Hops
Though industrial waste products are hard to find, the rise of instant coffee, even instant dandelion coffee, has made coffee wastes a possibility, as are spent hops. Both are worth exploring in case there is a local factory that is not yet selling its whole output for stock feed or as a filler for something unexpected.

	Moisture %	Ash %	N %	P %	K %
Coffee Grounds (USA)	62.9	0.5	1.84	0.03	0.12
Coffee Grounds (Britain)			2.69	0.30	0.95
Meadow Hay	15,0	6.2	1.50	1.40	1.60
Spent Hops	79.1	4.4	2.13	0.66	0.42

Analysis of wastes for mulches

The wide contrast between British and American grounds arose because the British sample came from Lyons Coffee Extract factory and consisted largely of chicory root, which is rich in minerals. (The large, white top roots of this crop can go three feet deep in the subsoil.) As coffee prices rise, more chicory will be used, and coffee waste will become better value—if you can get it.

Spread the grounds 2in (5cm) thick on the surface, where they are rather less attractive to slugs than lawn mowings and, though they do dry out, less inclined to exclude rain than peat, also breaking down rather more quickly. Never use coffee grounds thicker than 4in (10cm), or they can cake and exclude air. They have been layered 1½in (4cm) thick in compost heaps, but should not add up to more than 20% of the material, because they can block the air supply. If you have to take a full load, stack it to decay of its own accord for three years, when it will become a fine black compost of good quality, which can be used on the surface at any time, and is especially attractive to worms.

Spent hops are also excellent if they can be obtained from a brewery, and can be applied as thick as 4in (10cm) on the surface in the autumn to reduce the loss of plant foods from sandy soils, decaying slowly on the surface through the winter. They can also be used in 2in (5cm) layers between crops right through the season. The dried flowers of the hop plant are sufficiently thin to decay and release their nitrogen, instead of holding on to it as sawdust does. They decay fairly quickly, and again, if a full load has to be taken, stack them (if possible) with equal parts of lawn mowings or mixed vegetable wastes, plus a scattering of old compost and 4oz a square yard (150g/m²) of slaked lime at every foot (30cm) of depth. A carpet covered compost heap stacked around upright poles, that are afterwards withdrawn for better ventilation along the air control, would be ideal. Failing this, just provide the lime scattering and leave the heap to decay slowly for use as a mulching material. As spent hops vary in moisture content, hose the heap if it appears to be dry.

The analysis table shows that hay, even of poor quality is the best value of all, and home-made hay for no-digging potatoes is well worth the trouble of making.

Anti-weed Mulching

The easiest mulch to use against such weeds as creeping buttercups between bush fruit is newspapers. The more serious British newspapers are the best because they are large and their paper is of excellent quality to stand up to sun, wind and rain.

Wait till the weeds are growing well, run a rough grass cutter over them, rake off the cuttings for compost, then spread your papers eight to ten pages thick, opened out and overlapping each other all round by about 3in (15cm), and set a line of stones along each overlap. The object is to have them dead flat and held down in plenty of places so that there is no way for the wind to get under and tear them apart. They kill by excluding light. For this reason, clear plastic sheet is useless as an anti-weed mulch, and so are opened out plastic fertilizer bags, if they have a white background, although the aluminium-coloured bags are good (especially if there are enough to allow two or three thicknesses). Black polythene is excellent, but in large strips it still needs weighing down with stones, bricks and stakes, for once the wind gets under it the sheet can thunder and tear away like the topsails of a windjammer rounding Cape Horn.

Exclusion of light kills any weeds that are growing. But those which have deep roots and those designed to store energy, like lesser celandine (*Ranunculus ficaria*), wood sorrel, horsetail, convolvulus and comfrey can store themselves as if they were potatoes in a clamp. When the papers start to break up, yellowed with sunlight and sodden with rain· by their second spring, remove them for composting in a mixed heap, and replace them. The seeds in the soil will be lying dormant, like the charlock and another season under paper or polythene will kill out many more by bad storage conditions.

This method cannot be expected to kill weeds close round the raspberry canes, but it will reduce the solid carpet to something manageable. The canes themselves will keep on growing, and will not suffer from drought under either newspaper or black polythene, which will remain damp underneath from the condensation.

Black polythene is also used for suppressing grass and other weeds around willow cuttings, which are planted in holes made by driving a crowbar through the stretched sheet. There are gardeners who use black polythene with slits for planting seed potatoes, so that the haulm grows through the hole, and the tubers stay on the surface. This no-digging method may offer chances of publicity on television or radio, or in the press but it does not supply any fertility to the soil. The problem of all polythene mulches is that they attract such quantities of slugs to enjoy the moisture and feast on the decayed remains of slaughtered weeds.

Sawdust Mulching

Sawdust is the mulching material with the widest carbon:nitrogen ratio, and in Britain there is less to be gained from shielding the soil from the hammering of rain, or baking by strong sunlight than there is in countries with harder climates. Sawdust was first popularized as a mulch by the late F. C. King of Levens Hall, one of the many head gardeners more famous than their employers.

Because sawdust is always the result of sawing up trunk wood, not twigs, it is always low in potassium, as in the table.

The only materials that sawdust leaves behind in quantity are some of the lignins, which darken the colour of the soil and lighten its texture, though some of the plant foods are released as the celluloses break down. As regards their contribution to fertility,

	Moisture %	Ash %	N %	P %	K %
Oak Sawdust (Fresh)	45.6	2.1	0.12	0.002	0.12
Poplar Sawdust (Fresh)	43.5	2.5	0.13	0.001	0.15

Analysis of sawdust

sawdust or shavings give the best value in the deeplitter poultry house, using up the energy in their wide carbon:nitrogen ratio of 500:1, which falls only to 200:1 even after stacking for five years, when they will have rot down to a cocoa brown colour.

There are good gardeners who have use sawdust mulching successfully. One was Mr Victor Leroux of the HDRA Committee and the Soil Association Middlesex Group, who carried out a trial over a ten-year period, including carbon:nitrogen ratio testing and soil analysis (see Appendix 3i).

The problem of using sawdust or shavings as a weedkilling mulch is that all the worst weeds grow through it, leaving the gardener with the task of clearing away the sawdust and digging them out. Both have been used for making paths, confined by boards along the sides, and the small quantities of sawdust trodden on the beds do no harm. Shavings, especially as stable manure shavings, make rather better paths, but neither will decay enough to be dug in; both must stay on the surface.

Mounding

This is a new German system of composting, which began with the work of Alwyn Siefert, inventor of a compost heap based on layers of soil, which he called 'The Artificial Earthworm', for it broke down organic matter into humus and plant foods without wasting any vegetable matter on producing heat, just as earthworms do.

The theory behind this system is that Sir Albert Howard was on the wrong track for Europe and other temperate climates. Sir Albert was concerned to secure high temperatures, because he was dealing with human wastes as activators and aimed to destroy the eggs and cysts of tapeworms, hookworms and other tropical pathogens. In Europe, such heat is not needed, and it would be better to conserve compost material to produce more from small city gardens. Experiments on the HDRA Trial Ground, and Members, are proceeding and it remains to be seen whether the method can be established as worthwhile in terms of yield of vegetables for the time and trouble involved.

The following account was written by Mrs Jean Bollkaemper, one of the HDRA's German members, and appeared in Newsletter No. 76:

Advantages

Can save space (town gardens). Hot-bed effect can give increased yields per unit area. Uses up all garden rubbish. Eliminates some bending work. Simplifies watering. Applied ideally in a 4-year rotation, with one new mound—preferably running North/South —built each autumn as a special form of compost heap.

Construction

1) Dig out a shallow depression 5–6ft (1.5–2m) wide; length depends on space and materials available. If building on grass, remove turves first and incorporate them later upside down above or below autumn leaves. Earth removed must suffice for a 2½in (6mm) layer over whole mound finally.

2) Build mound roughly as sketched, not too loosely, and with material slightly moist. Sequence of layers is more important than their individual thickness, but there must be enough reasonably fresh compostable material mixed, e.g. with lawn mowings, to rot down, giving a hot bed effect, in the top layer beneath the soil. 'Inoculation' with comfrey, seaweed, chicken or other manure helps. Sides should slope not more steeply than 40°.

3) Surround for treading, placed where shown, is most useful. Strong stakes can be put in from top next to channel if tomatoes, for example, are to be grown.

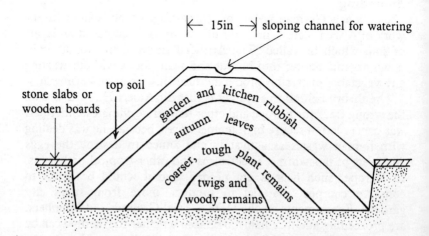

Cross-section of mound showing construction

4) Important: top of mound must be flattened off and 'gutter' must slope, preferably North/South to permit watering by hosepipe trickle, not any surface sprinkling.

5) Earth is kept loose by suitable small hand tool(s), such as a 'scratcher', to minimize water loss. Only a minimum of hand weeding is needed if suitable mixtures of crops for interplanting are grown.

6) Seeds are sown in parallel 'contours' round the mound, sun-lovers at the top, moisture-lovers near bottom. Along one row early crops (e.g. kohlrabi) and late (e.g. savoys) can alternate to use space optimally. Or try sequences such as early lettuces on top, followed by tomatoes. Plenty of chance to experiment with combinations of your own.

'In a four-course rotation, crops needing such nourishment as brassicas are best the first year, legumes second and potatoes the fourth, when the mound has flattened down.
One example:

Year 1
Top: radishes and early lettuce, then tomatoes.
Next: a contour of onion sets.
Lower still: spinach, then cucumbers.
Bottom row(s): cabbage tribe.

Year 2
Top: peas, then remontant strawberries.
Next: Onion sets.
Then: carrots (or these can alternate in same contour).
Next: dwarf beans, then remontant strawberries.
Bottom: broad beans.
Suitably mulched with garden remains, leaves, etc., strawberries stay in throughout.

Year 3
Spreading to cover mound. Harvest lengthened by plastic tunnel. Strawberries then removed, any unrotted remains in mound likewise. Flattened bed can temporarily receive earth waiting to cover this year's new mound (built on another plot), then be used for early crops before.

Year 4
Chitted potatoes are planted on flattish surface.'

This system does not abandon the spade, but involves the very hard work of making the mounds every four years. It replaces the hoe with hand weeding and very close planting to suppress weeds and grow more from less space. The question is whether the advantages of using material otherwise difficult to compost, which decays slowly without much heat in the mound, will keep up the supply of plant foods and humus to last four years. Basically it is an attempt to combine the garden with the compost heap, and the furrow along the top is very important, because it collects the water which soaks down inside, rather than being shed down the sides as from a house roof.

Chapter 3

1. LONG, D. B. *Selective Weedkiller Toxicity in Barley Straw* HDRA 1969

2. *The Complete Book of Composting* Rodale Press, Inc. Emmaus, Pennsylvania 1960

3. 'Dusty Answer' HDRA *Newsletter* No. 52 February 1973

4. HOWARD, Albert *An Agricultural Testament* Oxford University Press 1940

Chapter 4

1. HILLS, L. D. *Comfrey—Its Past, Present and Future* Faber & Faber 1976

Chapter 5

1. HUXLEY, Anthony *Plant and Planet* Allan Lane 1974 pp.333–335

2. OOSTERBRINK, H., KNIPER, K., and JACOB, J. J. S. *The Tagetes Effect* (translation) HDRA 1958
   The 1961 Tagetes Experiment HDRA 1962

6 Leaf-Mould, Peat and Mushroom Compost

Leaf-mould, peat and mushroom compost are not manures, because they contain a comparatively low level of plant foods and these are not easily available to crops or soil bacteria; they lack the tonic effect of good manure or compost which has its nutrients in forms that are ready for rapid recycling in the soil. They are usually classed as 'bulky manures', like wool shoddy (which does, however, release its generous supply of nitrogen readily, once it begins to break down).

All three supply the mechanical qualities of humus—making clays more easily dug, and holding moisture on sands—but leaf-mould is by far the most important, not only because it lasts longer in the soil, but for its eventually released plant foods. Above all, there is plenty available, so that we can use enough in our gardens to make a real difference to our soils, especially if we can reach out and gather the harvest of wasted humus from the street trees in every city.

Almost every garden large enough to employ a gardener will have well-matured leaf-mould from leaves swept off the lawns. But these are rarely used. Modern gardeners insist, quite correctly, that baled peat is free from weed seeds and disease. So, too, is leaf-mould. The difference lies in the fact that Nature does not advertise, and things that are free employ no public relations officers. So, today, autumn means the smell of burning leaves as we send our humus up in smoke and then buy peat to replace the wealth we have squandered.

The billowing clouds of bonfire smoke leaning away on the wind from almost every suburban garden are turning fertility into pollution. According to Professor F. C. Pybus, bonfire smoke contains about 350 times as much carcinogen as cigarette smoke.[1] Though we do not inhale the smoke to the same extent, our bonfires can make our neighbours' lives a misery, and are actively harmful to any emphysema, asthma or lung cancer cases who may live nearby.

Many years ago, Professor Pybus made a donation of £500 to the Henry Doubleday Research Association to pay for printing the leaflet on composting garden rubbish and making leaf-mould from dead leaves, *Give up Smoking Bonfires*. Designed to fold into a rate demand, this was given free to Councils, as well as gardeners who sent in for it. The Ministry of Health for Northern Ireland recommended all their Medical officers to ask for the leaflet as the only measure against air pollution that cost the ratepayers nothing. After distribution of half a million copies, only shortage of funds and the rising cost of printing ended the HDRA attempt to send the leaflet through every letterbox in Britain. An enlarged version is now sold to the many Councils and individuals who still apply for thousands every year at a price that covers the cost.

The only rubbish that should be burnt is rose cuttings (the thorns do not decay and retain their sharpness in the compost), tree, bush fruit and shrub prunings, yew or cypress hedge trimmings, and thick branches of any kind.

Street Tree Leaves

There is a legend that only oak and beech leaves make good leaf-mould. This began because the only leaf-mould that the head gardeners of the past would *buy* was the very best for special beds and potting soils. For everyday uses, such as digging into herbaceous borders and between shrubs, they saved the leaves that were swept from under every tree on every lawn in the great gardens of the past. They used peat only for rhododendrons, ferns, orchids and other plants that preferred it, for in those days every head gardener was a Mrs Beeton of the potting shed.

Leaves from oak and beech are richest in the tannins that preserve the plant foods (just as it is the tannin that makes old boots go three times through the compost heap before they decay). On sandy soils, mould from these leaves lasts longest of all, but as leaf-mould breaks down it releases its plant foods, so, provided we make and use plenty from the constant supply that is renewed every autumn, there is no need to rob oak and beech woods of the annual dressing that they have given themselves every autumn since these trees began.

There is a carefully fostered legend that plane and chestnut leaves are 'poisonous'. But there are no leaves or plants which are poisonous in leaf-mould or compost heaps. These two are simply the slowest of all to break down. They should therefore be stacked on their own in one of the systems described later.

A more modern fear is that street tree leaves will be contaminated with lead from petrol fumes. However, lead stays near to the ground in towns, especially at traffic lights, and is more likely to endanger dogs at pavement level and babies in prams. As well as providing oxygen and consuming carbon dioxide, town trees act as pollution filters, taking from the air 2–3 tonnes an acre of lead, rubber dust from worn tyres, asbestos from brake linings, sulphur from power stations, and smoke in London, New York or any other large city, and letting the rain wash these substances off their leaves and down the gutters with the storm-water, either into a river or to the sewage works. The leaves that we can gather for garden uses remain only briefly at ground level before they are swept up, and absorb little pollution. Our bodies absorb only 15% of the lead taken in by mouth, and the quantity that would be taken up from urban leaf-mould used on our vegetables would be infinitesimal. City dwellers are in more danger than their trees, for we absorb 70% of what we breathe, and there is nothing to wash the lead from petrol off the hundred square yards of lung surface in every adult.[2]

The usual procedure for importing leaves is to bribe the roadman who sweeps your street to empty his barrow in your garden, or the men who drive the Council lorry taking leaves to the refuse tip to dump their load by your gate. It would be far better to write to your local paper in August insisting on the right of ratepayers to share the street tree leaves, instead of having them burnt at their expense. Suggest that gardeners requiring full loads, or even plastic bags full, should leave their names and addresses at the Town Hall and pay a small charge. As leaves must be swept up, anyway, and taken somewhere at a cost to the ratepayers, reducing the distance they have to travel should contribute towards the cost of the scheme.

The only city in the Commonwealth that makes municipal leaf-mould is Toronto, but several in the USA put their dead leaves through large compost shredders and sell them direct to the public after only six months in the stack (few town areas have the space to allow leaf-mould to mature slowly in heaps) at a better price than any composted dustbin refuse.

Leaf-Mould Making

The site for a leaf-mould heap can be in dry shade under trees, next to a high wall, or anywhere with room for it to decay for at least one year, ideally two. Kew Gardens have stacks of vintage leaf-mould behind some of the green gates marked 'Private', for it improves with age. Level off the ground, drive in stout posts at the corners with extra posts every four feet and staple 1½in (40mm) mesh wire netting around them to contain the leaves. Because they will be packed firmly enough by their second autumn not to blow round the garden, the wire can then be unhooked, the posts (which should be well creosoted) dug out, and the enclosure removed to take next autumn's leaves.

Pile them in just as they are gathered, removing dead branches and paper litter if they are swept from the street. Hose the heap once or twice during the first summer, because it can get too dry.

Never include weeds or garden rubbish in the leaf stack, or dead leaves in compost; mould and compost making are entirely separate processes. The decay of leaf-mould is carried out, without the need for oxygen by fungi whose spores are present on all dead leaves, just as the bloom on a grape holds the yeasts that make wine. It is a process of acid decomposition that involves little heating because the leaves contain hardly any carbohydrate as fuel. Any weed seeds in the stack will therefore remain undestroyed, while leaves in a compost heap will have too little time to complete their own slow decay.

A small degree of heat is produced in the process, especially from the first leaves to fall, but they must decay in their own good time. Five cubic yards (3.8m³) of leaves as swept stack to three (2.3m³) with treading, and will decay by the autumn to two cubic yards (1.5³) or roughly a tonne. If the leaves are plane or horse chestnut, both of which decay slowly, first spread them on the lawn or any other flat surface and run a rotary mower at them repeatedly—the cheapest way to shred them and sweep them up for stacking. Where leaves fall or blow on mown grass under fruit trees, run the rotary mower over them anyway, so that the worms can take the shredded leaves right under, instead of just pulling the stalks down. More than 90% of apple and pear scab spores over-winter on fallen leaves, and if these are shredded the spores give the worms the equivalent of a breakfast of mushrooms on toast. Surplus leaves can go on the leaf-mould heap, where they will break down, but it is as well not to use the same mould under apples or pears.

After a year's decay, the leaf-mould heap can be chopped down with a spade and sifted for use in potting soil, but for this purpose it ideally needs another year, after which it will look more like flake tobacco. Year old leaf-mould is excellent for digging into a sandy soil, or spreading in a 2in (5cm) coat on the surface to be chewed up and turned in with a rotavator. Spread it on the lawn, and chop it up with the rotary mower, so that the worms can take it down and build up the humus to hold moisture under the kind of lawn which struggles on Surrey sands.

Leaves in the Garden
When a deciduous tree has returned most of the minerals in its leaves to storage in the twigs in preparation for the peak demand in spring, the hollow shells that fall to the ground are still of great value to it, which explains why no forester will allow them to be sold as leaf-mould. Dead leaves are a weapon against weeds and undergrowth, and they are also a sponge to hold surplus plant foods

that are washed off the upper surfaces of the living leaves above and, in a forest, there are surplus minerals from the tree's own root gatherings, as well as the dust that is blowing in the wind. In some areas, dust falls from the air at the rate of as much as 14 tonnes per acre (0.35 hectares), rests a while on the leaves and is then washed down to join the thick surface mulch for slow recycling. It is in the tree's interest to make the tannins that conserve its gathered minerals as long lasting as possible. A tree's best friends are its own leaves.

The following table shows the percentages of minerals retained in leaves from various trees:

	Nitrogen %	Phosphates %	Potash %	Calcium %
Beech Leaf-mould	1.80	0.10	0.15	0.80
Oak Leaves	0.80	0.35	0.15	—
Beech Leaves	0.67	0.10	0.65	0.99
Apple Leaves	1.00	0.15	0.35	—
Maple Leaves	0.52	0.11	0.75	1.81
Tea Leaves	4.15	0.24	0.29	—

Analysis of dead leaves for leaf-mould

This shows that leaves are generally slightly richer in nitrogen than well-rotted farmyard manure, with about 0.6%, (except of course for the fantastic figure in tea leaves, which is all safely held by the highest tannin level of all). The ideal use for tea leaves is to brush them over a lawn that is struggling on a sandy soil, for the individual leaves make a nice 'bite size' morsel for earthworms in the same way as chopped, partly decayed leaf-mould. Even tea bags can be dug in, or used in a compost heap, and a real quantity from a cafe would be excellent value rotavated into a very poor sandy soil.

rine bonemeal to provide steadily released nitrogen and phosphorus for herbaceous borders, herbs, shrubs and all flower-garden uses. It is good for the vegetable garden, too, provided that it goes on with compost, manure or other plant foods for immediate use, if the next crop is to be a greedy one like potatoes or brassicas.

Because dead leaves contain so few carbohydrates, they can be dug or rotavated directly, without first decaying, into poor soils and subsoils. Experiments on raw subsoil at the HDRA Bocking Trial Ground in 1969 showed that freshly swept dead leaves turned in like this, ideally with a mechanical cultivator that spreads them through the top 12in (30cm), provide the quickest and cheapest way of bringing humus-starved soil to life.

Where this can be done in a new garden that is mostly subsoil, spread up to 8oz a square yard (300g/m²) of slaked lime to correct the acidity from the leaves, as well as the same amount of bonemeal. It would pay to build a stack of leaves on the site ready for the time when you can at last get at the garden, and concentrate on getting the brickends and hard rubbish clear in order to make a clean sweep with a hired machine, rather than dig small beds in odd corners.

Apple leaves are the best top dressing for apples, but newly planted trees drop too few to provide for themselves. Therefore, when dead leaves are available from any tree other than chestnut or plane, it pays to give each apple tree an extra ration, about as many as a twelve year old tree would itself drop, to build up their root systems, rather than to provide the plant foods which should have gone into their holes at planting time.

Buy some 1in (2.5cm) mesh wire netting 1ft (30cm) wide, cut a 2ft (60cm) length and join the ends together to make a circle 8in (20cm) in diameter round the tree trunk. Then make a larger circle, almost 4ft (120cm) in diameter, around the first, with a 12ft (3.7m) length, and drive in short stakes to hold it firm. Fill the space between the circles with trodden leaves, just leaving them to rot and feed the tree, with perhaps a coat of farmyard manure on the surface of a poor soil before the leaves go on.

The inner circle of wire netting is intended to keep the leaves away from the trunk, for these can start the tree rooting from above the graft. A variation on this trick, known to organic fruit farmers as 'birds nesting', is to buy straw-bales, cut the string and break them into squares 1ft (30cm) thick, which can be built round the trunk into a square pile instead of a round one. Wire netting can be used around them to prevent birds from scattering the straw, but an inner circle is even more important, since mice can hide in the straw, and in cold weather they may feast till they kill the young tree by ring barking, unless there is the netting to keep them off.

Fast Leaf-Mould from Slow Plane and Chestnut Leaves
Our member, Dr Peggy Ellis, has invented the following method of hastening the decay of slowly rotting leaves:

'Start with some of the tallest 1½in (4cm) mesh wire netting, 4–5ft (120–150cm) high, in a 12ft (3.7m) length. Hook the ends firmly together and stand your wire netting cylinder upright. Drive in a stout stake at the back, or a length of 2×2in (5×5cm) timber, well creosoted, and staple the cylinder to it up the back. Then fill the cylinder with dead leaves well trodden. The post will prevent the cylinder from blowing over in the wind and scattering the leaves round the garden. Whatever type of bin you use take it up as high as you can to use less space than the traditional oblong stacks only 2ft (60cm) high.

'Then pour urine on it, which will, it seems, speed up leaf-mould decay just as it does composting. It cannot make the leaves heat much but it appears to help the fungi reduce refractory leaves to good humus in one year rather than three.'

Those who wish to recycle their own potassium and get the best value from their wasted nitrogen might build a battery of these tall leaf-mould bins, which could equally well be made, like Californian cylinders, from short ends of pig netting and lined with old carpet, to share their daily contributions throughout the winter. An adult male should be able to keep pace with four heaps, and the evidence suggests that the salt washes out without building up trouble.

Combining weeds with dead leaves in a compost heap results in the germination of weed seed because of poor heating and also because leaves do not hold enough bacterial food to make good compost. However, lawn mowings produce their swift heating by fungal action, and as leaves are also largely broken down by fungi, dead leaves obtained from the Council roadmen, combined with grassmowings from the local tennis club, can go a long way towards cutting out both bonfires and the use of expensive peat, without cost but that of your own labour and any journeys made to fetch the materials.

This idea of a mixture was tried out by two HDRA members, Mr Robert Sherman and Mr John Hunt, and the following account is a blend of their experiences:

Stack the leaves in the usual enclosure in the autumn with polythene, carpet or a layer of soil on top to prevent them from blowing away. In April or May, when there is plenty of grass available, turn the heap and mix in 25% of lawn mowings as the contents go back into the container. Both experiments applied QR Activator after mixing, but Mr Sherman made two heaps, only treating one with this herbal preparation, achieved nearly as good a result from the heap that had none. Both methods provided an excellent, finely divided, leaf-mould three to four months later.

This process distributes the mowings through the leaves, eliminating any risk of making slippery silage or loose, yellowed clippings, while the saving in space from producing in one year a result that would take three by traditional methods is especially important in small gardens without room for a row of maturing heaps. This quickly made leaf-mould is ideal for potting mixtures and as a replacement for peat in no-digging gardens. Because the lawn mowings have been composted under ideal conditions, there is rather more plant food available, and a good quantity can be dug into the root vegetable section of the gardening rotation, or on any ground low in humus.

Peat

The minerals in leaf-mould have been gathered from the subsoil by deep roots, and from the air, with the means of producing energy and humus provided by the sunlight of a single season. Peat, on the other hand, has built up very slowly, sometimes over centuries, in places where plant wastes that have increased through the summer have insufficient time to decay before production of the following summer's waste is ready, because of long, cold winters, or acid conditions under water in a peat bog.

Bracken can build a dry, acid peat, excellent for rhododendrons, but most horticultural peat comes from water plants, mainly sedges, hence the name 'sedge peat' for the brown type, between pH 4.0 and pH 5.0, which is used extensively by commercial growers. The Norfolk Broads are on the site of medieval peat digging for fuel, and there are extensive workings in Somerset and Ireland, rather like watery open-cast coal mines, which will be exhausted far sooner than oil or coal. In Ireland there are many power stations fired with peat, which still serves also as a domestic fuel; the ashes are low in plant foods, because fresh water offers fewer for the gathering than forest subsoils.

	Moisture	Ash free Dry Matter	N	P_2O_5	K_2O
	%	%	%	%	%
Average Graded Peat	40–60	40	0.50	0.07	0.04
Rhododendron Peat	—	—	1.20	0.15	0.10
Average Farmyard Manure	77.0	17	0.60	0.30	0.70

Comparative analysis of peat and farmyard manure

Peat will absorb up to fifteen times its weight in water, and is valuable both for its sponge-like effect on sandy soils and for facilitating the passage of roots through the kind of clay that bakes hard in summer. It is also a good surface mulch for no-diggers.

Peat is rather less rich in tannins than leaf-mould and so breaks down more quickly, especially on well-limed soils, but, as the table shows, it has less to release than farmyard manure. Rhododendron peat is more acid and lasts rather better, but it is more useful in the flower garden, to grow species that really enjoy it. Peat blocks, as used for burning, can even make a kind of 'rock garden' for those small shrubs and rock plants that hate lime, and there is an excellent example of this usage to be seen in the Edinburgh Botanic Gardens.

Baled peat, chopped finely, is the very best material in which to store root vegetables. When peat is dry, the air spaces in it provide excellent insulation against frosts, and this, with the absence of any spores of moulds or bacterial rots, as well as moisture, makes it superior to sand or dry, fine coal ashes. A bale of peat that has stored roots for three seasons, and is then mixed into potting soil or used as a mulch, has earned its keep in any garden.

Mushroom Compost
The great increase in commercial mushroom growing has made spent mushroom compost available almost everywhere. It is a humus material that has been used in the past to build up organic enterprises. For instance, Arthur Hollins of Fordhall Farm, Market Drayton, applied great quantities when he began to build up the soil after years of chemical agriculture, and Charles Hapgood, the organic apple grower at Ingatestone, Essex, used it throughout his early years. But the problem, nowadays, is that we are no longer dealing with a product which is largely horse manure.

Modern mushroom compost often includes horse manure, but it consists mainly of wheat straw composted with a chemical activator (usually 'Adco M') plus casing soil, peat, and large quantities of lime and lump gypsum.

An unfortunate feature of the ash is that the casing soil makes up a large part of the bulk, so that its silica and alumina are always going to amount to far more than the humus-forming material. If you apply 20 tonnes an acre (50 tonnes per hectare) on a farm scale, this adds about a tonne of lime, chalk and gypsum, which can cause problems from overliming where the compost is used repeatedly, especially on a garden scale.

For organic farmers and gardeners, the drawback in modern mushroom compost is the large quantities of BHC and DDT used against fungus gnats. Apart from the environmental hazards pointed out by Rachel Carson in *The Silent Spring*, BHC taints root

	Moisture	Ash-Free Dry Matter	N	P₂O₅	K₂O	Ash
	%	%	%	%	%	%
Average Spent Mushroom Compost (British)	64.0	13	0.60	0.50	0.90	—
Spent Mushroom Compost Horse Manure (USA)	37.0	—	0.50	0.12	0.45	28.0
Spent Mushroom Compost Synthetic (USA)	29.7	—	0.23	0.06	0.39	22.6

Analysis of mushroom compost

crops, and DDT is toxic to cucumbers, according to Ministry of Agriculture Bulletin No. 210 *Organic Manures*, which adds a caution that the total BHC may reach 1cwt an acre (125kg per hectare) from a 20 tonne dressing, in some cases. Organophosphorus compounds mainly diazinon and chlorfenvinphos, are now used, but since the Ministry of Agriculture has warned us that spent mushroom compost presents a risk of trouble from pesticide residues, it is clearly no product for organic gardeners or farmers. However, spent mushroom compost is often advertised merely as 'composted horse manure' in local papers and sold quite expensively in plastic bags. If a real quantity were available free, and you would be able to take the entire output, it would be worth having an analysis, and tests for pesticides, made (Aynsome Laboratories, Kentsford Road, Grange-over-Sands, Cumbria, will carry out a residue safety test for a fee), so that you could be sure that no persistent pesticides were present. Any such material obtained from an organic mushroom grower, who would control fungus gnats with derris or nicotine well before the time for harvesting the crop, would of course be entirely safe to use.

1. PYBUS, F. C. 'Cancer and Atmospheric Pollution' *Medical Proceedings* Vol. 10 1964

2. BRYCE-SMITH, D. 'Lead in Food—Are today's Regulations Sufficient?' *Chemistry in Britain* 10/6 1974 p.202

7 Manures

When every car was a carriage and pair and every lorry a dray, the carts that took the fruit and vegetables to market returned loaded with horse manure, spreading a fairy ring of fertility round almost every city. Carters were bribed 'as much as a *shilling*' to clear one livery stable rather than another, and the doomwatchers, if there were any in the 1880s, might have calculated that by the 1980s London would be buried ten feet deep in horse dung.

Raw materials delivered to factories, finished goods leaving them, commercial travellers and customers calling, all made every industry a source of manure that would find its way to gardeners by means of contractors with pony carts. The great houses used not only the produce of their own stables to keep up the supply for hotbeds growing cucumbers, melons and even pineapples, but bitterly-grudged loads of manure from the home farm for fertility-greedy head gardeners.

In those days, any farmer who sold manure would have found himself snowed under with bills from all his suppliers as the rumour went round that he must be nearly bankrupt, or he would never be selling the fertility that was the life of his land. Modern manure dealers will collect and deliver in plain lorries for cash and, in this permissive society, selling manure has become as respectable as using four letter words. But no organic farmer would sell the manure which has to go back to his land to keep the fertility cycle turning. The only sources, then, are the more old-fashioned orthodox farmers, and those with 'cowtels' or zero grazing systems, slatted floor broiler beef houses and 'sweatbox piggeries'. Because these establishments use antibiotics that cause a risk of infection by resistant bacteria, and often large quantities of persistent pesticides, the waste products of factory farms are not recommended.

Horse Manure
Perhaps the only freely available, non-factory-farm manure comes from the many pony clubs, riding stables and private owners who make up what is becoming known as 'Horsiculture', and now surround our towns with over-grazed paddocks that are slowly losing their grass, and gaining only docks, nettles, plantains and thistles, because of the selective grazing by horses that once made farmers either graze them with their cattle to gain a better balance, or scythe their horse pastures. Regular mowing and liming, as advised for those who cut these weeds for compost, will improve

the grazing for the horses and avoid the problem of complaints about blowing weed seeds, even if the cut material is not used for composting. Riding people are rarely good gardeners. They are too busy grooming and riding.

The drawback with this source of manure is the use of sawdust and shavings litter. Even when this is stacked for two or three years, it will still cause bad nitrogen robbery because breaking down a carbon:nitrogen ratio of 500:1 to about 400:1 (allowing for the lignins) needs so much more nitrogen than could ever get into the heap. Though there is nitrogen in the urine and dung, this will be spent long before even the sawdust has decayed, and the wood shavings with their larger, irregular surface area, will last to cause many years of trouble. Peat littered horse manure is far safer, and if it is stored for six months, it will become quite good manure, with the value of the peat thrown in.

The best litter is wheat straw, and anyone with a stable who wants to make sure of selling the manure, especially in bulk to mushroom growers, should use it, even if the cost is higher. Dry bracken is also excellent horse litter, although not so good as plain wheat straw. If it can be gathered when it is red-brown in the autumn and stored dry, it makes a useful saving in litter costs, and provides rather more potassium than any straw. As horses avoid grazing round their own dung, because of the instinct that protects all grazing animals from parasitic worms, tie brushwood along a heavy stake and tow it round the pasture to scatter the droppings, if you haven't time to gather and take them in a barrow to the manure stack.

If you are fetching manure from a paddock by the bag, it is as well to remember that fresh horse dung without any litter at all is an excellent compost activator and, even if the heap from the stable is filled with dangerous shavings, there may be enough loose in the paddock to be worth the trip. When I was very young, my mother and a retired bank manager who was a neighbour used to watch for the contribution of the milkman's horse and dash out to collect it with a shovel and bucket. In case horses ever come back into wide use, it should be recalled that the right of dung gathering used to extend to the middle of the road in the area exactly in front of your house, and non-gardeners would often pass on this right to their neighbours.

Storing Manure

The process of storing manure is the very reverse of making compost. Here we are concerned with material that is already very near the carbon:nitrogen ratio of good compost (about 14:1) and, having paid a high price for it, have no wish to reduce its bulk. The object is to reduce it from the raw, fresh state to what used to be recommended as 'well rotted manure', still retaining enough nitrogen to activate a compost heap.

The following methods are modified from those used in the 1920s and 1930s by the more old-fashioned head gardeners, and the key to modern manure conservation is the clear polythene sheet that nursery-men use when they steam or liquid sterilize the soil in their tomato houses. Black polythene as used for weedkilling is just as good, but clear will do and is often free.

Build up the heap in an oblong, tapering from the base to the top, and whack the sides and ends. No air passages are required at the base, for you are trying to make something nearer a silage than a compost. When the heap reaches about 4ft (120cm), sloping in from a 5–6ft (150–180cm) base, cover it with the polythene, and weigh the sheet down at the edges with stakes and stones or bricks, bearing in mind that if the wind lifts it the sheet will flap and tear itself to pieces.

Within four to six weeks the whole pile will have broken down beautifully, with steam from the manure fermentation condensing on the underside and draining back to keep any rise in temperature under control, while shortage of oxygen prevents further break-down. There will be some drainage from the heap, and if the manure has first to be wheeled into the garden, rotate the site, always stacking it where cabbage-type crop will be planted, or in the poorest area, so that any liquid seeps where it will do most good.

There is no need for the heap to be in contact with the soil, and where a lorry must back in through a gate, a concrete floor is a good idea, though it may well break up under the weight unless it is thick, which today is expensive. Old gardens frequently had a place where the manure was shot off the cart against a brick wall and protected with sheets of corrugated iron. But these blow off easily, and are not such good condensers as polythene.

So few modern stables know how to stack their manure, that barrow loads are frequently tipped in a loose heap and allowed to become too dry in summer, or when kept under cover. This invites infection by the fire fang fungus, which spreads as white mycelia, reducing manure to a dry and dusty looking mass. If the manure heats up rapidly there is always a risk that this fungus will break down much of the material to carbon dioxide and gaseous nitrogen. While a compost heap should heat, the temperature of a manure stack should never go higher than 115°F (46°C), which is the reason for excluding the air and firming the heap by treading.

The traditional remedy for badly fire-fanged manure is to spread it in a layer 1ft (30cm) thick and pour on cold water, in which half a pound of common salt has been dissolved to each full two gallon (25g/lt) can. Wet the surface thoroughly with this brine, leave it an hour to cool and stack it firmly as described above. The best way to make sure that the stable supplying your manure does not ruin it by letting it overheat is to give them a polythene sheet to cover it, which can be used even if the manure is stored under cover, but not if it is to be sold for mushroom growing.

The Analysis and Use of Stable Manure

	Water %	N %	P %	K %
Fresh Strawy Horse Manure	66.2	0.54	0.31	0.67
The same rotted—Stable Manure	75.4	0.59	0.45	0.49
Peat Litter	76.1	0.54	0.33	0.45
Peat Litter After Storing	53.8	0.64	0.49	0.58

Analysis of stable manures

Peat litter manure was stored under cover and heated enough to dry out; both samples would have been good value for any garden.

It is difficult to suggest exact quantities of any manure to apply to the soil because there is so much variation in analysis, and the carbon:nitrogen ratio will balance itself by bacterial action. Horse manure that has been two months stacked is usually applied at the rate of one barrow-load to five square yards (4m^2) on clay soils, or four (3m^2) on sands. Well-rotted horse manure of this type, supplemented with leaf-mould, was the main fertility source for all our greatest gardens in the past.

Horse manure will keep under polythene without any loss of quality for at least six months, and is always worth collecting regularly from any source. There is no need to make the whole heap at once so long as the cover is replaced after each addition.

Cow Manure

Once, the manure from bullocks fed generously on roots and lavishly supplied with straw provided the plant foods and energy to run the old Norfolk Four Course rotation, but increasingly this lasting fertility is turned into pollution. Much manure and urine from unlittered cattle is washed from the cow stalls into tanks and spread as a slurry on the fields. But more and more often it is discharged into an aeration ditch, where air is pumped through it to break it down by a kind of sewage treatment so that it is sufficiently low in oxygen demand to be poured into a river.

Organic matter tipped into rivers causes robbery not only of nitrogen, but also of oxygen, for only a limited amount of oxygen is dissolved in water (from splashing and the photosynthesis of aquatic plants), unlike the ready supply that passes in from the air through the ventilation channels of a compost heap. In hot or thundery weather, the water is capable of holding less oxygen, and the discharge of silage effluent, and the drainings of cowsheds and over-loaded aeration ditches, grabs the oxygen and kills the fish with the eutrophication that poisons so many lakes and rivers today.

It is not possible to use slurry in private gardens, for it is too dilute, making transport costs too high, and is both raw and smelly, but the manure that is now sold as 'farmyard manure' will have the minimum litter with it. Frequently, only sufficient is added to make it hang together enough to load with a foreloader, and gardeners should try and buy it with as high a straw content as possible. Ask to see a sample and refuse anything that is sloppy. A 'short' manure, which is supposed to be well rotted should have straw well distributed throughout. Unfortunately, it is a case of buying what you can get, in this 'take it and like it' age.

Manure dealers prefer to sell in full loads, and this is the cheapest way to buy, but a ten or twelve tonne load stacked high costs about £60 in 1980. Such a quantity is more than any small garden can take —the best way is for neighbours to club together and share it out by the barrowload if it is shot outside one house. Wash the pavement afterwards and remember that if you cannot clear the whole load in one day you must put out red lights to warn anyone walking along the footpath—legally the smell is not warning enough. Battery powered cycle rear lamps would do.

Farmyard manure, which is so called because it is not only cow manure, but heifer, calf and bullock too, should be stacked just like horse manure, though there is little risk of fire fang. During experimentation on manure storage at Rothamsted in the past, it was found that, when firmly stacked, manure lost 4% less dry matter and 7% less nitrogen, and that protecting it from the rain saved a further 4% of dry matter.[1] The polythene covered heap makes these savings, and removes one of the major problems of manure buying: every gardener wants to buy in the early spring or in the autumn, and also wants delivery on a Saturday when he or she is not at work. But arranging, instead, to take a load on some Saturday in the summer, with the idea of stacking it on any available spare ground, could make it much easier to get a delivery.

It should be said that the farmer's manure dressing for a greedy crop like potatoes of twenty tonnes an acre (0.4 hectares) works out at about 8lb a square yard (4.4kg/m²), perhaps 12lb (6.6kg/M²) on a poor sandy soil. Cover the scales with polythene to weigh this amount, then you can guess it as you spread the forkfuls. A cubic yard of farmyard manure weighs 12–16cwt (800–1070kg/m²) and barrows of course vary, but up to 1cwt (50kg) is a comfortable wheeling load for most people.

Like everything on the land, the analysis of farmyard manure varies, but the following modern figures from the Ministry of Agriculture and Fisheries Bulletin No. 210 *Organic Manures* make a good guide for anyone who can find a farmer who is not too old-fashioned to sell manure, or too up-to-date to have anything worth buying.

	Dry matter %	N %	P_2O_5 %	K_2O %	Magnesium %	Calcium %
Bullock Manure	25.0	0.57	0.36	0.88	—	—
Dairy Cow Manure	20.0	0.48	0.30	0.47	—	—
Average F.Y.M.	23.0	0.60	0.30	0.70	0.04	0.20

Analysis of cow manure

The average ash-free dry matter was 17%, which is the total of available energy releasing and humus forming matter together with the plant foods or 'macro-nutrients'—the minerals that are required in quantity. Bulletin No. 210 also includes a table of the trace elements essential for nutrition that are recycled via the manure.

If that trace of molybdenum is missing, a serious deficiency condition called 'Louping ill' arises in lambs; without the trace of cobalt there can be no Vitamin B_{12} in the milk, and the iodine is the vital growth-controlling factor in our thyroid glands. Too much zinc or boron, and crops are poisoned. Every one of these substances, from the fast and frequent sodium chloride to the slowly distributed iodine, is repeatedly recycled in the blood and body fluids of living creatures. The manure of our cattle is too good to waste, not because the world is likely to run out of iron or

	Parts per Million	Weight in 10 tonnes manure
Sodium	1,000	20lb (10kg)
Chlorine	2,000	40lb (20kg)
Iron	180	4lb (1.8kg)
Manganese	45	1lb (450g)
Zinc	20	7oz (200g)
Copper	4	1½oz (40g)
Boron	4	1½oz (40g)
Cobalt	0.3	1/10oz (3g)
Molybdenum	0.3	1/10oz (3g)
Iodine	0.05	1/60oz (0.5g)

Trace elements in farmyard manure

manganese, but because it spreads vital trace elements in the appropriate quantities. The land does not live by NPK alone, and the purity of chemicals supplements can add up to the deadly refinement of white sugar or white marble tombstones.

Pig Manure

There are still some farmers who rear pigs on straw, rather than bare concrete washed down to replace the hard work of mucking out with the easy job of pumping slurry, and they may have a good (but very strong smelling) manure to sell. Ever increasing rail charges have made it uneconomic to move hundreds of thousands of tonnes of baled straw across from the drier grain-growing counties of Britain, so that straw is scarcer and more costly, but no-one should buy pig manure with any other type of litter, because shavings and smell together would be the worst bargain of all.

The original garden method was to stack the manure with a 1in (2cm) thick layer of garden soil between every 6in (15cm). This provided denitrifying bacteria *Nitrosomas* and *Nitrobacter* that are also supplied in the dry earth bin for bucket sanitation. Cover down with polythene, and the result will be good manure which is worth the trouble if it is free cartage or from your own pigs.

	Moisture %	N %	P_2O_5 %	K_2O %	Magnesium %	Copper p.p.m.
Pig Manure, Average	76	0.6	0.6	0.4	0.13	350

Analysis of pig manure

Compare the 4 p.p.m. of copper in average cattle manure with the level for pig manure, and there is a strange contrast. Modern pigs suffer a shortage of copper when they are not allowed to balance up their minerals by snouting up a pasture after the fat cockchafer grubs and other delicacies that they hunt by scent, and instead live on concrete with an entirely man-provided diet. Copper is added to their food, but as with the ground chalk added to our bread, only 2–6% of their intake is absorbed; the rest passes through them and can build up in a pasture to toxic levels. Pig slurry that is 99% water can contain 100 p.p.m. copper, which accumulates with every dressing to a level that could permanently poison pasture on which it is sprayed for, though even the organo-chlorine pesticides break down in time, toxic metal pollution stays in the soil.

Beware of pig manure unless you know where it comes from, and are certain that the pigs concerned have not been fed copper supplements.

The Dry Manures

These are all rich in plant foods, but it is only rarely they can be bought; they are included to help keepers of rabbits, sheep, goats and dogs (for the disposal of dog manure can be a problem for people who keep kennels, especially with the larger breeds).

	Moisture %	N %	P_2O_5 %	K_2O %
Rabbit Manure	58	0.5	1.2	0.5
Sheep Manure	68	0.8	0.45	0.35
Goat Manure	64	1.44	0.22	1.0
Dog Manure	—	1.97	9.95	0.39[2]

Analysis of the dry manures

The really remarkable phosphorus level in dog manure is the product of whole bones broken down by their digestive juices. All carnivores have the ability to release the calcium phosphate in bones and thus maintain the fertility of the pastures grazed by their vegetarian prey. It is just one of the many cycles of fertility which redistribute minerals gathered by the roots of plants and trees and stored in the bones of grazing animals.

Dog manure is an excellent compost heap activator, for whatever goes into the heap stays there, unless it is washed out by rain, and, with plenty of nitrogen available, there will be quick heating for all summer heaps. During the winter, when there will be a few weeds and no lawn mowings, the dog manure can be shovelled into a plastic dustbin between layers of garden soil to make about a 50–50 mixture. This will ensure that the denitrifying bacteria prevent all smells, and though most of the nitrogen will have gone off as odourless gas, the phosphorus and calcium will be ready to add as 1in (2cm) thick layers to spring and summer compost heaps.

The cat's tray of earth can also be used as an activator, and it should be added that cat litter sold in bags for flat dwellers is based on fuller's earth, a mineral containing 53% silica, 10% alumina, 24% water, with the balance made up of calcium, magnesium and iron compounds. This, too, can be added to the compost heap, together with contributions from parrots, canaries, budgerigars and other pets. The amount may be small, but it can all be recycled.

The best of this group of manures comes from goats and, if it can ever be bought, is a bargain, because goats are browsers as well as grazers, digesting twigs, even branches, as effectively as dogs digest bones. For choice, they strip potassium-rich bark wherever they can reach it, and their manure is a splendid source of trace elements. Goats, sheep and rabbits are drought resisting, unlike cows and pigs; not only do they live under dry conditions, but their grazing activities make these conditions worse as their numbers increase—for there is a very great difference between the few gentle well-behaved 'nubes' or Saanens of the British goat keeper and the desert-making beasts of Africa and the East.

All three animals produce activators rather than manures to be spread as tons to an acre, but where their dung is available in quantity with straw litter, stack it like horse manure, but hose the heap well after completion and cover down with polythene, for there may well be too little water in relation to the dry straw. When the manure is broken down, use it at about the same rate as other kinds, bearing in mind that any good farmyard manure shows an effect for at least five years after application.

Poultry Manure

According to the Ministry of Agriculture, there are about 220 million chickens in England and Wales producing 4–5 million tonnes of droppings. Of these, about 41 million are laying birds, the majority in batteries, for the numbers on free range and deeplitter are now too low to show in the statistics. Like all factory farming, keeping broilers and battery birds is really a commercial process for converting large quantities of imported protein foods, such as fishmeal and soya feeds, plus maize from overseas, into a very much smaller quantity of human food, while the fertility in the manure is wasted, so far as gardens are concerned.

Though there is an excellent method that would fix the nitrogen in battery manure and reduce it to a dry and easily spread 'semi-organic manure'—by adding superphosphate from a hopper as the droppings go by on an endless belt for a perfect mix—most of the manure is now added to cattle cake, which is an economical but unattractive answer to an increasing problem.[3] Several large poultry firms have installed driers, but rises in the cost of the fuel oil that they burn make the price that must be charged to gardeners to cover drying and carriage prohibitive.

There is, however, an enormous quantity of good plant food and humus going to waste in Britain because of the conversion of so much agriculture into industries that draw together the fertility from all over the world and waste it as pollution. This is apart from any consideration of the cruelty of factory farming, or the ethics of importing fishmeal that should feed hungrier countries.

	Moisture	Ash free dry matter	N	P_2O_5	K_2
	%	%	%	%	%
Fresh poultry droppings (battery manure)	71.0	20	1.7	1.4	0.7
Dried poultry manure	14.0	61	4.2	4.3	1.6
Broiler shavings	28.0	21	2.4	2.2	1.4
Deeplitter (straw)	31.0	18	1.7	1.8	1.3
Deeplitter (peat)	17.7	—	4.4	1.9	1.9
Deeplitter (straw & peat)	52.0	—	3.0	2.5	1.5
Deeplitter (softwood shavings)	20.4	—	2.25	2.5	1.5
Deeplitter (hardwood shavings	31.0	—	1.0	1.98	1.0

Analysis of chicken manures

In the past there were problems with the acidity of battery manure, or any raw poultry droppings, but as today's battery birds are fed plenty of fine ground limestone, their droppings contain 2–3% of calcium, which is enough to correct this. They will also contain up to 400 p.p.m. of zinc from the galvanized wire of the cages, which the birds peck out of boredom, and up to 30 p.p.m. of copper from their rations.

No gardener should buy battery manure—especially beware of any that has been stacked with just enough straw to hold it together for mechanical loading. Battery manure is a 'manure silage', preserving itself from decay by both the exclusion of air and the presence of acids from the breakdown of its proteins. Therefore, when it is dug in, it can stay undecayed for even a year, and will always rot anaerobically—which means that it smells. Any dried poultry manure, if it can be bought bagged, is a good compost heap activator and general fertilizer, especially for the comfrey bed. The heat of drying would have destroyed any risk of antibiotic-proof bacteria, rendering these dried by-products of factory farms safe (apart from any risk from the litter), but expensive. The toxic metal level is well below Ministry of Agriculture safety limits, especially if the dried manure is used only as an activator or lawn dressing.

Deeplitter Poultry Manure
The deeplitter system became popular in the 1950s, but was employed in 1976 by only 6% of poultry farmers, and the figure is probably still lower today, because of rising labour costs and feed prices. Some day there will be million-bird 'egg factories' entirely controlled by micro-chips, but consumers who can afford them will recognize the difference and still buy free range eggs at an astronomical price. The deeplitter system allows more space to the bird—3–6 square feet (0.28–0.55m²) in a large building, with room to walk about, instead of cages in which they can hardly turn round—and it is about the best way yet discovered of converting wood shavings to humus.

Birds, unlike mammals, expel their urine as a dab of white, on every dropping, which includes nitrogen as urea and ammonium carbonate, and all their surplus potassium, so that there is nothing liquid running to waste. Therefore, all bird manures are rich in potash, but also in 'fierce', or readily available nitrogen. A 1ft (30cm) deep layer of straw, constantly replenished through the 12–15 months the litter stays down, and with scratching by the birds to keep up the air supply, enables Hutchinson's spirochaete to convert the nitrogen to more stable substances and provides good humus. Deeplitter compost should always be dry, and the traditional test is to walk across the chicken house then see if you can clean your boots by dusting them. If the litter is wet, it lacks air and should be forked up and mixed with new straw.

The heat produced by breakdown of the cellulose in this fast 'composting system' dries out the moisture in the manure, but demands just as much oxygen as would be needed to burn it, so the house should always be well ventilated. Deeplitter compost made with wheat straw is a first-class manure, and a 1in (2cm) thick surface coat dug in is a good tonic for any vegetable garden or comfrey bed.

Peat litter, of the type also used for horses, preserves the nitrogen, because its cellulose is protected from bacteria by tannins, and remains a mixture of peat and strong poultry manure, which is still a good comfrey dressing, but less desirable for vegetables, except where a green manure crop is to be grown first. A mix of straw and peat gains both heating and high analysis, but on the whole straw is best from the viewpoints of both poultry farmer and gardener. If you buy straw deeplitter compost, ask what selective killer has been used on the grain crop. If the answer is TBA, refuse it, for this lasts in the straw and passes through the process unchanged, unlike MCPA, which breaks down safely, as described earlier.

The hardwood shavings sample in the Table above came from a poultry farm next door to a furniture factory; it was all from hard woods, not pine, and contained no wood ends. The nitrogen was low because so much had been spent on breaking down the cellulose to achieve a carbon:nitrogen ratio of 9:1, from a starting point of 500:1, which kept the chickens warm through the coldest winter. This system is popular in Zimbabwe and Zambia, where the houses must have wire netting sides and the right situation to let the trade wind blow away the heat from the breakdown process.

The softwood shavings sample was provided by a farmer near Hull who fetched the shavings from a fishbox factory as return loads. He used all his deeplitter compost as top dressing for grassland and grain crops and used to say that if he ever sold any, three generations of his ancestors would cause an upheaval in the village churchyard by turning in their graves.

Broiler Manure

Broiler manure is from day-old chicks reared to 9–10 weeks old on shavings or sawdust litter, with an average throughout of 270 million a year, producing about 1½ million tonnes of manure. *This should be avoided by all gardeners.* The material is high in nitrogen, because the birds are fed a very high protein diet, and has a low moisture content because Hutchinson's spirochaete has no chance to get going before the house is cleared and another load of chicks and shavings goes in. It also contains a high proportion of shavings to droppings because, unlike deep litter, it derives the raw material from young chicks, whose output is much lower than that of 18–20 week old pullets.

It undergoes none of the intensive scratching that mixes enough oxygen into each layer to keep bacteria thriving and composting. (One of the reasons why shavings-littered horse manure should be avoided is that horses do not spend their time busily scratching and pecking.) Do not buy broiler manure, even if it has been shredded until it heats under cover. It is far better burnt, as it usually is today.

Other Poultry Manures

Turkey farming is increasingly popular, now that the idea of selling cut turkey joints through supermarkets is developing. In the USA, where they have Thanksgiving Day and Christmas as traditional turkey eating days, there are million-bird ranches; they may be copied elsewhere, for large turkeys are the most economic to feed, though they do not fit small families.

Turkeys are kept in yards on a deeplitter system, usually straw, but though they scratch as vigorously as chickens, they are much heavier and crush the manure into a firm, dry, brown material that is easily loaded mechanically. If the yard is covered, the manure will be far drier and better in quality; because the birds stay so much longer on the litter than broilers, it has time to break down very well. Litters of shavings still need caution, so if there is a supply going locally, insist, before you buy, on an analysis, including a Black and Wakeley Test to determine the carbon:nitrogen ratio. Anyone in the poultry business can afford to make sure that the manure he is selling is free from pesticide residues, provides value in plant foods, with a level of toxic metals below Ministry of Agriculture safe limits, and also is sufficiently rotted to be used without nitrogen robbery in gardens or on farms.

	Moisture %	N %	P_2O_5 %	K_2O %
Duck manure (fresh)	32	0.8	1.4	0.6
Goose manure (fresh)	75	0.6	0.6	0.8
Pigeon (fresh)	61	3.4	1.4	1.2
Turkey on straw litter	64	0.5	0.6	0.4
Turkey on peat litter	10	3.8	2.5	1.4

Analysis of duck, goose, pigeon and turkey manures

Duck and goose manure is spread as the birds range freely, and geese grazing an orchard leave their droppings on the ground for quick breakdown with an ample air supply, on the ground as do free range poultry, benefiting the owner's pasture rather than his or her pocket. Until the price of free range eggs goes high enough to pay for farms made fertile by the 'golden claw' (like the 'golden hoof' of the folded sheep on the Wiltshire downs), the best way to enjoy the best eggs is to keep your own chickens, and this equally provides the best poultry manure.

Wood Ashes and Poultry Manure

The officially recognized stocking level for free range poultry is two hundred birds an acre (500 per hectare), but no chicken will range very far. They are flocking birds, each flock with its territory, which they maintain even in a deeplitter house, like the Pensioner who said at my first Chelsea Flower Show, 'There aren't many of us Crimea Boys left, and we stick together.' So the hut that provides their sleeping perches and the nest boxes has to be on wheels for moving at intervals, or the chickens will reduce the grass to bare soil with dust-bathing hollows under the house. The Farm and Food Society standard depends on the number of birds that can run on an acre without damaging the grass, provided the poultry hut is moved at intervals (usually hitched to a tractor).

Even if dropping boards are fitted, they have to be slid out and scraped, and today the usual policy is to have the perches above the bare floor, making one rather messy job of the scraping. HDRA member, Mrs MacArthur of Pitlochry, has a woodburning cooking and heating stove of the widely popular controlled-draught type that has now been used even for central heating. She spreads all her wood ashes on the poultry house floor, enough for the chickens to dustbathe in. This prevents any unpleasant smell, stops flies in summer, and makes it possible to sweep the dried manure out of the house at intervals instead of scraping the floor, turning a slow and smelly chore into a quick and easy one. Although the mix of ashes and droppings is about half and half, she merely throws each morning's ash accumulation in, without bothering about proportions.[4] Samples of the dry, grey-brown powder, 'poultash', were analysed.

A reaction between potassium carbonate, which is a powerful alkali, and the acid nitrogen compounds had produced enough heat to dry the poultry droppings to dust. The chemical process happens as follows:

	Fresh Poultry Droppings %	Woodash Treated %
Moisture	72.00	16.70
Organic matter	20.00	89.85
Nitrogen	1.66	0.90
Phosphoric acid	0.91	1.50
Potash	0.48	2.12

Analysis of poultash

The potassium carbonate (K_2CO_3), in the woodashes dissolves in the moisture of the poultry droppings and forms an alkaline solution which destroys both bacteria and the smell-producing molecules, and drives out the nitrogen as ammonia (NH_3). The chemical reactions, for the benefit of those who are interested in chemistry, are:

$$2K^+ + CO_3^{--} + H_2O \rightarrow 2K^+ + HCO_3^- + OH^-$$
$$NH_4^+ + OH^- \rightarrow NH_3 + H_2O$$

There is thus a loss of about 40% of the nitrogen to the air as ammonia, and a fall in pH to a more neutral level. The decrease in moisture in our samples was such that the organic matter had increased 4½ times, while there was a four-fold rise in potassium, partly because of the extra in the woodashes.

What happens to the potassium (K^+) and how is it converted to a form in which it will be less easily leached? The answer is that the potassium ions (K^+) which are positively charged are held on the negatively charged sites of the organic matter, i.e. the poultry manure. These are collectively known as the 'cation exchange complex' and are mainly provided by carboxyl groups ($RCOO^-$). They are usually occupied by the ions of calcium (Ca^{++}), magnesium (Mg^{++}), potassium (K^+), sodium (Na^+), ammonia (HN_4^+) or hydrogen (H^+), all of which can displace and replace each other. As an exchangeable ion, the potassium is now available to plants and will only be slowly removed from the 'exchange complex' of the organic matter by leaching. Rainwater and humic acids will provide hydrogen ions to displace it. Liming the soil would displace it with calcium ions, and addition of nitrogen fertilizer salts would also displace it.

A second sample taken in December to test whether the reaction had gone any way towards solving the problem of rapidly soluble potash on sandy soils, showed rather less phosphorus and more potassium, because with more wood burned there were more ashes in relation to the droppings. Experience will show exactly how much will produce the reaction, for those with more birds than ashes.

	%
Total phosphorus	0.84
Citric soluble phosphorus	Nil
Water soluble phosphorus	Nil
Total potassium	3.04
Citric soluble potassium	2.66
Water soluble potassium	2.13

Solubility of poultash

This shows that all the phosphorus is locked up as oxide, just as in woodashes, and rather less than a third of the potassium is held in a form that will not wash immediately out of a sand. How long it will stay within reach of a hungry gooseberry bush is another matter, but potassium sulphate and potassium chloride (sulphate and muriate of potash) are as readily dissolved as common salt or washing soda.

It is going to pay any gardener with a chicken house to clean out a woodburning stove to make as much as he can of this high potash general fertilizer, with its nitrogen nicely 'tamed', which is of considerably better value than any dried battery manure. Use it at the rate of 8oz a square yard (300g/m^2) on most vegetable crops, especially tomatoes and broad and runner beans on sandy soils. It could also serve as a compost heap activator, at about 1lb to the square yard (550g/m^2) of surface layer, because it may well be relatively slow in starting, compared with other organic manures.

Laying Arks
These are movable poultry houses complete with a run that were once moved every day across pastures, which they improved greatly. Left to themselves, chickens will eat the young grasses, leaving the old, and also scratch holes, unlike sheep and cattle, but the laying ark kept them in one place and distributed their droppings over a small area. It is now extinct on the farm because of the cost of replacing arks after rapid determination from the shock of being hitched to a tractor and towed to the next position, which was in itself fairly expensive in fuel and labour. However, an HDRA student, David Lacey, has designed a small mobile ark with

two wheels which can be pushed round the garden and weighs only 25–30lb (11–14g), including hens. It holds up to ten birds, and plans can be obtained from the Association for 20p, plus stamped addressed envelope.

This ark can be used on lawns, where a tray underneath the sleeping section prevents the concentration of droppings at one end during the night. The droppings can be removed for use as a compost activator or, with the addition of wood ashes, a fertilizer. The ark is also suitable for moving across a weedy area, or one that has been dug and could benefit from insect searches by the chickens.

The Addie Ark is a heavier model, about 6ft wide, 8ft long, and 5ft high (180×240×150cm), made with a rope in the middle to fit across your shoulders. To move it you shut up the chickens in their separate small hut, then walk inside the ark to carry it to its new position, replacing the nest box and sleeping compartment afterwards. This ark is roomier and serves to accomodate birds that are used to clear weeds or search rough ground for pests, because it does not need smooth ground to run on. Either type can be used for folding rabbits on nettles that are just recovering after a cut. Young nettles up to 4in (10cm) high are excellent green food for rabbits, and after experience has shown how often the ark needs moving to keep pace, there will be more grass than nettles by the second spring and only a few scattered nettle shoots by the end of that summer. Plans of the Addie Ark are also available at 20p, plus stamped, addressed envelope, from the HDRA.

Rotational Chickens
The standard organic rotation depends on four squares, with potatoes, legumes, brassicas and root crops following round the years. Anyone with sufficient room for a fifth square can try a rotating poultry run, which needs a minimum of fifteen square feet (1.4m^2) per bird. This is the rather scornfully regarded bare-soil run system which, continued for a long period makes land 'poultry sick', but is one way of building up poor soil and clearing weeds.

Fence your area, using either wire netting or the cheaper nylon, which does not last so long, and install a small poultry house of the old, intensive type that allows about three square feet (0.27m^2) per bird, with nest boxes on the outside, and perching room and floor space for dustbathing in wood ashes also extending under the perches. The best type of house, of which drawings are available in any backyard poultry book, should stand clear of the ground, with room underneath for a boarded-in enclosure of ashes for dust-bathing, where the birds can also shelter in wet weather.

If the bed were sown with winter tares the previous September or October, the poultry could go on it in the spring, lay through the summer, and be eaten or sold in October, leaving behind enough eggs in waterglass to last through the winter. The birds will have pecked bare the winter tares, and should have as much as possible in the way of vegetable wastes thrown in to them during the summer. It pays to dig or rotary cultivate the plot up to three times during the season, to give the poultry a chance to eat as many soil pests and weed seeds as possible, and to keep the droppings mixed into the soil.

After the poultry have either been slaughtered and put in the deep freeze or sold to someone who will kill and take them away, sow the land with grazing rye to hold the nitrogen, and dig it under in spring before planting potatoes or the cabbages. The soil will be so rich that it is not advisable to plant spring cabbage, kale or broccoli immediately after removing the chickens for they would be too overfed with nitrogen to come through the winter. Another square should be sown with tares in September or October for the following season's poultry.

This is the poultry equivalent to turning in a car after one year's running, for to start with point of lay birds and kill them at the end of their first season means maximum production and minimum trouble, while if you are willing to eat eggs from waterglass until the next year's pullets start laying, you cut out all problems of keeping the flock through the winter. Carrying the birds on until their second autumn means a smaller egg yield in relation to food, and a lower price for them as table birds, though of course buying pullets every year instead of every other year incurs more outlay.

In the country, it is often possible to buy battery hens cheaply in the spring, after they have spent the winter under artificial daylight, and to run them through to the autumn, giving them a spring, summer and early autumn holiday of scratching and pecking like real hens. They will be what are known as 'boiling fowl', and sold as such, but make far better food than 'broilers', though they take longer to cook.

This rotation is a good one for reclaiming a neglected garden, if you cut down the weeds and run the birds on the young shoots that are starting through, also turning the ground with a rotary cultivator once or twice to give them a good go at the wireworms and weed seeds. It should be said that a proportion of the 1cwt (50kg) of droppings that each chicken produces in a year will have been converted to fertilizer, or scraped out as compost activator, but the land will have had a reasonably heavy dressing of nitrogen-rich droppings, so apply lime after the potatoes, or before brassicas, as the soil will be on the acid side. Do not expect to grow crops on land that has been under chickens for long enough to become crowded with nettles, docks and thistles rejoicing in the manure and the acid conditions. Lime generously, and weed by repeated mowings.

The same routine of rotation can be carried out with ducks, and khaki Campbells are splended slug eaters. Their webbed feet puddle clays, so they are best on sandy soils. There are many books on poultry keeping and plenty of advice is available. The HDRA can supply plans for making a very effective automatic poultry feeder which cuts down considerably the attention required.

Chicken Compost
This is a variation on the rotation system for those who can accumulate quantities of coarse compost material—straw, sweet corn stems, tomato, pea and bean haulm, and such cut weeds as rosebay willowherb and tall nettles. Spread them in a 1ft (30cm) thick layer over the plot, then turn the chickens out of their intensive house on what will be roughly a one-layer compost heap, with poultry manure the activator, and scratching claws the ventilation. Add more material—weeds of any kind and further straw—forking the surface at intervals to keep it from becoming matted with mud and droppings.

This system suits anyone who would like to run some birds on for another season, because so much good material is available in the autumn, and it is rather better for the birds' feet than muddy bare soil. In the spring, when the flock might be transferred to winter tares on a weedkilling area, the surface material, which should have broken down to about 6in (15cm) of near-compost, can be forked aside for no-digging potatoes to be set on the soil below.

Lawn mowings spread along the rows and round the potato plants as soon as they show through will cake solidly together, reducing the number of potatoes which turn green from exposure to light as they thrust up through the surface compost, and add still more humus. The autumn should see a good crop of potatoes and a complete breakdown of the material in what is, in effect, an outdoor deeplitter system. This can either be dug in, or followed by other no-digging mulches. The limitation is that it does demand quantities of compost material.

References on p. 146.

8   The Broken Cycles

Today, only one Authority in the whole of Britain sells municipal compost. This is Leicester, where a battery of Dano composters are still slowly converting dustbin refuse and sewage sludge to a fine, dark product bought by local gardeners. The famous compost plant on Jersey has been replaced by an incinerator, and the last Dano in Denmark (where the process was invented) has been silenced by changing conditions.

The Mogden Works at Isleworth processes bodily wastes, bath water, industrial effluents and everything that goes down the sewers for a million and a half Londoners, and still sells 400 tonnes a year of its famous Morganic   gardeners who call between 8 a.m. and 4 p.m. on weekdays and collect it in 56lb (25kg) bags. In the North of England, the Yorkshire Water Authority is selling Dewmus, which alone survives out of the long list of splendid dried sewage sludges whose analysis figures were once proclaimed in the long out of print booklet that began as *The Observer Sludge Guide* and finished as the HDRA *Fertility Finder*.

Once, every local sewage treatment works was proud of its sludge, and conservationists campaigned for Municipal Compost rather than incineration. What happened to the prospect of unlimited humus for organic gardeners and farmers from city refuse, for which so many people hoped? Just why has the glory departed?

The Toxic Metal Problem

Like many natural questions, this has several complicated answers, and the truth takes time to tell. The most important reason is the decision in 1974 of the then Conservative Government to continue the Local Government reforms begun by the Labour Party, and merge all the Sewage Authorities and Water Authorities into ten huge area boards covering the whole country. This increased the cost greatly—for small is not only beautiful but usually far cheaper—and also increased the salaries, but reduced the independence, of the local sewage works managers who were working enthusiastically to keep their effluents clean enough to go in the river without harming fish, and to produce dried sludges that did them credit in their ratepayer's gardens.

Then came the Six Day War, the oil crisis, and price rises that have made drying and grinding the residue from the heated digesters on about 5,000 sewage treatment plants in Britain too costly for the rates to meet the losses. Mogden Works and the cities that sell their dried sludges under the banner of Yorkshire Water Organics, dry their sludges with the heat from methane gas released by the digesters that is left over after production of the electricity needed to power everything from mighty sewage pumps to typists' tea kettles. So, for the time being, two good dried sewage sludges can still be bought for use as compost activators, and for lawn feeding, which includes dressing sports grounds, football pitches and golf greens as recommended by the Sports Turf Research Institute at Bingley in Yorkshire.

The final blow was the result of investigation by Professor Derek Bryce-Smith of Reading University, whose work on lead pollution is known in all countries. In 1972 he was called in as an expert at Leicester, where it was proposed to build houses on the site of the old Beaumont Leys Sewage Farm. Here, he found an average lead level of 171 parts per million (p.p.m.) and 400 p.p.m. in places. The Lead in Food Regulations (1961) insist that the maximum level of lead should be 2 p.p.m. and 0.5 p.p.m. for tinned baby foods. Lead in food is far more dangerous to the under-fives than it is to older children or adults, because they absorb more lead from what they eat, and are more susceptible to brain damage, since a young child is building bone and brain cells, and these are where concentration of lead occurs. About 90% of children having even a mild attack of lead poisoning before the age of five suffer a degree of damage which shows in later years as educational disabilities and such emotional abnormalities as hyperactivity and tendencies to cruel or violent behaviour.[2]

There is evidence that the build-up of lead in our bodies can cause mental and health problems. There is still none that eating vegetables grown on a soil with a high lead level has ever harmed any human being of any age, from the present householders on Beaumont Leys to the healthy inhabitants of Shipham, the Somerset village where lead was mined from the time of the Romans to the 1930s, whose soil has higher levels than any sewage farm. Cadmium is dangerous in far smaller quantities than lead and caused an outbreak of the painful itai-itai bone disease among the peasants of Fuchu in Toyama Prefecture in Japan, when waste from cadmium mine polluted the river that flowed through the town.[3]

The present (1980) safety limits for sewage sludges set by the Department of the Environment are 2,000 p.p.m. for lead and 20 p.p.m. for cadmium, which is taken up far more readily by vegetables, especially lettuce. The figure for lead is set too high, in the opinion of many authorities, for a sack of dried sludge that reached that level (far beyond any made in Britain) would be more dangerous than any lead painted toy. It should be possible for parents to prevent children eating manures of any kind, organic or inorganic, and there are very few garden chemicals that can safely be consumed in quantity.

There are many old-fashioned sewage farms of the same type as Leicester's Beaumont Leys, that came into use up to a hundred years ago, when this method of sewage treatment first became popular, and they have had up to half a million gallons an acre (11 million litres per hectare) a year of sewage sludge poured on to them. For the first seventy years they could not only cope with this flood (though not very efficiently in terms of fertility) with the help of soil bacteria, but were serving the main purpose of every local Authority, which is to dispose of the sewage as cheaply as possible.

Then industry began to pollute the sewage with toxic metals, especially with the effluent from electro-plating plants. There is a disused sewage farm in Essex with a cadmium level of 1,400 p.p.m. because the metal is now used in electroplating the bright parts of cars before the chromium is applied. Lead, mercury and cadmium are toxic to human beings but it has only rather recently become possible to measure accurately their level in the soil. Other metals such as zinc, chromium, copper and nickel are needed in small quantities by plants, so are readily absorbed, but excessive amounts kill crops. They are described as 'phyto-toxic', and sewage engineers worry less about them because they destroy plants before they endanger ratepayers.

The sewage farm foreman says 'So long as you give the land plenty of lime, there is no trouble' and he is right, because lime '*chelates*' these metals, locking them out of root reach. It has been possible for Beaumont Leys to produce wheat yields of 3½ tonnes an acre (8.7 tonnes/hectare) for stock feed, with the straw sold for bedding and finishing perfectly safely on the manure heaps of the farmers who bought it. The sewage works managers used to say, 'Perhaps the Professor is right, he must know more about chemistry than I do, but can he tell me what to do with tomorrow's twenty million gallons of sewage coming into the works, and the next day's, and every day more of it as the town spreads? Can he tell me what it will cost in £100 millions, and how much more it will cost when the clever scientists have worked out the answer?'

The immediate problem, as at Leicester, is that towns have grown round the old sewage farms, which are flat, empty and worth vast sums as building land. They also present a chance to cut the waiting list for Council houses, and plan splendid new estates. Children at the age when lead can do them most harm can have a habit referred to as 'pica' which is deliberately eating soil; they also get their hands muddy and lick their fingers. If the soil in the gardens where they play holds lead, cadmium and mercury in any quantity, this can be dangerous. Though lime locks up the toxic metals, the human stomach produces hydrochloric acid, which unlocks them again, but there is no evidence, so far, that any child has ever suffered from metal build-up on sewage farm soils.

Chewing flaking paintwork in old houses, or drinking water that has come through lead pipes, yes, but toxic metals in sewage, no. This may be merely because the build-up is not yet high enough, making the present risk only a small fraction of that from the lead in petrol, of which children absorb even more than the 70% taken in by adults through their lung surfaces, where it does them even more damage. Should we therefore have a Government Health Warning on every petrol pump, other than those selling leadless blends as in the USA?

Adding 10–15% of ethyl alcohol to petrol would produce all the advantages of tetra-ethyl lead, without the pollution, and as petrol prices rise higher the alcohol additive becomes relatively cheaper. In this way, motorists and petrol companies could not only save money, but save damage to the brains of children. In a saner society, lead in petrol would be banned immediately, and oil companies would use existing refining methods that do not need added lead, bit cost about two pence a gallon more. The increase would be more gladly paid by motorists than the OPEC-caused price rises.s.

The immediate toxic metal problem remains a minor ris.., but feelings against the recycling of sewage are strongly reinforced by the prejudice that we share with most other living creatures against our own excreta as a potential carrier of the eggs of parasitic worms and possibly disease bacteria. This is why we brush-harrow pastures to spread the cowpats so that cattle will graze again.

The heated digestion process that produces methane gas lasts 21 days at a temperature of 90°F (32°C) under anaerobic conditions, and destroys all tapeworm eggs other than those of *Taenia saginata*, the beef tapeworm. When liquid sludge is sprayed on pastureland, cattle are by law kept off the field for three weeks so that the eggs of the 1% which may survive the heat digestion process die in the open air, and there are no pathogens affecting human beings that will survive as long outside our bodies. Our safeguards against beef tapeworm are the veterinary inspections at slaughter houses, and the fact that we do not usually eat our meat raw (for cooking kills the larval stage, the only form in which this parasite is transmitted

133

to humans). However, it can be passed on in dung from infected cattle, so they too have reason to be instinctively cautious.

The Official Attitude

The Department of the Environment has to make official decisions on the use of sewage on the land, because new treatment works must be built as old ones wear out, and as cities grow, with the baths and flush toilets of every modernized terrace house adding another 22 gallons (100lt) a day. The basis for the Department's decisions is the account of a Working Party, chaired by Mrs Lena Jeger, MP, on sewage disposal, which was published in August 1970 and is available from HMSO under the title *Taken for Granted*.[4]

Like most Working Party reports this recommends modest and cautious proposals, because its members hope that their endeavours to gather the facts before they change for the worse will not be entirely wasted. Caution, however, is not enough. Much more is needed when we must deal with problems that will double themselves in twenty years, and cost five times as much to solve. Ten years ago, no one could have foreseen our present concern with toxic metal, for research and scientific discovery today are far more likely to lead to new warnings than to solutions for old problems, with the doubling and redoubling of fuel costs which were not even considered at that time.

The Department of the Environment has now considered the questions of toxic metals, fuel, and a great many more, including inflation and ever rising wage and salary rates. To quote an Official Spokesman, writing before a report expected during the 1980s 'It is likely to recommend the eventual phasing out of the supply of sludge to the general public because of risks, albeit very low, of pathogenic infections through handling the material and also because there is no effective means of ensuring that the recommended application rates are not exceeded with the risk of the addition of toxic metals to the soil. Current opinion is that sewage sludges that contain less than 20mg/kg (p.p.m.) of cadmium in the dry solids and have been subjected to some form of heat treatment, heat conditioning or drying, are acceptable for supply to the general public. The trend is for more liquid sludge to be tankered to farm lands where records can be kept of amounts applied so that the recommended maximum permissible amounts of toxic metals added to the soil should not be exceeded.'

Tankered sludge is pumped straight from the digesters and spread by special lorries on pasture land. The liquid looks like thin tar, smells faintly of unwashed socks, and contains about 5% of dry matter, which is usually about 6.8% N, 4.7% P_2O_5 and 0.3% K_2O. The nitrogen and phosphorus are mainly in the bottles of the methane-making bacteria, which alone can survive three weeks' digestion, and this makes them very ready for release by soil bacteria, so that the grass leaps ahead, leaving no loose nitrates to wash into drinking water.

Ever since 1968, Professor Barry Commoner of Washington University has been warning of the danger of nitrate fertilizers, which can be changed into poisonous nitrates by bacteria present in the digestive organs of a baby. High levels of nitrate also reduce the oxygen carrying capacity of a baby's blood, dangerously starving the brain. For three months in 1970, wells in North Lincolnshire had a level of nitrate above the World Health Organisation safety limit, and mothers were supplied with bottled water from safe areas.[5]

The tanker system not only saves the ever-increasing cost of fuel oil for drying sludge from about 65% moisture in drying beds to 10–20%, but also the labour cost of this process. It rather more than doubles the plant foods, because so much nitrogen and phosphorus go up the drier chimney with the steam. Though there is the cost of diesel oil to run the tanker lorries, it is worth the money, because of the advantage of spreading the metals thinly in 5% of moisture in 6–12,000 gallons (65–130,000lt) on an acre of farm, where the man from ADAS (Agricultural Development and Advisory Service) can test at intervals and stop supplies in the event of a further warning from the research stations, or if the level is rising too high.

Municipal Compost
Processed municipal rubbish has always had a good image because of the magic word 'compost'. On the other hand, it may contain much higher level of toxic metals than sewage sludge, and has the additional problem of plastics and broken glass. Unless the glass is smashed very fine, it can endanger footballers falling, or children tumbling, and far more children play bare limbed on lawns than ever eat soil.

The composting process is made very rapid by the constant turning of huge steel cylinders, as in the Dano machines, mechanized stirring in the Fairfield, and many devices for pulverizing, spreading in windrows and turning by tractor-mounted appliances. The main difficulty is in persuading farmers to buy a substance that varies between 18% and 40% organic matter with an ever increasing quantity of plastics, when inorganic farmers are even unwilling to spread their own farmyard manure. The Leicester plant, the largest and most modern in Europe, screens its product so well that this holds only 3% of fine glass 1% of plastics, and can be spread as easily as a chemical fertilizer.

Today, the composition of our dustbin refuse has changed from 40% of cinders and ashes in the 1950s to what can be 10% of plastics by weight. This means vastly more in bulk, when the expanded polystyrene packing for TV sets, hi-fi equipment and other fragile goods is added to the clear plastic blister packs surrounding almost everything stationers and ironmongers have to sell.

The proportion of compostable food wastes has shrunk, with the rise of convenience foods, TV dinners and Chinese take-aways, all of which add aluminium foil, cardboard, paper and plastics, in place of peelings, which are now a factory waste. Old clothes that once provided nitrogen in wool now provide undecayable man-made fibres, with battered shoes made of PVC. Paper and cardboard are now the main organic wastes, and as their cellulose breaks down in the composting process it results in a concentration of the yellow and red inks used in colour magazines and packaging that can reach up to 29,000 p.p.m. of lead and 4,000 p.p.m. of cadmium.

The higher our standard of living, the more we throw away, and the less of our rubbish is material that will break down to humus in the soil. Though black and white TV sets are quickly shredded, soon to be followed by computers as these are replaced by smaller and smaller models, these only mean more glass, plastics and assorted unusual metals. There is nothing here that will compost and feed the land.

The future probably lies in using our refuse as a source of raw materials for re-use, as these grow more expensive and scarce, rather than for compost. Doncaster has recently installed a complete recycling plant to handle 60,000 tonnes of refuse a year. This starts by removing the cans and scrap iron with a magnet, to sell at £15 a tonne; the broken glass also fetches £15 a tonne after powerful washing; the large papers and plastics are sorted out by laser beams that distinguish materials by their reaction to light, then separate them, while the dirty and small portions of paper and plastics, plus the food fraction are compressed into pellets that sell as low grade industrial fuel. One of the major factors in deciding to recycle in the city rather than run the refuse lorries to a still further away tip has been the cost in fuel of taking more and more loads of lighter and bulkier wastes.

The long-term answer lies in throwing away less, with the help of paper and cardboard collections either by councils or voluntary organizations, the disposal of food scraps either in compost or as poultry feed by gardeners, and municipal recycling rather than composting. The prohibition of aluminium cans and foil (which cause endless trouble by beating the magnets), and a regulation that all Government forms should by printed on recycled paper would be two inexpensive but far-reaching measures that any Government really concerned about conservation should enforce.

Municipal Compost and Sludge for Gardeners

Among the claims made for the Leicester compost, marketed as 'Lescost', are that it produces a 30% increase in vegetable yields, and that it is superior to farmyard manure on analysis, like most domestic composts, rich in organic matter, and lasts as a soil conditioner for up to three years. It is recommended for application at 3lb a square yard (1.6kg/m²) to lawns, vegetable and flower gardens, and in 1980 cost 70p for a 56lb (25kg) bag collected from Wanlip works, or £6.90 a loose tonne, including VAT delivered in bulk to farmers and other users of large quantities. It is also sold through agents and garden centres beyond the 50-mile delivery radius.

The toxic metal level is very low, and the following table compares Lescost with average farmyard manure, and Dewmus and Morganic dried sewage sludges.

	USA standard	FYM	Lescost	Dewmus	Morganic
Zinc	1,500	20	350	2,631	1,520
Copper	750	4	310	492	820
Iron	—	180	21,860	29,523	8,550
Nickel	150	—	20	54	265
Chromium	500	—	trace	2,344	815
Lead	500	—	410	862	600
Cadmium	50	—	13	12	50

Metals (p.p.m.) in sewage sludges and municipal compost

The iron level does not matter—there is plenty in sand or clay, and all plants need some, but take only as much as they want. The USA column refers to the Federal limits of safety, and it will be noted that Dewmus has well over 1,500 p.p.m. more of chromium and 238 p.p.m. more lead, while Morganic reaches the US limit for cadmium and exceeds the level for lead. It is well above the British 20 p.p.m. for the deadly cadmium, while Lescost comes through safely on all standards.

Though there are only (to the best of our knowledge) these three sources for gardeners, there may well be organic farmers near small plants for the treatment of sewage from rural residential areas, where the only zinc would be from cosmetic residues when well made-up ladies take baths, and the lead from the insides of water pipe, where the supply is peaty or soft. Any prospective large-scale user should ask for an analysis of what is locally going free and insist on knowing the lead and cadmium figures. If the lead is below the US limit and the cadmium below the British, consult the nearest ADAS branch for an analysis of your soil for toxic metals, because the safety of any supply depends on the levels already present. It might well be possible to buy a small slurry tanker for towing behind a tractor and be paid to take the whole output, or to persuade the council to provide a larger model, enabling pastures to be sludged every three or four years in turn, starting with the poorest field. Organochlorine pesticides used in sheep dipping may cause contamination of the sewers in rural areas, but as the advice of the ADAS man is free, and the Council should pay him to take the samples and have the analysis done, keep on the safe side and check for safety. If it were not for industrial pollution, sewage would be a bargain, and your local treatment plant could provide good value in fertility.

Using Dried Sludge in the Garden

The organic gardener needs sewage for two purposes: as a compost activator, and in feeding his lawn organically to produce the maximum of material for making compost and mulches. The quantity needed is so small that it pays to buy in 56lb (25kg) bags, even with carriage, and though a child would be in great danger of lead or cadmium poisoning if he or she ate a whole bag of Morganic in a week, 56lb (25kg) of basic slag would contain more minerals and taste just as nasty.

The analysis figures in the following Table do not add up to 100% each, because both Dewmus and Morganic contain silica, alumina and other substances lumped together as 'ash'. These do no harm, and both materials contain a useful supply of humus, mostly as lignins, however, and they therefore supply rather less energy in proportion than farmyard manure or ordinary compost (though the total energy production is greater, because they are so much drier).

	Dewmus	Morganic	FYM
	%	%	%
Moisture	13.0	10.0	77.0
Ash free Dry Matter	40.3	50.0	17.0
Nitrogen	2.5	3.0	0.6
Phosphorus (P_2O_5)	2.5	2.3	0.3
Potassium (K_2O)	0.46	0.2	0.7

Analysis of sludge and municipal compost

Gardeners who wish to try Morganic should write to The Engineer and Manager, Mogden Sewage Treatment Works, PO Box 7, Isleworth, Middlesex TW7 7LP. The address for Dewmus is: The Manager, Yorkshire Water Organics, Mitchel Laithes, Clough Lane, Earlisheaton, Dewsbury, West Yorks WF12 8LL. To obtain Municipal Compost, apply to The Manager, Wanlip Composing Plant, Fillingate, Wanlip, Leicester. It is a sad reflection on present methods that there were once twelve municipal compost plants selling to the public (as distinct from using their compost to fill up holes), and thirty Councils selling dried sludges; today there are only these three.

Dried Sludge as an Activator
Dried seaweed, when used as an activator for veganic compost (see the section on activators in Chapter 2), makes bacteria, as distinct from fungi, multiply very rapidly. However, apart from the disadvantage of high cost, it provides very little nitrogen, which is a problem when the compost heap consists of woody stems rather than sappy young weeds high in protein.

A long time ago the HDRA carried out a programme of trials extending over three years on the use of dried sludges in the garden on behalf of the Upper Tame Main Drainage Board. Part of our brief was to explore the possibilities of sludge as an activator. It turned out to give a slow start and a low temperature limit, probably because the heating process slows the release of the nitrogen and phosphorus and makes it last longer. The addition of 25% of dried seaweed, however, improved the effect of both activators and lowered the cost considerably (see Appendix 3j).

Dried Sludge for Lawns
On many lawns, sand is coals to Newcastle. On still more, there is a shortage of humus, as well as a lack of plant foods arising from constant mowing and clipping. In these cases, it pays to substitute a

dried sewage sludge for the sand in the lawn sand recipe given in Chapter 3 (see the section on Lawn Mowings as Compost Material). There will be a gain as the sludge's more slowly released nitrogen feeds the roots when the ammonium sulphate has spent the tonic effect which follows its weedkilling action. No gardener wishes to use chemical nitrogen on his lawn in quantity because it means more mowing in a rush in the spring, but this 'lawn-sludge' maintains a steady production of mulching and compost material throughout the season.

Since the mixture is so fine that it rapidly washes down among the grass roots, out of the reach of any child, the lead and cadmium levels are not important, while the heat used for drying the sludge will have destroyed any possible pathogens. In the past, dried sewage sludges were favourites for golf courses, football fields and tennis courts. Those who happen to be honorary secretaries of sports clubs could save the clubs' money by buying sludge, making their own lawn sand, and sharing out the grass mowings, free of any selective weedkillers, among the members who are organic gardeners.

Septic Tank Effluent

The cheapest water sanitation for an isolated house is one of the modern plastic septic tanks. These take the human wastes, and the water from baths, washing-up, laundry and other household uses, and ferment them under anaerobic conditions so that much of the organic matter breaks down to such gases as nitrogen and carbon dioxide, and liquids. Older, brick-built tanks are larger but all work on the same principle, and the HDRA supplies Odorcure, which is a culture of bacteria to start off a new tank, or reactivate an old one that has started to smell because something has upset the inhabitants of what is, in effect, a water compost heap.

Eventually the lignins and other lasting solids, including the heavy metals that pass through our bodies, accumulate in the bottom of the tank, and they can be removed by the Council. Otherwise, it is possible to fit a small hand pump with a hose reaching down to the bottom, so that it will suck out the sludge that has accumulated after at least a year.

Septic tanks hold about 600 gallons (2700lt) and, as baths and wash-days build up the level, there will be an overflow, which should not go straight into a river. Its biological oxygen demand will be about 600–750mg per litre, compared with only 10mg per litre from a good sewage works, and there is a health risk.

Liquid from the tank should not be used on lettuce or any salad crop, or on lawns or sports grounds, for these may involve personal contact with people, but has been used successfully to irrigate black currant orchards, grassland grazed by cattle or sheep, and plantings of willow, alder and poplar. The tank should be sited where there is a fall that will allow the effluent to flow along shallow channels across the area to be irrigated. It should be realized that however much you cut down on water use, so as to use less than 32 gallons (144lt) each day, there will be a considerable bulk of fluid to dispose of. Therefore you cannot run it into any ditch that will lead it direct to a river. It must filter through grassland or woodland, and woodland is to be preferred, because the soil will not freeze badly in winter, allowing a soakaway effect.

Willows are the ideal trees for an effluent irrigated 'mini-wood' because they do not mind standing in the wet all the winter, and will drink up to 6pt of water a day for every square yard (4lt/m²) grown for firewood, with bark for goat feeding, to be cut down every three years about 2in (5cm) from the ground. Plant the cuttings 1yd (1m) apart each way. Goats will eat willow twigs rather thicker than pencils, and it pays to cut a weekly ration, turning the branches to let them bark both sides of larger shoots. Expect to burn willow wood felled between October and February a year later, sawing to burning size and stowing it to save space and to season better. Bowles Hybrid is the fastest variety.

Where it is impossible, or very expensive, to have your tank cleared out, pump it to fill one or several trenches dug in a vegetable plot that can be rested for a summer. Let the water soak away and then fill in the trenches. In the spring, sow sunflowers as recommended in Chapter 3 (see the section on Home-Grown Compost Material) for an area where bucket sanitation results have been buried, take several crops for compost, then lime the soil and plant the cabbage tribe through the winter. The advice of the suppliers who fit the septic tank should be taken; they want their product to work well, with minimum trouble, for if it creates difficulty with smell and other problems, they will find it less easy for their customers to get planning permission to install one. To quote an authority in the field of water research: 'There is no handbook that recommends the practice of using septic tank effluent for irrigation because of the possible health risk. I am bound to endorse this view officially, but of course there is no doubt that some people actually do this in violation of the consent conditions of the Water Authorities, and, with care and good luck do not suffer any harm.'

The Detergent Problem

Detergents contain phosphates, and at one time there was a racket in which a type containing nitrogen was sold as environmentally safer, although it caused just as much oxygen depletion. All are now biodegradable, but all contain borax, and release the element boron, which can build up to danger levels in the soil. It is toxic to conifers, but not to broadleafed trees.

Smallholders who have the opportunity to have a liquid sludge sprayed on their land should check that it does not contain more than one milligramme per litre of boron if it is to be used on plums, pears, apples, cherries, blackcurrants, strawberries and raspberries. The safe limits are 2mg/lt for potatoes, tomatoes, redishes, peas, sweet corn, barley, oats and wheat and 4mg for asparagus, beet, broadbeans, onions, turnips, cabbage, lettuce, carrots and lucerne. If you have a sceptic tank, stop using detergents; soap flakes break down better and leave no toxic metals.[7]

The Broken Cycle

The basic difference between organic and inorganic thinking is that we, in the organic movement, think further ahead. Not only to the organochlorine compounds accumulating in the body fats of our children, but to toxic metals building up from the pollution of our sewage sludge by industry, which is more important than the oil tanker disasters that kill countless seabirds, because it means permanent pollution of the land that should be growing the food that the more crowded world of the future will need in ever greater quantities.

Even the organo-chlorine compounds, such as DDT, dieldrin and aldrin, break down eventually. But there is no way so far known of taking toxic metals out of the soil. Research may find crops or trees that can gather the deadly traces with their roots and toss them away on the winds, or hold them in stems or timber for recycling, but we dare not gamble on the success of untried methods of dealing with man's oldest wastes, as the greedy gambles with his newest and most deadly.

If we decide that sewage sludge is too dangerous to use, and that the only way to dispose of it is by drying and burning it with costly fuel, or discharging it into the sea, we impose a limitation on the future of humanity by breaking cycles that return the plant foods and trace elements we gather together in our daily food and should then restore to the soil, like every other living creature. We should all think ahead, not only to the fossil fuels, but also the fossil fertilizers, running out.

We wash the world whiter than white with detergents (even more wastefully soluble than superphosphates) that we have made with phosphates from the rich beds of fossilized fish left, in North Africa for example, by only a limited number of primeval seas, when we might have been conserving them as the lasting ground minerals needed by so many tropical soils. In the long run, we are bleeding to death the farmlands of the world through our haste to pour into the suffering seas the residues of plant foods we have eaten, mixed with ever increasing quantities of industrial pollutants. The sea has no subsoil to hold plant foods and trace elements in readiness for tree roots to reach them. Substances that we should return to the land we are diluting in the vastness of the sea, and it will take a very long time to come back in seaweeds, fish and fishmeal to the cycles we have so wantonly broken.

We cannot gamble the 55 million inhabitants of Britain, and the other 700 million people who are also prosperous, will be alone in their use of a standard 60 gallons (270lt) of water a day. It is only too probable that the 3,000 million-odd other people with whom we share the world will develop towards using modern sewage systems to solve their far worse problems of pathogens and parasites, and follow our wasteful roads to pollution and resource exhaustion. If this happened, the world would be faced by far worse preoccupations than our Western worry of having no wild life left to look at. Man's most important task of all is to conserve the world's fertility on which all life depends.

Taken for Granted sets out the 1970 totals of plant foods in sewage, calculated by multiplying the NPK in average dried sludge by the 1.1 million tonnes a year of dry solids in the vast quantity of sewage that passes through our treatment plants each year. When the figures are calculated from tanker sludge analysis they show a different picture.

This kind of assessment, easily made with the right adding machine, can only be an informed guess, because of the figures that cannot be included. The sludge figures are about 20% too low because in 1970 there were 10 million people whose sewage went into the Tyne and other heavily polluted rivers, and 148 seaside resorts that discharged theirs direct into the sea. Manchester, Glasgow and the Great Becton Sewage works that serves 3½ milion Londoners, take their sludge out in specially constructed ships for dumping at sea, though about half of the sludge that is produced finds its way back to the land.

The really disastrous waste is in effluent, which is run off into rivers on a scale large enough for the Upper Tame Main Drainage

	Average Dried sludge analysis %	Tonnage in 1.1 million tons a year tonnes	Tonnage of chemical fertilizers used in UK tonnes
Nitrogen	2.4	26,400	600,000
P_2O_5	1.3	14,300	350,000
K_2O	0.3	3,300	350,000
	Average Tanker sludge dry matter		
Nitrogen	6.8	74,800	600,000
P_2O_5	4.7	51,700	350,000
K_2O	0.3	3,300	350,000

Plant foods in sludge

Authority to boast that before the river Tame reaches the sea its water will have been used five times. Each sewage works is pouring its effluent into the river, and every waterworks lower down stream is pumping water out again for purification and returning it to the mains supply, to become sewage again.

This saves the water that is another of our limiting resources, for the reason why we cannot go on feeding a repeatedly doubling world population on synthetic foods is that they take far more water to produce than natural foods do to grow. Even though 30–50 gallons of water as rain or dew will grow 1lb of wheat (60–100lt/kg), and 2,000 gallons (9000lt) produce a tonne of meat, this is distributed by the rain and dew, and held by sponges of fertile farms and forests. The 2,500 tonnes of water to make a tonne of synthetic rubber must be pumped, purified and piped before discharge, often with polluting chemicals dissolved in it.

In 1970, the daily flow of sewage to British treatment works was 5,000 million gallons (22,000 million litres) a day, quite apart from that discharged direct into rivers and the sea by local authorities and industry. Multiply that figure by 365, and the 1.1 million tonnes of

	Analysis of Effluent mg. per litre	Plant foods in total British Effluent tonnes
Nitrogen	30–40	151,800–202,500
P_2O_5	8–12	40,500– 60,700
K_2O	10–30	50,600–151,800

Analysis of effluent

dry matter contains quite a small fraction of plant foods, compared with the bulk there is in the wasted flood of effluent.

The most important of these plant foods is phosphorus, as the Third World countries are going to need increasing quantities as their populations double, and its cost has increased five-fold since 1970. The following table shows Britain's phosphorus balance sheet:

Annual Gains by Imports	Tonnes	Annual Losses to Agriculture	Tonnes
Mineral Phosphates:			
Fertilizers	210,000	Sewage	54,000
Detergents	26,000	Animal wastes	26,000
Feed additives	7,000	Bones in refuse	23,000
Food additives	4,000	In drainage water from land	20,000
Industrial chemicals	8,000		123,000
Organic materials:			
In fishmeal	3,000		
In stock feed	53,000	Retained in soil	213,000
In human food	10,000		
	336,000		336,000

The phosphorus balance sheet
(Adapted from *Phosphorus—A Resource for UK Agriculture*, Centre for Agricultural Strategy, Report No. 2, University of Reading, Earley Gate, Reading, Berks. 1978).

All the phosphorus wasted in detergents and human wastes goes straight down to the sea, growing algae and blanket weed on the way, while that which is used on the land has a very good chance of staying in the soil until it is unlocked by the action of root fungi and soil bacteria. In fact, the opinion of the Centre for Agricultural Strategy, and many other orthodox authorities, is that British farmers are using far too much phosphate fertilizer for the health of their soil.

Just as orthodox gardeners burn their leaf-mould and buy peat to replace it, factory farmers waste their manure and buy more unnecessary superphosphate to replace what they have squandered.

As a cow produces about 16 times as much bodily waste as an adult human, the aeration trenches that are used to destroy manure (working on the same principle as septic tanks) release far more plant foods into rivers and the sea than get there in human sewage.

Today there is a world phosphorus shortage because so many Third World countries have soils that are low in this most essential plant food, and they need ground rock phosphates that will stay in the soil, despite the leaching of tropical rains. In Britain, we are building up more than we need from the animal feeds and fertilizers we import, but in the future we shall have to reform our methods of sewage treatment to close the broken circle that is the fertility of the world's soils.

Chapter 7
1. HALL, Sir Daniel *Manures and Fertilizers* John Murray 1928 pp.107–217

2. *The Complete Book of Composting* Rodale Press, Inc. 1970

3. THOMPSON, Alan *The Complete Poultryman* Faber & Faber 1952 pp.417–422

4. 'Poultash' HDRA *Newsletter* No. 79 1979

Chapter 8
1. BRYCE-SMITH, D. 'Review of the Analytical Findings for Beaumont Leys Development Site, Leicester' Department of Chemistry, University of Reading 5th January 1972

2. 'Behavioural Effects of Lead and other Heavy Metal Pollutants' *Chemistry in Britain* 8/5 June 1972

3. TUCKER, Anthony *The Toxic Metals* Earth Island 1972 p.182

4. *Taken for Granted.* Report of the working party on sewage disposal. Ministry of Housing and Local Government, HMSO 1970

5. COMMONER, Barry *The Closing Circle* Jonathan Cape 1972

6. SHIPP, Raymond F., and BAKER, Dale E. 'Pennsylvania's Sewage Sludge Research and Extension Program' *Compost Science* 16/2 1975

7. 'Organic Manures' Ministry of Agriculture *Bulletin* 210 HMSO 1976 p.35

9 Organic Fertilizers

Organic fertilizers are the many substances which are of animal or vegetable origin, but contain little humus and provide a more concentrated source of plant foods than manures. Though many are dried and ground, they still have their molecules arranged in forms that soil bacteria can easily take apart. In recycling terms, they are like returnable bottles that need only washing and refilling, as opposed to beer cans with iron smelting complications from the ring-pull aluminium top.

This probably explains why they are different from all chemical fertilizers in terms of cost. Experienced market growers in many countries, for perhaps a hundred years, have paid between four and six times the amount for the plant foods they contain that they would for the same amount from chemical sources. The prices per unit of nitrogen in the textbooks change faster and faster, but dried blood is still worth four times as much per unit as sulphate of ammonia. It may be the presence of auxins, or some side-effect of the bacterial breakdown, but there is always enough difference to be value for money.

The Nitrogen Fertilizers
Organic gardeners and farmers see their crops standing still in cold, dry springs, while those of their inorganic neighbours rush ahead. Until the soil warms up enough for bacteria to release the organic nitrogen contained in it, there is not enough to start the crop into full growth, but the ammonium sulphate, sodium nitrate or nitro-chalk used as a spring top dressing for grain crops is taken up directly, producing the lush, dark green growth that is so attractive to aphids in inorganically cultivated crops. Organic farmers, however, know their crops will catch up as warmth in the soil brings into action a full team of micro-organisms; and so do experienced organic gardeners.

A trial by Dr Hamence and Dr Owen at Cheshunt Research Station reported in *The Fertilizer and Feeding Stuffs Journal* for 25th June 1952, compared the amount of nitrogen released as nitrate, and available to plants within 21 days, by a given quantity of dried blood, which was taken as 100, with the other nitrogen-containing organic fertilizers, sulphate of ammonia and synthetic urea.

Great care was taken in the experiment to have the pH of plots, as well as their moisture, aeration and temperature at the ideal balance for nitrification with the maximum bacterial activity.

	Availability[1]
Dried blood	100
Meat and bone meal	102
Fish Meal	129
Hoof and horn meal	100
Shoddy	90
Rape meal	60
Leather dust	50
Sulphate of ammonia	112
Urea	170

Availability of nitrogen from organic fertilizers

Therefore, the hoof and horn meal sample scored level with the dried blood, while the urea would have produced the fast, sappy growth which is typical of overfed crops.

Dried Blood

This is the most rapidly available of any organic fertilizer, for it begins releasing its nitrogen four days after application. It is a summer tonic for laggard lettuces, celery plants that have had too many leaves picked to get rid of leaf-miner, and best of all in a cold, dry spring for frame-raised plants that just sit flat on the ground and sulk. Dried blood should never be applied later than mid-August, and even that is wasteful, for it is best scattered on the surface along the lettuce row, and in cold weather may go furry with moulds that live on its protein, which should be feeding soil bacteria. It will keep releasing nitrogen for more than 70 days, and if it is used to start a slow crop into action there will still be enough left in the soil to help a fresh planting along the same rows.

Many commercial growers use dried blood at the rate of 1–5cwt an acre (125–625kg/hectare) on tomatoes or cucumbers under glass, and it is extensively used for lettuce by inorganic growers because, unlike soluble chemical fertilizers, it will not 'burn' crops with foliage close to the ground. The greatest value as far as shops are concerned is the gain in keeping quality. Lettuces fed with dried blood last longer in the greengrocer's shop without going flabby like those grown with chemicals.

Feathers

Feathers are a neglected source of nitrogen, making over 15.3% available quite quickly, for they decay rapidly in the soil if they are wet enough. In a compost heap they break down very fast, and much of their nitrogen is wasted. One of the best uses is for black-currants and rhubarb, and here again, old bolsters, pillows and eiderdowns provide a supply to empty cautiously into your fruit planting holes (without letting them blow about) and cover with top soil. A good stock of old eiderdowns rotavated into a new garden on sandy soil in the autumn can be better value than an expensive load of manure, or polythene bags of something dried and costly. Do not use feathers on subsoil because they need bacterial action to break them down, and suitable organisms are short on this kind of soil, which builders so often leave behind.

In America, it is estimated that about 100,000 tonnes of feathers are available annually, and even in Britain the broiler industry must be responsible for thousands of tonnes. The US Department of Agriculture have developed a process for converting feathers into a dry meal providing slowly released nitrogen. The feathers are pressure cooked with steam for 30 minutes, dried to 10% moisture and ground. The average nitrogen content is between 12% and 13.5%, and no nutrient appears to be lost. Organic gardeners will naturally want to be satisfied that no persistent pesticides are present in the feathers, but there is no reason why a supply from free range flocks should not be put through this process.

Hoof and Horn
The availability of nutrients depends on the fineness of the grind, for the material in the table above was a 'meal', with particles under ⅛in (3mm), but the grades go up to chips averaging ½in (12.5mm) across. The value of the larger pieces is in holes dug for fruit trees at planting time, where their 12–14% nitrogen released at a steadily increasing rate during the first three years is a great asset, especially under walls, where the soil is usually poorest.

The fine grade is used commercially by tomato growers at the rate of 10cwt an acre (1.25kg/hectare), because the nitrogen will be released from eight to ten weeks later.

Leather Dust
This is the slowest nitrogen source of all. Today, pure leather dust is very scarce, and there is the risk that any supply will contain chromium from the chrome tanning process, or some of the many 'composition' materials used, that are mainly plastic. If a sample with about 9% nitrogen can be bought from a fairly old-fashioned factory or, better still, from a craftsman shoemender, it is good value as lasting feed for fruit and other trees. The provision of nutrients to sustain long-lived crops is the main value of organic

concentrates, and it is worth any gardener's while to spend the price of a garden goblin on such good, slow plant foods that can mature like an endowment policy to pay for the 'education' of fruit for the future.

Rape Dust and Castor Meal

Rape cake, which is the residue left after crushing rape seed for oil, was once regarded as a first-class 'portable manure' for mangolds and barley, because of the organic matter it supplied and the nitrogen which was available slowly through the season—'as effective as sulphate of ammonia or nitrate of soda', to quote Sir Daniel Hall, Director of Rothamsted Experimental Station in *Fertilizers and Manures*—a classic reprinted many times since it appeared in 1909. Another residue of the same type is castor cake, the by-producr of castor oil making, but this is scarce now that flying and motor racing have moved away from the era of leather helmets, shouting, and the smell of this first of the high-speed engine lubricants.

There is now a return to growing oil seed rape, which shows in fields solid with the yellow flowers of this close relation of mustard in early summer, and cattle cake manufacturers buy most of the residue, though they cannot use the poisonous castor cake. Both are worth finding, especially for veganic gardeners who are otherwise without a quick nitrogen tonic to use in dry springs, because they refuse to use any animal manure. Both used to be used at the rate of 18cwt an acre (1.4kg/hectare), about 6oz a square yard (200g/m^2), and the speed of availability depends on a fine grind to allow plenty of working surface for the soil bacteria.

Wool Shoddy

Modern shoddy varies, because it sometimes contains man-made fibres and cotton, which can cause nitrogen robbery. One of the best sources of useful fibre is in old mattresses, which can often be gathered from dumps or bought very cheaply from second-hand furniture dealers. Test by lighting some of the contents. If your sample frizzles and burns slowly with a smell, it is nitrogen-containing wool, silk or hair. If it burns quickly with a clean flame, it is cotton, coconut fibre or other useless material, while man-made fibres can produce black smoke. Wool wastes, known as 'dags', that include sheep dung, are excellent, but expensive. If you can find a few old mattresses, they will start a garden off with an effect that lasts for years.

Apart from being a source of nitrogen, shoddy retains moisture very well on sandy or chalky soil, and it should be dug in, tucked well down in the bottom of the planting holes for fruit. Quantities are difficult to estimate, but the traditional dressings for hops were 1–2 tonnes an acre 2.5–5 tonnes/hectare) or up to 1lb a square yard (550g/m²). Shoddy was always ploughed under in the autumn, which is also the best time to dig it in, so that it can become saturated, like a sponge, with winter rain, making the moisture last some way into the summer. Fruits, especially blackcurrants and rhubarb, gain most from shoddy.

Soot

Soot has always been regarded as an 'organic' manure, although the only plant or animal material it contains is unburnt carbon from the smoke of burning fossil fuels. It has been used for centuries as a spring top dressing for wheat, not only for the nitrogen it contains, but because it is disliked by slugs. It was also used for onion beds in the days when every gardener had special recipes for assorted fertilizers, both for its supply of nitrogen and because the darkening of the soil surface increased the soil temperature through the absorption of more heat from the sun.

Bedfordshire growers formerly used soot extensively for Brussels sprouts, at the rate of a tonne an acre (2.5 tonnes/hectare) before planting, and as a top dressing of 10cwt (1.25 tonnes/hectare). The temperature gain in the daytime is about 2°F (1°C) and, though this is not significant in the open, it helps under cloches. As soot fresh from the chimney is so rich in freely available sulphur compounds that it is dangerous to plant life, bags of soot were stored under cover for three months to weather before use.

Soot was valued in the past because it contains between 5% and 12% of ammonium sulphate, which explains the need to keep it off the leaves and to prevent its getting too close to the crop. It is really a chemical fertilizer that was used long before any others were invented. Anyone who wants to use ammonium sulphate can buy it pure, at much lower cost and with fewer side effects than soot. Flue dust is also sold as a source of potassium, but again, its purity depends on the factory process that provided the smoke going up the flues, and this is not organic either.

Fly ash from power stations is also recommended, but this, too, is merely an example of the willingness of those who sell industrial by-products to unload them on the organic movement. There is a far greater risk of soil pollution from using any of these materials than that from sewage sludge or municipal compost, because the toxic substance present may be concentrated, and in an active form.

The Analysis of Nitrogenous Fertilizer

Soil and fertilizer analysis grew from the need to measure the cash value of consignments of seabird guano from rainless islands off the coast of Peru. Some samples were heavily adulterated with sand, some were fresh and some reached back to the days of the Incas, who were the first people to use concentrated organic fertilizers. When measurements started, great stress was laid on the 'Unit Value' of a fertilizer, which is the cost per tonne delivered, divided by the percentage of the plant food present in the greatest quantity.

This does not apply to organic fertilizers, for the gardener is not aiming to buy nitrogen from the cheapest source, but simply to obtain relatively small quantities for help with specific problems, such as a temporary shortage of nitrogen in lettuces in a cold spring, or the need to provide plant foods for newly planted trees during their first five years. Because a market gardener does not have the advantage of stock to graze and build up the leys or produce manure for spreading on arable land, he or she must import plant foods and humus, and concentrated by-product organic manures are of value because of the transport costs they save. Therefore, market growers are often forced to use them when organic gardeners need only green manures, composts and manures to provide all their nutrient requirements, except when they are building up a poor soil in a new garden.

In theory, all the plant foods our crops take from the soil can be provided in bags of chemicals. The following table is designed only to show what proportion of plant foods there should be in the nitrogenous fertilizers. One of the important differences between organic and inorganic fertilizers is that, by law, the inorganic type

	Moisture	Nitrogen	Phosphorus P_2O_5	Potash[2] K_2O
	%	%	%	%
Dried Blood	—	9–13	0.8	—
Feathers	10–18	2.15–13.1	0.1–0.4	0.1–0.7
Hoof and horn meal	—	6.5–13.2	0.8	—
Leather dust	19	0.5–7.5	0.1–0.2	0.2–0.3
Rape dust	—	5.1–5.3	1.6–2.5	1.5
Shoddy	7–17	3.2–14.9	0.3–10	0.1–12

Analysis of nitrogen-rich organic fertilizers

must show the analysis on the bag—organic sellers are not bound to give one, because by their nature, all organic materials vary—and the two figures given show the possible variation.

Phosphate Fertilizers

Nitrogen is available from the air in unlimited quantities, needing only the energy to fix it, but it is merely the cheque book that enables you to draw on the world's strictly limited reserves of other plant foods, and the more nitrogen fertilizers you use, the larger the cheques the land must cash.

In 1972 an American chemical combine signed a contract with the USSR to supply a million tonnes of phosphoric acid annually for 21 years in exchange for urea and ammonia nitrogen fertilizers, and at Christmas 1979 they agreed to send a further 350 million tonnes. The 'New Lands' of Southern Siberia are evidently running out of plant foods, their fertility wrecked by the kind of greedy, stockless farming that has made the North American grain states so heavily dependent on chemical fertilizers.[3]

Canada and the USA have been the world's greatest grain exporters, with surpluses available for famine relief, wars, disasters and crop failures. They have been able to maintain the yields that make this possible only because America's rock phosphate deposits have been spent on a massive scale. However, these deposits are now running low.

The need to open up new areas for strip mining means the desecration of tens of thousands of acres of mountain and hillside country, and farmlands are stripped of their fertile topsoil well before the grabs go in. The lower the phosphate level of the rock, the more land must be bared and pulverized for every million tonnes of finished superphosphate—which results in choking fluoride fumes, poisoning plants and stock, from the factories that process the ground rock—and the more energy must be spent in grinding it.

Since phosphate chemical fertilizers are only about 20% available to crops, men must mine and haul to the fields about four times more than they need. This excess stays locked out of the reach of roots, and can be released only with 'adequate liming and organic matter'. Some day in the future, the American corn belt, the Canadian wheat plains, and the Soviet steppes will have to be split into millions of mixed holdings farmed organically in order to tap the phosphates and keep them recycled to feed the world of the future, that must be One World. Gathering back the phosphates from the seas, where modern sewage treatments have squandered them, will be less easy.

Bonemeal

Just as trees concentrate potassium and calcium all through their long lives, we vertebrates hoard phosphorus and calcium in our bones. Though deer cast their used antlers for recycling on the mountains, most species give back their hoard only at the end of their lives. Bonemeal from the millions of animals slaughtered for food every year remains our most concentrated phosphate source. It is one of our oldest organic fertilizers and was mentioned in John Evelyn's diary in 1674; it was used extensively as a pasture dressing, feeding the famous Cheshire pastures that would fatten a bullock to every acre, even as late as the 1920s.

Raw bones, even crushed, are of little immediate value, because their phosphate is too slowly available, and they cannot be finely ground. The gardeners of the past used beef bones from butchers to bury in the holes where they planted their vines, and from Hampton Court to Chatsworth and the great houses of the Victorian age, the resulting 50–70 years of good phosphate feeding for vines planted outside the greenhouse and led in through the brickwork sides, or grown against sun warmed walls, have given us grapes of quality, and vines that last. It is possible to break large bones by hammering, but any form of grinding needs so much power that a hand or electric mill would be impossibly costly.

Domestic bones can be hoarded, week by week, for planting under vines and stone fruits, to provide benefit in the distant future, because they will not be much help to the trees for at least ten years. Burning bones produces a charcoal, but wastes most of the phosphorus in the gases driven off. The bone charcoal used for refining sugar is sometimes sold, and will be 70% calcium phosphate, but it usually goes direct to the makers of superphosphate. If it can be bought, it is a bargain. In the past, bones were collected and stored in layers of wood ashes in barrels, with water added to the full barrel, and left six months to ferment. This was reputed to make the bones easily crushable with a spade, producing a 'do-it-yourself' bonemeal. The process has recently been repeated, but it needs a large container and a quantity of bones and ashes to start the process.

Bonemeal, as we buy it today, is made out of bones collected from butchers and slaughterhouses, treated with high pressure steam to remove the glycerine and fats, boiled to extract the glue, and then very finely ground. This destroys all bacteria, in particular those of anthrax, which were dangerous in the less risk-conscious past, and leaves plenty of working surfaces for organisms in the soil to make the plant foods available.

Fine bonemeal, which is used to be called 'steamed bone flour', is the ideal phosphorus manure for strawberries, also providing useful nitrogen and calcium, which will last for the full three or four year life of the bed. Spread it at the rate of 8oz to 1lb a square yard (280–550g/m²) with compost before planting the bed, using the greater quantity on poorer soils. A certain warning of a shortage of available phosphorous can be seen in the weed 'fat hen' (*Chenopodium album*), a species of goosefoot—if it shows a maroon tinge in and around the growing points, use more bonemeal for the strawberry bed.

The other crop that is hungry for phosphorus is sweet corn, which is why the American maize belt needs so much rock phosphate. Because even fine bonemeal lasts at least two years, and maize ('corn', in the US) does not have any disease like clubroot that builds up in the soil, it is safe to grow it in the same sunny bed for two or even three years running. Apply bonemeal at the rate of 8oz a square yard (280g/m²) up to six weeks before planting sweet corn, and sow winter tares after harvesting the first crop, to grow humus and hold on to the plant foods until you dig it in before sowing the second crop.

Coarse bonemeal can sometimes be obtained, and is worth finding for its value when planting fruit trees, especially stone fruit, with 1–2lb (0.45–0.9kg) in every hole, plus an extra pound (0.45g) of dolomite limestone for such fruit as cherries and plums. Both types of bonemeal are of special value on sandy soils, as clays usually have plenty of phosphorus. The fine grade is a better bet for organic gardeners than ground rock phosphate, because it is available steadily over a short period and throws in calcium and some nitrogen, too.

Bone and Meat Meal

Also known as 'tankage', this is a blend of bones and slaughterhouse wastes including condemned carcases. The material is steamed for several hours at such high temperatures that all possibly pathogenic bacteria are destroyed, and all the fats come off for soap making. The meat proteins, amounting to as much as 50%, are then dried and ground for poultry food, but the lower grades go for fertilizer. They have the advantages of being cheaper than dried blood, providing phosphate as well as nitrogen, and lasting longer in the soil. They are used commercially at the rate of 10cwt an acre (1.25

tonnes/hectare), in the open or under glass, and on a garden scale at about 4oz a square yard (150g/m²), to provide a tonic for an aging strawberry bed or for lettuces grown for both speed and flavour.

Bone meals and blood are essentially a tonic, and a really healthy soil does not need one. They are no replacement for compost and well rotted manure, but if all you have been able to dig into a new garden on poor soil is raw dead leaves for humus, some blood and bonemeal in the spring will start your vegetables moving.

Fishmeal

Today, fishmeal is far too expensive to use as a compost heap activator, because of the rising cost of cattle cake and the ever increasing demand from factory farmers for proteins for pigs and poultry. Where it can be obtained reasonably, or if you can afford it, use it at the rate of 4oz a square yard (150g/m²), dug in as a general fertilizer before sowing vegetable crops. It is quickly available, but continues to break down in the soil for about six months.

Always dig it in, because if it is scattered on the surface it will be eaten by birds and slugs. Do not use it before March, for it can go mouldy on the surface or in the soil, as will bone and meat meal, and the rest of this group of organic fertilizers; they cost too much to use merely to feed soil-scavenging fungi.

Seaweed Meal

Dried seaweed is the only genuinely complete organic fertilizer in the sense that it holds a full set of plant nutrients and trace elements. The value of seaweed, especially in liquid preparations as a source of trace elements will be considered in Chapter 11 (see the section on Foliar Feeding). Seaweed meal is, however, an excellent fertilizer in its own right, although it holds such a supply of minerals that it is added to cattle feeds, and therefore the price is kept relatively high by that demand, apart from the cost of drying and grinding. It is rather low in nitrogen, and provides far more

	Moisture	Nitrogen	Phosphorus P_2O_5	Potash[4] K_2O
	%	%	%	%
Bone meal	0.2–14	0.3–4.6	14.1–33.2	—
Bone and meat meal	6.0	3.9–12.3	0.9–19.0	—
Fish meal	—	6.3–8.9	6.0–8.9	—
Seaweed meal	—	2.80	0.22	2.29[5]

Analysis of organic fertilizers

potash than phosphorus, thus making an excellent tomato fertilizer. As it contains quantities of alginates which form a 'gel', it should always be forked in, for if it is left lying on the soil surface, it can cause a thin, sticky layer that is extremely awkward for seeds.

Hydroponics

This technique of growing crops in a sterile medium fed with chemical salts dissolved in water is not, of course, in any way organic. Nor is it of any value to replace the soil and all its living organisms with manufactured products and human labour. It can be done, just as good crops can be grown with chemical fertilizers, but they cannot by any stretch of the imagination be called 'organically grown'.

There have been attempts to make up hydroponic solutions using only organic fertilizers of the type described in this chapter, but though there are a number of aquatic species of our common soil bacteria, such as *Azotobacter agilis*, the free-swimming nitrogen fixer, they are equipped to break down only what they are likely to find in water. Therefore, adding the mixtures of plant food contained in all organic fertilizers will produce shortages of trace elements and some plant nutrients, simply because some bacteria will fail and others succeed. What the vitamin and mineral content of the resulting crops will be is anyone's guess.

1. *Organic Fertilizers* Fertilizer Journal Ltd, London 1954

2. 'Organic Manures' Ministry of Agriculture *Bulletin* 210 HMSO 1976

3. CALDWELL, G. 'Phosphates Deal' *Acres USA* April 1980

4. 'Organic Manures'

5. Chase Organics, Chertsey

10   Wood Ashes and Mineral Fertilizers

Fire is Nature's chemical fertilizer factory, and forest blazes were breaking out long before there were cigarette ends, or broken bottles to work as burning glasses and focus sunlight on dead leaves. Trees struck by lightning, or dead branches rubbing together in the wind that fans slowly charring wood into flame, could result in a heavy dressing of a very unbalanced compound 'artificial' on the land where a forest had been slowly recycling its wastes and feeding the hosts of living creatures that depended on its energy and mineral-gathering ability through the centuries.

Burning forests concentrate the minerals that the roots and leaves have gathered into roughly one pound of ashes for every 2cwt of timber (500g for every 100kg). When leaves fall and become leaf-mould, or trees flatten out at the end of their lives, like dropped gloves on the forest floor, their minerals are dispersed in forms that are ready for recycling and re-use. But fire destroys all the humus, releases the hoarded nitrogen into the air, and reduces potassium to the powerful alkali potassium carbonate, which is highly soluble. It washes away quickly when the rains come and causes a number of complications in the soil.

As every inorganic gardener knows, tomatoes need potash, but when a generous supply of potassium chloride has been given for several years on end to the one bed that is sunny enough to ripen fruit on a dozen or so outdoor plants, the bottom leaves may well turn yellow while the veins stay green. This is because the presence of too much potassium has the effect of increasing the solubility of the soil's magnesium content, so that it washes away in the rains, together with boron and manganese which are both essential trace elements. To a forest, wood ashes are not a dressing of fertilizer but a disaster. Furthermore, this disaster may take more than fifty years to repair, with the help of the pioneer weeds, shrubs, and trees with winged seeds that await their opportunity to sail in and start the cycles turning again.

Wood Ashes in the Garden

Accurate comparisons between the ashes of different trees are almost impossible to find, for there is so much variation between twig and trunk wood that the only sound method would be to analyse a set of ash samples from woods of the same age or diameter. The following table gives the general picture.

	Potash K_2O %	Phosphorus P_2O_5 %	Calcium CaO %
Beech	12.50	8.65	39.27
Birch	8.66	3.99	36.25
Elm	21.92	3.64	17.80
Larch	15.24	3.06	27.00
Lime	37.84	5.12	31.60
Oak	8.34	3.46	75.46
Pine	12.98	7.24	45.29
Spruce	19.70	2.40	60.70

Comparative analyses of wood ashes

Wood ashes are, therefore, mainly a source of calcium, with a variable quantity of potassium, and a relatively small amount of phosphorus (though vastly more than there is in any manure). If, however, you used wood ash apply two tonnes an acre (5 tonnes/hectare) of lime, you could well be adding the equivalent of half a tonne (or 1.25 tonnes/hectare) of potassium chloride, which far more than a safe dose and likely to reproduce the soil problems that beset forests swept by fire, or tomato beds whose owners have piled on the potassium. Incidentally, apple prunings are one of the richest potassium sources, making with a level of 40%—plus 20% calcium, 6% phosphorus and 15% sodium chloride (common salt).

It is the presence in quantity, of common salt, that adds yet another difficulty in the use of wood ashes in the garden, for it can cause trouble on heavy clays. When hops were first grown in Kent and Surrey in the reign of Henry VIII, the ashes from an almost entirely wood-burning London went back to the land on return loads to feed this potash greedy crop. So much sodium then built up in the soil that it gave Britain its first problem with an excess of chemical fertilizer. The Kentish clays in the hop gardens became permanently sticky, because the calcium molecules in the middle of each clay particle were replaced with molecules containing sodium, just as they were, by the same reaction, when parts of Essex were flooded by the sea in 1953.

The Romans had the best answer, because wood ashes were their only concentrate, and they were well aware of their behaviour on heavy clays. They applied gypsum (calcium sulphate) at the rate of about 1lb a square yard (550g/m²), which reversed the reaction, producing sodium sulphate, which washes away in the rain, as it did for the farmers of Essex in 1953, and the hop growers of Kent at about the date when Henry VIII was marrying his last Queen. The knowledge of gypsum lived on in the Latin textbooks that survived the fall of the Roman Empire.

Organic gardeners produce relatively little wood ash, because all material that will decay fairly rapidly is far better value in the compost heap, or as a mulch. Ashes from tree and shrub prunings—which are about all that a gardener needs to burn—should be collected and stored in a metal dustbin or other large non-plastic container, for they will melt plastic if they are still hot when they are fetched in from the rain.

Their major use is for crops that need potash, lime and salt, such as asparagus, beetroot and onions, for which they are spread at the rate of 4–6oz a square yard (300–400g/m²), in February or March, and at the same rate in November for broad beans. Gooseberries appreciate the same amount every autumn on the sandy soils where regular wood ash dressings are desirable. On clays, where potassium is more readily available and the salt can be a long-term problem, there is no need to use wood ashes at all. As the quantity of lime in the ashes causes scab in potatoes, that crop is always better without them.

The other use of ash is as a substitute for lime layers in Indore type compost heaps, scattered thinly like slaked lime, enough to whiten, or rather 'grey', the surface, which is about 1lb to the square yard (550g/m²) of layer surface. The extra-alkaline potassium makes ash rather a good addition where heaps consist mainly of lawn mowings from tennis clubs, and remains in the finished compost, while the sodium is well diluted. All living material, including all our bodily fluids and those of every other living creature contains a small amount of sodium. The problems only arise when the sodium is concentrated. Like muck and money, it is, as William Cobbett used to say, 'best well spread'.

Wood Stove Ashes

Ashes from wood burning cooking and central heating stoves are far more completely burned than those from any bonfire, and are available in greater quantities than any garden can use purely as concentrated ashes. The best method is to use the poultry manure treatment described in Chapter 6 (see the section on Wood Ashes and Poultry Manure).

The mixture of ashes and poultry manure provides us with a good source of lasting potash for sandy soils, in a far better balanced compound than any wood ashes, with lime and concentrated organic material as a bonus. We need to work out both how many chickens balance how much wood ash, and study more closely the possibilities of a waterless sanitation method for the isolated 'self-sufficiency' families who are likely to be growing their own wood in Britain, and in other countries where wood is the major cooking fuel. The disinfecting and deodorizing effect would be of value in many countries, but the experimental work will have to be done by an individual or the Henry Doubleday Research Association, for no major company is likely to be interested in carrying out research to replace chemical fertilizers with two by-products which offer nothing to patent or sell, but are available free in small quantities almost everywhere in the world.

Bonfire Ashes

Bonfire ashes are even more variable than wood ashes because they usually contain weed clumps with soil on their roots, although the weeds themselves would be far better value on the compost heap. Unfortunately, the kind of grass clod that should go on a stack to decay slowly for potting soil, is usually part of the kind of bonfire that sends clouds of smoke across gardens and allotments, and has been deliberately lit with plenty of wood at the start, to smoulder for days, producing 'burnt earth'.

This is clay baked with plenty of air, which becomes a reddish powdery substance, rather like a hard tennis court dressing. Before modern fertilizer analysis, it was greatly valued for lightening clay soils, and for its tonic effect on the soil. Heating any soil kills off all the bacteria within reach of the temperature, leaving their bodies, like oxen roasted whole for a banquet, as food for the smaller new arrivals that increase enormously, to release quickly spent nitrogen. The tonic effect from the partly baked clods lasts only briefly, and to burn sods is to throw away their fertility, transforming them into a clay-lightening substance which is inferior to builder's sand.

To produce enough burnt earth to make a real difference to a clay garden covered with couch grass would involve stripping the turf and burning the best of the surface soil. A summer spent lying fallow and several rotary cultivations to kill the couch would be far more effective. So would stripping the turf to stack and decay, then rotavating in dead leaves.

Peat Ashes

The minerals in wood ashes have been gathered by roots and leaves from the soil and air, but the plants which went to make up the peats used for burning had to obtain their trace elements and plant foods from the very small quantities in fresh water. Peat ashes are very high in calcium, and when they are fresh or kept dry, this is in the form of calcium oxide or quick-lime, which will be slaked quickly when scattered, but should never be allowed to come into contact with living leaves.

An average sample of the ashes from peat burning power stations contains 47.3% calcium, 18.2% silicates, 11.2% iron oxides, 8.8% magnesium, 1.9% phosphorus and 1.1% potassium. The high calcium content comes from the 'hardness' extracted from the water, and the iron oxides are partly responsible for the dark colour of the peat. Vegetation under water does decay to some extent, and recycles some of the potassium, which is the most soluble of the nutrients that the water plants have collected during the uncounted life cycles that add up to the peat bogs of Ireland and Somerset.

Peat ashes are therefore lime rather than fertilizer and are best used instead of lime layers in compost heaps, or as layers at perhaps 4in (10cm) intervals in stacked leaves, which is perhaps the easiest way of slaking their lime to calcium hydroxide. In rural Ireland, a bucket of peat ashes has been part of the furniture of the 'outhouse', with a small shovel provided for its addition, together with dry soil, to the human wastes; this recycles the calcium and magnesium and has a certain disinfectant effect from the quicklime.

Coal and Furnace Ashes

One of the worst gardeners to follow is one who had the vague idea that 'ashes are good for gardens' or, even worse, one who kept chickens and threw all his ashes into the run for their dustbaths. Coal ashes contain about 1% potash, 0.1% phosphorus, but consist mostly of alumina and silica, with quantities of sulphur trioxide varying from 0.3 to 10%, plus 4% to even 40% of iron oxide. Any moisture will make the sulphur trioxide become sulphuric acid, and this produces a number of unwanted reactions in the soil.

Generally speaking, the end result is nettles and a soil that may be easier to dig where the ashes have been used to lighten clay, but needs lime and humus in quantity to get back even to moderate fertility. London gardens that are black, poor and pebbly are all too often further bedevilled by ashes that have been added to them since manure became scarce because mews no longer held horses but Jaguars. Furnace ashes from coke or anthracite central heating are rather worse in one respect: they have burned at a high temperature, producing tiny, hard, glassy clinkers, which cause even more potato scab than coal ashes. All potatoes have to swell in the soil, and the odd shapes they sometimes assume are not inheritable deformities, but result from expansion along the lines of least resistance in a soil of varying hardness. Minute clinkers and glassy particles make every swelling tuber resemble a fat man eating biscuits in bed. The irrigation damages the skin, letting in the spores of common scab (*Actinomyces scabies*) until almost every tuber is badly attacked and looks very unappetizing.

So keep your coal, coke and anthracite ashes for paths, the bottoms of cold frames or to cover greenhouse staging. Do not spread them anywhere on the soil and never use them in the compost heap.

Sweet and Sour Soils

In the past, soils that were acid were called 'sour' and alkaline soils 'sweet', but today we refer to the 'pH' or 'pH value' which is an accurate measure of the difference from pH 3.5, for an extremely acid moorland soil that will grow nothing but some of the heathers, to pH 8.5, which denotes a highly alkaline chalk downland pasture or limestone formation.

To know the soil pH is of special value in a new garden, both one inherited from an inorganic gardener who may have used quantities of chemical fertilizer, and any that consists mainly of subsoil, or is low in humus, for any reason. An organic gardener with plenty of humus rarely needs to test the soil, but the grower who adds 4oz a square yard (150g/m^2) of slaked lime before almost every crop can be using far too much. This can make phosphorus, potash, iron, magnesium, copper and zinc less available to plants, while an over-acid soil can also put these elements out of root reach, except to species adapted to grow with a low pH.

The ideal pH for most horticultural crops is between 6.0 and 8.0, with the neutral pH 7.0 exactly at the middle of the scale.

Organic gardeners are concerned with feeding the soil and the micro-organisms that make the minerals in it available to crops, rather than supplying plant foods direct, which is much like selling dried babyfoods to black Africa, where there are plenty of loving breasts available. Therefore pH is important, because pH 6.0–8.0 is ideal for most soil bacteria, including the nitrogen fixers, both free living and in legume roots, as well as the organisms which convert ammonia from manure into the nitrate forms that most plants prefer, and the many species that break down vegetable wastes into plant foods. At lower pH values, most of this work is done by soil fungi, including nitrogen-fixing mycorrhizas in the roots of pine trees, heather and other acid soil loving plants.

		pH
Injurious to most crops; favours many harmful bacteria; only a few mosses and algae grow.	Extremely acid Very strongly acid	Below 4.5 4.5–5.0
Favourable for heather, azaleas, rhododendrons and lime-hating shrubs and gentians.	Strongly acid	5.0–5.5
Favourable for tomatoes, potatoes, cucumbers, raspberries, strawberries.	Medium acid	5.6–6.0 Clubroot common
Favourable for lettuce, cabbage, beans, peas and most garden plants.	Slightly acid	6.0–0.5 Potato scab rare
Favourable for asparagus, beet, broccoli, cauliflower, asters, carnations, dahlias.	Neutral	6.6–7.3
Too alkaline for most common vegetables. Ideal for aubretia, campanulas and other lime-lovers.	Slightly alkaline Medium alkaline	7.4–7.8 Potato scab common 7.9–8.4 Clubroot rare
Injurious to most plants, except for those specialized to grow in this kind of soil.	Very alkaline Very strongly alkaline	8.5–9.0 9.1–

Soil pH

Lime is not a fertilizer—except as a source of calcium which is an important plant food. It merely makes available the plant foods and trace elements that are already there, by what used to be referred to as 'sweetening' the soil. Hence the old saying from long before soil analysis or chemical fertilizers were discovered, 'Lime and lime without manure, Make both farm and farmer poor' (which rhymes better when said with a Scottish accent).

Inorganic gardeners add acidity to their soils by the use of sulphate of ammonia, sulphate of potash, and superphosphate, but if a soil is high in humus and has not been unbalanced by the continued use of quantities of chemicals, it is in no more need of continuous liming than any forest. Farmers are, of course, constantly taking calcium off their land in grain, meat, bone and milk, and gardeners remove some in their vegetable crops. But compost and manure have what is called a 'buffering action', and, without going into the chemical details of pH, this means that there is less need to bother about keeping to the lines suggested by soil analysis if you have used plenty of good muck or compost.

A soil testing outfit for measuring pH is cheap and simple to use. It consists of a small scoop in which to place the soil sample, a bottle of liquid to pour on the sample, which will change colour according to how acid or alkaline it is, and a strip colour chart, so that the exact shade can be matched on the pH scale. Take at least five samples down to a depth of 8in (20cm) and mix them very carefully to make sure that the small test portion shows a true average for the bed.

With the chart, there should be a table to show approximately how much lime, in the form of slaked lime or ground limestone, you need to bring your soil back to neutral. There are a number of weeds that indicate an acid soil, such as sheep's sorrel (*Rumex acetosella*), annual knawel (*Scleranthus annuus*) and corn spurrey (*Spergula arvensis*), but they are common only in acid soil areas, and the gardener who wants to know whether his new garden would be improved by liming is not likely to be able to recognize them.

Dolomite

By far the best form of lime for amateur gardeners is ground dolomite limestone, which is now sold to organic farmers and garders in Britain, as it has been for the past thirty years in Europe and America. It contains 50–60% calcium carbonate and 30–40% magnesium carbonate and has the great advantage of lasting longer in the soil than slaked lime, since it is made slowly available by the action of bacteria and secretions from plant roots under the conditions of moisture and temperature at which plants need it, so that they can take it as required; the magnesium that most soils need today is thrown in as a bonus. If the magnesium is supplied in sulphate form (Epsom salts), it washes very quickly from the soil, but the effect from dolomite can last five years, even on the sandiest soils that suffer most.

If your supply of dolomite gives the analysis on the bag, you can use the table with your soil tester to calculate how much your soil needs in terms of calcium carbonate alone. With a mix of roughly half each of calcium and magnesium carbonate, use twice as much as the table says for ground limestone, and do not apply another dressing before carrying out a careful soil test after four years.

In Tasmania, there are soils that are by nature very low in phosphorus and normally grow plants specialized to recycle the little they have. To grow our British farm crops and fruit in a climate that is very near that of Cornwall, superphosphate has been applied in vast quantities until almost every mineral and trace element has been locked up in the soil, and still larger quantities of fertilizers and trace elements have been added to replace what is already there but unavailable.

Fortunately, 'Tazzy', as Australians call it, possesses a deposit of dolomite about twenty-five miles long, two miles wide and about a mile deep ($40 \times 3.2 \times 1.6$km), and this is being ground for use by the 150 organic farmers of the country (out of a population of 400,000 people, the highest proportion anywhere in the world.) So the best answer to a soil that has been farmed or gardened with too many chemicals, is dolomite (as well as more humus) and one pound a square yard ($550g/m^2$) is a good average dolomite dressing for a garden that may be short of both lime and magnesium.

Ground Limestone

This is used extensively by farmers in Britain, but is rather hard to find in small quantities for garden use. Because you need about half the quantity, it is cheaper than dolomite, but today the cost of the carriage is often more significant than the price of the product itself. The cheapest way to obtain ground limestone is from an agricultural sundries supplier, whose address can be found in the yellow pages of your telephone book. If you can, buy several bags and share them with neighbours, because it is vastly cheaper to have one lasting dressing delivered on a lorry than to buy a 56lb (25kg) bag of garden lime every year.

Both dolomite and ground limestone go on in the autumn, forked into the upper 8in (20cm) of soil. You will find that they do not have an immediate effect on the pH, but if you apply the dose shown on the scale, the soil bacteria and root secretions will release lime slowly over the years. Another test in two years' time should show that your soil is about right.

If there is a very wide differene between your soil pH and neutral, do not try to correct it by more than a single pH unit each year. If your soil is pH 5.0, for example, and you are aiming at pH 7.0, apply the ground limestone in two successive autumns. It should be added that ground limestone does not react with farmyard manure as slaked lime will, for it is too slowly available, which is one of the many reason why farmers use it.

Slaked Lime

This is easily bought in any garden shop or centre, and is excellent for use in compost heaps, as its particles are so fine that it is immediately available. It is calcium hydroxide, with some calcium oxide, but both in the compost heap and in the soil, there is so much carbonic acid about that it soon becomes calcium carbonate, like a very finely ground chalk.

Slaked lime is best for correcting excess acidity caused by the use of raw dead leaves or lawn mowings to build up soil organic matter quickly, and 4oz a square yard ($280g/m^2$) dug in with the material will also help it to decay. In the 1930s, the late C. H. Middleton, the first, and perhaps the most famous, BBC gardening correspondent, recommended this amount of slaked limed spread in the spring as a cure for moss on lawns, and London's suburban front gardens turned white in a night. It does remove the moss, but it makes the clover grow faster. However this is no disadvantage to organic gardeners who value their lawns as a source of compost and mulching material.

Bad moss on any lawn, like rushes and moss in any garden, is a sign of poor drainage, and digging a sloping trench, which you then fill with stones, broken jam jars and other rubble, to lead the water to an outlet or soakaway is a permanent answer, though liming every few years may be cheaper and easier.

It has been authoritatively stated that 50% of British gardens are short of magnesium, which is needed in such relatively large quantities that it is nearer to being a major plant food than a trace element. This is largely due to the fact that at one time every newspaper gardening correspondent recommended 4–6oz a square yard ($150–220g/m^2$) of slaked lime for almost everything, because they knew that most of their readers lived in towns, where their gardens received a steady rain of sulphur-rich soot from coal fires which lowered the pH values by reacting with calcium carbonate to make chemically neutral gypsum.

Today, all gardens need less lime, and a change to slowly released ground dolomite and limestone would mean a great improvement in soil health for inorganic as well as organic gardeners, and especially for beginners who feel that because ordinary garden lime is not an 'artificial fertilizer' they can use plenty to make up for what their gardens are lacking. For them, the old saying could well be brought up to date: 'Lime and lime, without good compost, Makes your minerals good as lost'.

Gypsum

Though such crops as potatoes, as well as rhododendrons, ericas and some other plants need a low pH, they also need calcium as a plant food. This is where gypsum is of value, at the rate of about 4oz a square yard (150g/m²) and it should also be used instead of slaked lime or wood ashes sprinkled between the layers of Indore-type heaps when the compost is intended for lime-hating plants. Mushroom growers always use gypsum—which is a fine, powder that is best bought from builder's merchants—because their fungi need some calcium, but prefer an acid medium.

Apart from its value in dealing with sodium clays caused by excessive wood ashes, it is also useful where the stickiness results from the use of quantities of kainite (hydrous chlorosulphate of magnesium and potassium), nitrate of soda, or common salt, for beet or sugar-beet. It is worth trying on any very sticky clay, for sodium clays are permanent and a particularly bad area may be a legacy from an over enthusiastic inorganic gardener working when chemicals were a new craze and kainite the latest cure-all.

Gypsum was also used as a substitute for lime at the rate of 4–8oz a square yard (150–300g/m²) to solve a problem that is rather unlikely today. Kitchen gardens, especially in London, were manured year after year with the supply from carriage horses and the ponies of local tradesmen, until they became too rich and too 'sour' for good crops, despite liming. It was found that using gypsum instead of lime every three years brought greatly improved yields, and this could well be equivalent to a fortnight at a health farm for overfed soils, such as those enriched with too much farm slurry, poultry manure, or bucket sanitation disposal.

Maerle

Maerle consists of the finely ground fragments of *Lithothamnion calcareum*, a seaweed that concentrates calcium into a system of branches almost like a cold water coral and is dredged up off the coasts of Brittany and Cornwall. The Breton market gardeners use it in very large quantities, and it is employed as a compost ingredient in many parts of Europe.

The calcium content varies between 45% and 50%, but maerle is mainly valued as a source of trace elements and organic matter. It is now sold in Britain, but it is too expensive to use as a substitute for ground limestone, or even dolomite, because it contains only 5–8% magnesium, and if this is lacking, a half-and-half mixture of magnesium and calcium carbonates is a better bargain. Many organic gardeners are convinced that the tiny traces of manganese, boron, copper, chromium and nickel are of value when spread via their compost heaps, but a dried meal or foliar feed made from seaweed would provide the traces that are missing from British soils only in exceptional cases, without adding calcium in quantities that may not be required. Scatter enough to whiten the surface of every layer, even on top of any manure, if you are set on using maerle in a compost heap.

Ground Minerals

Perhaps the clearest line we can draw is the one between ground rock phosphate (only slowly soluble, and present in the soil as fine rock particles, which can be made available to the roots by soil bacteria and fungi, as in nature) and superphosphate (manufactured by treating the same rock with sulphuric acid to make it quickly soluble, and therefore to be classed as a chemical fertilizer). However, making advertising space available in *Organic Gardening and Farming* to sellers of ground minerals has resulted in the sale of a great many ground minerals of doubtful value to organic gardeners and farmers in the USA.

The question here is not whether a substance is organic or inorganic but whether it is worth using. Low-grade rock phosphates take energy to grind, pack, and transport, and if they are composed mainly of silica, alumina and iron oxide, you may be paying for a dressing that will supply even less phosphorus than you already have in your own surface soil, and much less than the reserves in the subsoil.

The latest branch of the great river of organizations and ideas that began in the 1930s with the ideas of Rudolph Steiner and Jerome Rodale, is 'Eco-Agriculture' introduced by William Albrecht, a soil scientist and a Professor at the University of Missouri, with a publication *Acres*, started in 1971, that circulates mainly to farmers. Here, the emphasis is mainly on ground minerals rather than on compost, and *Acres* campaigns strongly in favour of small farmers swamped by the advance of agri-business, and against pesticides and pollution, a far greater menace in the USA than in Europe.

In many of the States, there are soils that may be so low in some mineral plant food or trace element—just as New Zealand is low in phosphorus—that ground minerals can give lasting results once the soil has been given a supply to recycle. But there is little evidence of British soils with similar deficiencies. Moreover, in America there are beds of rock containing resources of a variety of plant foods that can be profitably tapped, but Britain has no such deposits, and to import them would be entirely uncommercial.

Some Europeans insist that fertility comes from the rock fragments ground fine by the Ice Age glaciers, and that our only alternative to waiting for a new Ice Age to provide more is to send a considerable sum to an advertiser for a bag of something that he claims will work wonders, although it has only rarely been tested on replicated plots with yields weighed and recorded.

Potassium-Containing Minerals

If there were a good, slowly released ground rock source of potassium to use on sandy soils, it would be worth buying. In the USA, the favourite is Glauconite or Greensand, which is found as a geologically remote seabed deposit in New Jersey. (The Greensand Ridge running beside the North Downs of Kent and Surrey is an entirely different formation.) The New Jersey deposit contains 6–7% available potash, 50% silicon, 23% iron oxides, 7% magnesium, and many trace elements. It merely needs sufficient drying to let it pass through a fertilizer drill.

Basalt rock contains a trace (about 1.29%) of potassium, 0.78% of phosphorus, and 8.21% calcium. In Germany, ground basalt is spread by organic farmers one year, then ploughed in the next. It is also mined and ground in Oregon and a number of other American states, but its low level of plant foods and the energy required to process it make it less attractive than farmyard manure. Granite dust, too, is used extensively in Europe and the USA, but has the same problems. In Britain it is ground for use as a filler in the paint that rust-proofs the underbodies of cars, but no gardener could really afford the price that is asked for this finely ground product.

Far more likely sources of lasting potash fertilizer are orthoclase felspar, with 17% potassium, which is found in Cornwall, or leucite felspar with 22%. Because of the cost of grinding, these are more expensive than the soluble salts from dried up seabeds which make chemical fertilizers. Neither is available for sale, however, and the felspar used in the pottery industry, which is mined and available as a calcium felspar, is more expensive and no more useful than ground limestone.

Phosphorus Minerals

Ground rock phosphate from Gafsa in Tunisia, of the type used for making superphosphate, is available in Britain, but it is relatively expensive compared with bonemeal, which supplies some nitrogen and some calcium as well, in forms that are broken down readily in the soil. On the other hand, the phosphates from rock phosphate last well in the soil, and their availability is good, especially when they are finely ground. The question is always, 'Does the soil really need the extra mineral, or can I manage on compost or manure?'

Basic slag was formerly used in great quantities on Scottish, Welsh and Pennine hill pasture to replace the calcium and phosphorus taken by generations of sheep flocks off treeless mountain sides with high rainfall and thin soils covering the rock. It comes from the ground linings of blast furnaces of a type invented by two British chemists, Thomas and Gilchrist, and contains 12–20% phosphorus pentoxide (P_2O_5), and 45–55% quick lime (CaO). In Europe it is still known as 'Thomasmeal' after its British inventor, but in Britain modern methods of making better steel produce worse slag.

This is a borderline substance, regarded as organic on the grounds of low solubility, which is an asset on wet Welsh hillsides. However, its composition varies with the compensation of the ore that was smelted, and it can have even higher levels of toxic metals than dried sewage sludges. It is not recommended for gardeners, and can be regarded as doubtfully organic. Ground limestone and rock phosphate, moreover, can produce the same effect, using less material, and present no risk of toxic metals.

Soil Analysis

The soil test for pH is easy and accurate, because it is measuring something simple—it is the only one that is useful to organic gardeners. There are also tests for nitrogen, phosphorus and potassium, but these can be actively misleading.

Nature is not like a shopper constantly driving down to the supermarket for something the advertisers claim to be indispensable, and there is no need to balance the soil figures on the last Friday in the month. The analysis of the top layer of any soil varies according to what minerals the soil bacteria and plant roots have made available. The late F. W. Newman Turner calculated that soil tests taken in

January would have cost him about £100 more (1955 prices)[2] on fertilizers to correct the shortages disclosed by analysis than tests done in June or July, at the peak time for bacterial activity. This variation in analysis, with often a greater increase in a plant food on land that has not had a chemical fertilizer than on one which has, is quite common on organic farms, and was discovered on the Soil Association Research Farms at Haughley by Dr R. F. Milton.[3]

Provided the soil is kept near neutral and contains plenty of humus, most garden soils will balance themselves. In Chapter 11 there is a discussion of the symptoms of mineral deficiencies and the many ways in which they can be corrected. The use of mineral additives for this purpose is like taking medicines for specific complaints. Compost or manure supply the staple diet for a fertile soil, while comfrey, green manures and organic fertilizers can be regarded as its teas, herbs and spices.

Organic farmers who want to know just how little calcium and phosphate is left in their hillside pastures should get in touch with their local Ministry of Agriculture Advisory Service and have an analysis made and interpreted, using the long experience of these experts rather than relying on do-it-yourself methods. They may well advise improving the drainage rather than spending money on lime, but whatever the recommendation, it will cost money to supply the fertilizers.

1. HALL, Sir Daniel *Manures and Fertilizers* John Murray 1928 pp.136–141

2. NEWMAN TURNER, F. *Fertility Pastures* Faber & Faber 1955

3. BALFOUR, Lady Eve *The Living Soil* Faber & Faber 1975

11 Mineral Deficiencies and

Seaweed Sprays

Many organic gardeners believe that with sufficient compost you can cure all plant diseases. This is because very many gardeners do not know the difference between the symptoms of a virus and signs of the many mineral deficiencies that are far more common in inorganic gardens than on soil that is well fed. There are genuine viruses, and very genuine diseases, such as clubroot and potato blight, but there are also many conditions that can be 'cured' with a better diet. This of course applies to human beings, too.

The mineral deficiency that everyone knows is magnesium shortage. Every year, you cut out the fruited canes of raspberries and take away minerals, until the shortage becomes apparent as leaves on the new canes turn yellow, while the veins stay dark green. In an attack of mosaic virus, whole leaves will be mottled with light and dark green patches; this will be accompanied by a slow reduction in the size of leaf, stunting of the canes, and a steady fall in the crop, in which case, you have to dig up and burn your crop, and start with another planting, at least 3ft (1m) away to be clear of the roots.

If the leaves stay normal on the edges and just go plain yellow, without any of the mottling that resembles markings on the leaves of the variegated laurel, spare your canes. Prune them in the usual way, but when you fork in the surface mulch and tidy up the weeds, spread 4oz a square yard (150g/m²) of dolomite and fork it in. This should last for at least five years. The older method of using 1oz (28g) of Epsom salts dissolved in a two gallon can (9lt) of cold water applied along 12ft (4m) of row in April should show a quick cure, but it does not last when fruited canes are cut out every year. Either method should have the young growth back to normal by the summer.

The commonest place to see magnesium shortage is in the tomato border, where inorganic gardeners pile on potassium fertilizer and lock up the trace element that plants need in the greatest quantity. Magnesium is vitally important in the making of chlorophyll molecules, in enzyme reactions, and as a carrier for the energy-supplying phosphorus. It is very mobile, and when the supply runs low a plant will move it from old, nearly worn out growth to new shoots that are growing and need chlorophyll urgently.

Magnesium shortage is the commonest deficiency in Britain today, because so much potassium is used in chemical fertilizers, but there is evidence also that unless plants have plenty of humus in the soil they cannot take up the mineral even if it is available, especially in a dry summer. The worst magnesium deficiency symptoms I have seen in lettuce were in a virus resistant variety on soil without humus at the Trial Ground of Britain's most famous seedsman.

No gardener should dig up a cherished tree or shrub because he or she is told it has a virus and there is nothing for it but burning. Wait till the spring, and try Epsom salts, which may be the answer. Where magnolias, rhododendrons, lime-hating gentions and other low pH plants have leaves turning yellow-green all over, also use Epsom salts to lock up the lime they dislike, but use it every spring; the lime in dolomite would be harmful for them.

If you have too much nitrogen available at once, you 'lock up' your potassium as well as wasting nitrogen. With a slow-nitrogen organic fertilizer there is no trouble. Fill the transpiration stream with a chemical salt, and only a fraction gets used. The rest just gets in the way, preventing other plant foods from working till it washes to waste. Use too much phosphorus, and this also locks up potassium, while excess calcium locks up the boron.

The worst case of boron deficiency I have ever seen was in a cauliflower field in Brittany where they had grown the crop for the English market year after year and held off clubroot with quantities of lime. When I realized what they all meant by excited cries of 'Payach-sept' (pH 7) the explanation of the small brown hearts and hollows in the stem was clear. The cure would have been ½oz (14g) of ordinary borax, used for gargles, dissolved in a two gallon (9lt) can of water and applied to 5 square yards (4m²). This would have needed skilled assessment, because too much boron can be equally dangerous, but the field had so much lime in it that the battle of the boron must have been a long one.

The reason for the rise of the mineral deficiency as a serious 'disease', is the decline of farmyard manure on farms and in gardens. Not only does manure contain NPK, but it holds traces of many minerals. Compost holds many more, for it returns to the soil substances that the plants took out, not products sold to the farmer or gardener by the chemical industry. These supply only the major plant foods, to make heavier crops which take more of the dwindling trace elements out of the soil.

Organic farmers who argue that kainite is 'natural', and potassium chloride is not, have some reason on their sides, for kainite contains magnesium as well as potassium and sodium. With more knowledge of what goes on in the soil, replacing this swiftly wasted source with a lasting one, in dolomite or tufa, is an answer to the extreme symptoms. Good compost, good manure, rotation of crops and good husbandry, in the sense of 'husbanding' the resources of the soil, provide the long term solution.

At the risk of worrying every gardener into mistaking the natural changes in foliage as the year goes round and crops ripen, or the effects of weather, for deficiencies, I give below the main symptoms of the more usual shortages in ordinary crops. The answer to most of them is more and better compost, but not just peat and fertilizers, for even organic fertilizers can cause deficiencies if used in excess. The other answer is foliar feeding with one of the liquid seaweed preparations.

Just as organic gardeners often insist that more compost cures all disease, those who sell these seaweed liquids believe that their products will do the same. Again, they are right in cases where gardeners (and even some experts) do not know the difference between virus and deficiency symptoms, or where a particular disease attacks only when a mineral is in short supply, like chocolate spot fungus, which strikes broad beans when potassium runs low.

The ability of plants to feed selectively through their leaves, taking the substances they need and leaving the rest to dry and blow off their leaves, or wash down to the soil, makes foliar feeding the ideal way to correct trace element deficiencies. This method of providing food can also correct shortages of major plant foods like potassium or phosphorus, but it is less valuable in these cases, because of the quantities required; compost, manures, or organic fertilizers remain cheaper and more effective answers.

There are purists who insist that the heat treatment applied to convert seaweed into the familiar brands of liquid foliar feed qualifies them as 'inorganic', while a trick that is common in Western Australia, of filling a clean oil drum with seaweed, topping up with water and leaving it in the sun, is 'organic'. But this is hair splitting. Seaweeds, fresh for direct use, dried as meal, or as liquid foliar feeds are one of the fertilizers of the future, for they are one way in which we can return plant foods wasted through our sewage systems back into circulation via the living soil.

Because tomatoes are the crop most likely to suffer trace element trouble from generous and repeated doses of artificials, I shall deal with them first. For a comprehensive, fully illustrated account of mineral shortages in plants we can look forward to the new, four-volume edition of *The Diagnosis of Mineral Deficiencies in Plants by Visual Symptoms* by Dr T. Wallace, which is now in preparation, and hope it will not be too expensive. It will be valuable to the horticultural and agricultural libraries of the world, whatever it costs, and available from HMSO.

Tomatoes

If the leaves are pale green, with yellow or purplish tints, small and erect, and the shoots thin and stiff, as they are in plants that have been starved in the pots before sale, this denotes nitrogen deficiency, rare in the garden, but common in nurseries. Do not buy these plants, for they will waste valuable growing time in recovering.

Thin, dwarfed shoots and leaflets that are small, blue-green turning dull purple, and curling backwards (also common in starved plants) show phosphorus shortage.

A deficiency of calcium is shown by fruit with flat brown patches, known as 'blossom-end rot'. The trusses die back, the leaves take on a purple-brown tint, and the growing points wither and die. When fruit develop the warning brown patches, the soil should be tested, and limed if it is below pH 5.5, which is moderately acid. Ground gypsum at the rate of 4oz a square yard (150g/m²)should be applied when the greenhouse is cleared. By the time you see the symptoms in the leaves, it is too late to do much about it for that crop.

Magnesium shortage, on the other hand, shows sufficiently early in the lower leaves for you to use dolomite at 8oz a square yard (300g/m²) as a long term answer, but always with compost, to provide the humus required.

Leaves with brown margins that curl forward, and patchy ripening of fruit mean potassium deficiency. Leaf blotches that are sharply defined would indicate a virus, but the green and yellow areas merge in the case of a deficiency. Watering with comfrey liquid manure can be effective if you see the lower leaves show these symptoms in time, but the best answer is more compost, or a comfrey leaf mulch between the plants, as for gooseberries (see Chapter 4, the section on Comfrey Mulching). Low night temperatures and over-watering can show as 'potassium deficiency', so be sure that these are not responsible. Try feeding with comfrey liquid before you dig out the soil and replace it with new for next year, which may save all the hard work.

If the leaves have small yellow spots scattered among the veins, this means manganese deficiency; if the dots are small and few at the start, but increase until whole leaves become pale yellow, almost white, then iron is lacking, and in both cases a seaweed foliar feed is the answer. Boron shortage shows in fruit with brown pits and corky areas in the skin and uneven ripening. This could be caused by an excess of lime, especially after attempts to supply the potash needs of the crop by over-dosing with wood ashes that happen to be high in calcium.

One way round the problem is to 'unlime' the soil, by watering on 2oz of Epsom salts dissolved in a two gallon can of cold water (60g in 10lt) and applying it to two square yards (2m²) of greenhouse soil surface. The result is a chemical reaction between the magnesium sulphate and calcium carbonate to produce magnesium carbonate and calcium sulphate (gypsum), which is slowly soluble. This could save some of the crop. Test the soil, which should be between pH 5.5 and pH 5.9, and apply the Epsom salts after clearing the house for next year.

If only a few fruits have been affected and other symptoms (purple and brown tints in the foliage, with leading shoots dying back) have not occurred, try a seaweed feed, which might cure the trouble, but use less lime.

Potatoes

If the foliage yellows while the veins, as well as the leaf edges, stay green, and there are dark brown patches between the veins, this is magnesium shortage. By the time it shows, it usually too late to do much about it, but more compost is one answer, so is dolomite, or Epsom salts as for tomatoes. Beginners often take this condition for potato blight (*Phytophthora infestans*), but an attack of blight starts at the edge of the leaves and spreads, in rounded, dark brown patches.

Lack of calcium shows in thin shoots, small leaves, which are pale green and roll inwards from the edges, and quantities of very small tubers. This can happen after the use of too much potassium, but more often results from holding back the lime to avoid potato scab. Compost, comfrey and bonemeal are the remedies. Very small tubers, accompanied by yellow, stunted leaves that die off early, are due not to a mineral shortage but to potato eelworm. Try Maris Piper for a maincrop and Pentland Lustre or Pentland Meteor as earlies, then rest the ground from potatoes.

Dark bluish-green leaves, brown spots and margins, with leaf edges curling backwards instead of rolling, show lack of potash which can happen from too much nitrogen. Very thin brown margins, leading on to grey-green leaves that yellow and die prematurely, show boron deficiency, perhaps arising from too much lime.

All these symptoms matter when they show in the growing season, from September onwards, but sooner for earlies. Foliage that changes colour as the minerals are returned to store in the tubers can be ignored. Compost or comfrey will give balanced feeding.

Cabbage and Related Crops

Their main problem is boron shortage from too much lime, which brings distortion or death of growing points and failure to heart in kales, cabbage and brussels sprouts, with hollows visible in the stem when it is sliced down the middle. Broccoli and cauliflower have small curds which go brown, leaves that are mottled at the margins, and again hollows in the stem. Use borax as recommended earlier, apply less lime and grow brassicas less often.

Lack of calcium, too, can be a problem, causing yellow mottling on the leaves, and distorted foliage with browning and curling of tips, but this is complicated by the fact that too little lime and an acid soil may cause a shortage of manganese or iron. The usual problem is clubroot, as cabbages rarely lack lime. See if a foliar feed helps. Nearly all these symptoms can show when a cabbage cannot get at minerals because the roots have been damaged by clubroot. Compost, lime within reason, and rotation of crops are the answers.

Magnesium shortage shows as marbling on the leaves in pale yellow, then orange, red or purple leaf tints, and as usual this is caused by too much potassium, but dull purple mottlings show phosphorus shortage. Fishmeal is a good answer here, for nitrogen as well as phosphorus. But the old-fashioned 10–20 tonnes an acre (25–50 tonnes/hectare) of good farmyard muck generally cured all these troubles in the past.

Beetroot, Spinach Beet and Chard

If the old leaves of any of these show yellowing between the leaf veins, beginning at the tips and margins, this is magnesium shortage, easily cured by the Epsom salts trick. If young leaves show distortion or backward hooking of the tips and death of the growing points, followed by dwarfed new leaves, then there is too little calcium, and your soil needs lime.

Garden beet can suffer from salt shortage, which will show in thin, dull green leaves, scorched leaf edges, and wilting in hot weather. Give 4oz a square yard (150g/m²) of wood ashes or 1oz sea salt in a two gallon can (30g in 10lt) watered over three square yards

(3m²). But, as always, it is rather late to correct the shortage if the growing point has gone. The best policy is to use the wood ashes before sowing next year's beet, or water with the salt solution when they are strong seedlings.

The indications of boron shortage are dead leaves at the centres, with small leaves trying to replace them, and wilted, scorched older leaves. Use ½oz borax in 2 gallons (17g in 10lt) on ten square yards (10m²). But the best preventive is to use less lime, plus compost.

Peas and Beans

Broad beans can suffer from too much lime, which causes boron shortage, and shows in squat growth, yellowing of leaves near the growing point, and shoots starting from the base. French and runner beans become similarly stunted, with stems thick, brittle and inclined to split. Use the ½oz borax treatment in the spring of the following year, when the broad beans start to grow and the others are well up. If they do not have just a trace of boron, they cannot fix nitrogen. It is the minute quantities of all the necessary minerals, contained by compost in readily available form, that prevent so many problems from starting.

Because broad beans are known to need potash, they are sometimes given too much and suffer from a lack of magnesium. As with tomatoes, the signs appear first in the older leaves, which go yellow, while their veins and margins stay green. French beans and runners suffer much the same symptoms, but runners can show purple tints and brown patches, like potatoes.

Runners and French beans might suffer from too little calcium. This deficiency gives rise to pale green leaves with brown spots near tips and margins, wilting pods and falling flowers. If the soil is acid, this also cuts off their supply of manganese, producing yellowing and, finally, dead brown patches on the leaves. Bonemeal provides a good, lasting answer and, in addition, takes care of phosphorus deficiency, which can cause dwarfing, small leaves and early leaf fall.

Peas can suffer badly from a lack of boron, showing stunted growth, thick stems and bushy habit, or from magnesium shortage, showing yellow leaves with green veins and margins, first on the old foliage. Stunted growth with thin stems and dull leaves indicates a deficiency of phosphorus. Young stems, and leaves which collapse after turning yellow-green mean calcium shortage, and brown hollows in the middles of the seeds are the sign of a condition called 'marsh spot', which arises from manganese shortage, caused by too much lime; this can also happen with beans. The remedies are to mix ¼oz of manganese sulphate in a two gallon can (8g in 10lt) and water it on over seven square yards (7m²), or to feed through the leaves with a seaweed spray, following the 'unliming' procedure with Epsom salts, or using dolomite instead of slaked lime, which is the easiest way round. Manganese sulphate should be obtainable to order through good chemists or agricultural merchants, but only very small quantities are needed.

Carrots, Parsnips and Celery

Carrots can have purple tints in the foliage from phosphorus shortage; old leaves go yellow with green veins if magnesium is scarce; squat growth and leaf tips which become brown and dry usually mean that potassium is running out. Dark maroon, often almost crimson, leaves mean that carrot fly larvae are attacking the roots.

Nitrogen shortage in parsnips causes small, pale leaves turning yellow, and stunted, thin growth, while similar symptoms, but with dull green leaves, show that phosphorus is running low. Leaves that have limp stalks and eventually die mean calcium shortage. Squat growth and leaves with scorched edges that roll forward indicate that potassium is missing; an excess of potassium brings the familiar early sign of yellowing in the older leaves, while the veins and margins remain green, that denotes locked-up magnesium. Thick leaf stalks that crack, and older leaves that turn yellow and then scorch brown at the edges mean boron shortage.

Celery with stunted growth and pale foliage lacks nitrogen; stunting, with purple tints on dull green leaves, is due to shortage of phosphorus; calcium shortage restricts the growth of young leaves, whose tips go brown and the growing point dies. Bonemeal to correct the calcium and phosphorus shortage without making the soil too alkaline provides the answer. The celery growers of the Norfolk Fens, where I once grew a million plants to go out on fifty acres (20 hectares), had no trouble—they just ploughed in muck. Distorted stems that split with young leaves browning and dying off (a condition known as 'stem crack') show boron deficiency. The borax treatment cures the problems for years, even on chalky soils.

Lettuce

Lettuces need slightly acid conditions (pH 6.0–6.8), but they can also suffer from calcium shortage revealed by distortion and scorching of the young leaves, which turn yellow and are increasingly susceptible to *Botrytis*. This is the reason for the organic grower's belief that plenty of compost 'cures' this grey mould fungus. Compost does provide calcium without increasing the pH, but it is a good idea to use ground gypsum instead of lime for lettuces, especially under polythene tunnels.

Bonemeal is also an answer, as it offers calcium and phosphorus to correct the similar stunting (accompanied by bronze or purplish foliage tints) that occurs when too much potassium has locked up the phosphorus. Magnesium deficiency in lettuces arises more often from low humus than excess potassium, because there is thought to be a soil fungus that helps to make magnesium available, and needs decayed vegetable matter in the soil to 'power' it. The lack shows up in the expected pale yellow, with the veins still green, on older leaves, as the plant moves the scarce mineral to young growth in order to get the best value from chlorophyll not yet crippled by magnesium shortage. If you think only in terms of NPK, leaving out magnesium and the humus it takes to make it available, you are heading for trouble, which you will see most strongly in dry years.

Possible answers are Epsom salts at the rate of ½oz in a two gallon can (15g in 10lt) watered over six square yards (6m²), if the deficiency shows when the lettuce crop has about a month to go before harvest, or a seaweed foliar feed to save a crop, but the best policy is to check the lower leaves of the last of the crop for symptoms, and use dolomite and compost to save trouble next year.

Shortage of potassium also increases the risk of *Botrytis*. It shows in dark green leaves, with brown scorching on the older ones beginning at the edges, and is often caused by locking up the potassium with too much nitrogen. On a garden scale, or in a greenhouse, the best answer is comfrey liquid manure to save the crop and grow it out·of trouble, with more good compost to solve the long-term problem.

Onions and Leeks

These can suffer from nitrogen, phosphorus, calcium, potassium and magnesium deficiencies, but the chief symptom in every case is yellowing at the leaf tips during the growing season—not in August, when yellow tips are part of normal ripening. The leaves are a dull green, in cases of phosphorus shortage, and a paler yellow when the plants lack magnesium.

The modern tendency to use onion sets, which allow the crop to be rotated instead of kept in a specially firm bed, has reduced these problems, which were mainly caused by heavy dressings of wood ashes in the same place year after year. Quantities of soot, giving variable amounts of ammonium sulphate and sulphur compounds, produced acid conditions which also prevented many minerals from being absorbed. The cure is to make sure that next year's onions go on ground that has had good compost and dolomite rather than lime. Foliar feeding is not easy with onions, because the spray runs down the smooth, round leaves, and the onions will ripen early, giving a crop which will not keep well, though it will be perfectly eatable.

Sweet Corn
Phosphorus deficiency shows in strong, dull-purple tints, starting at the tips of the leaves and creeping back along the margins. Potassium lack brings short-jointed stems, and long leaves, more slender than normal, with brown tips and margins. Missing magnesium means red and purple streaks longways down the leaves with interrupted lines of yellow dots between the leaf veins. The answer for all three is more compost, with bone or fish meal for the phosphorus, and dolomite for the magnesium.

Turnips and Swedes
These are usually grown fast and kept small when cultivated on a garden scale, and are thus less likely to show shortages than farm crops for cattle feed. Excessive liming can give rise to hollow hearts, or watery areas in the middles of the roots, from boron lock-up. Phosphorus shortage shows in dull green leaves with purple and bronze markings, and in the case of these two crops, magnesium deficiency can cause dull-red or brown, as well as yellow, patches between the still-green veins of the older leaves. The answer are, again, bonemeal for phosphorus, more compost for potassium, and dolomite for magnesium.

Apples and Pears
When the symptoms of fire blight struck Laxton's Superb pears in the Southend area of Essex, the County Horticultural Advisers had many telephone calls from gardeners worried that this deadly bacterial disease, carried by bees, had reached their gardens. However, despite suffering the blackening and dying back of blossoms and shoot tips as though burnt, which give the disease its name, most of the trees examined merely had magnesium deficiency. The ban on growing Laxton's Superb, which was a popular pollinator for Doyenne du Comice, and the destruction of trees of this variety stopped the disease in its tracks. It is now just a battle honour in the records of the Ministry of Agriculture, Fisheries and Food, but it incidentally showed that magnesium

shortage in fruit trees is commoner than we think. It is, in fact, the most common shortage of all, and one that is normally easy to recognize. In both apples and pears, the striking feature is early leaf fall, first from the base of the young shoots, and finally at the tips, where a bunch may hang on till normal leaf fall although the rest of the tree is clear by August. The shortage usually starts to appear as rather purplish brown patches between the veins in the middle of the leaves, with the edges staying green longest. A dressing of 8oz a square yard ($300g/m^2$) of dolomite, either forked in lightly or spread on the grass, over the entire orchard in the autumn is a lasting answer. Spray the trees, after the blossom petals have fallen, with 1oz of Epsom salts in two gallons (30g per 10lt) of cold water, aiming at wetting the leaves thoroughly.

Phosphorus shortage in apples brings short, thin shoots, small, dull green leaves and an early leaf fall, but the purpling of the leaves starts at the edges, leaving the midrib green, and the leaves come off the young shoots together. Spreading a coat of manure on the square yard ($1m^2$), or even four square yards ($4m^2$), round the tree is a good answer.

This applies especially to nitrogen deficiency, which is indicated in all fruit trees by small, pale green leaves that fall early after developing bright orange, red or purple tints, and by small but brightly coloured fruit. Apples betray a lack of potassium through brown, or grey-brown, scorching at the edges of the leaves, which are rather blue-grey, but do not fall early, as in magnesium shortage. Manure on the surface is the answer, with seaweed spraying to help next year's crop.

In apples, yellow leaves with veins staying green, the symptom you would normally expect from magnesium deficiency, occur in the tips of the young shoots when there is a lack of manganese, usually caused by an acid soil. Seaweed spraying is useful. The same appearance in leaves over most of the tree shows iron deficiency; 2oz of sulphate of iron dissolved in a two gallon can (60g in 10lt) watered round the tree can help.

On very limy soils there can be boron deficiency, which shows in malformed fruit, skin cracks and, possibly, brown spots in the flesh near the core. The leaves at the shoot tip may be stunted to form a rosette while the rest fall early, without colouring normally. There is such a small difference between too little and too much boron that 1oz of borax in a two gallon can (30g in 10lt) is enough to use. A safer way round both the iron and boron problems is to apply 2oz Epsom salts in two gallons of water (60g in 10lt) round each tree in the early spring, to look up some of the excess lime in the soil.

183

Potassium shortage shows in pears as dark brown marginal scorching of the leaves, while a lack of iron turns the leaves almost yellow all over, with dark brown scorching, and also results in very highly coloured fruit. Give the trees generous helpings of manure.

The advice to use coarse bonemeal, hoof and horn, leather dust, shoddy, feathers and oystershell at planting time applies to all tree and bush fruit. Trees stay longer in one place than any vegetable and, on poor soils, need a slowly released store of nutrients, which will help them to build an efficient root system, capable of searching a wide area for what is scarce.

Cherries

The shortages from which cherries suffer are almost all associated with excessive lime, because, though they thrive where the chalk joins the clay in the Kentish countryside, it is easy to give them too much of the lime that is immediately available. Magnesium deficiency shows as dull purple tints on leaves with veins remaining green, followed by brown patches between the veins, that start in the middle of the leaf, still leaving the edges green. The leaves fall early like those of apples. Potassium lack shows in blue-green leaves with scorched brown edges, and iron shortage brings pale yellow leaves, with veins staying green. With manganese shortage, the yellowing starts at the edges of the leaves and works in.

The answer is to 'unlime' the soil with Epsom salts. Watering it on in early spring and again the following year should achieve some improvement from the first season. At the same time, the trees should be fed with manure on the surface, because this will correct any lack of potassium and feed the bacteria in the upper soil layers, further increasing mineral availability.

Plums

Like cherries, plums usually suffer from the consequences of too much lime, which shows as iron deficiency in yellowed leaves with the veins staying green. Manganese deficiency, however, also causes this yellowing, though it works in from the leaf edges, and the green areas are wider. Here, the problem can be acid conditions, perhaps from too little lime, or it may be poor drainage. Potassium deficiency produces scorching of the leaf edges, which roll in towards the midrib, and can be corrected with manure under the leaf or straw mulch.

It should be said again that symptoms are significant only when they are early in the season. The colours of autumn may look like mineral deficiencies, and in fact probably are, but only because the tree has thriftily put its minerals away for the winter.

Blackcurrants
The symptoms of phosphorus deficiency are small leaves, dull green and covered with small, dark purple-brown spots, new shoots that are few in number and small, and a poor show of blossom. The shortage can be corrected with fishmeal forked in during the spring, or more generous manuring. Leaf spot fungus (*Gleosporium ribis*) also produces dark brown spots, but on normal-sized leaves and with shoots of the usual size; it causes a loss of leaves in wet seasons in June or July. In this case, gather up all the fallen leaves and burn them, to prevent the fungus developing into its wintering stage and attacking again the following year. Phosphorus shortage, too, cause early leaf fall, but late in August and September.

Magnesium shortage shows in leaves that turn a very distinct purple with clearly marked green margins, and fall early. Again, Epsom salts watered on the soil in early spring (about March) is the answer. This is also the remedy for iron deficiency, which causes pale yellow leaves with veins still green at the shoot tips, because again the likely cause is excess lime. Iron sulphate solution in spring may also be used.

Blackcurrants are always said to need nitrogen, and are therefore likely to suffer from potassium shortage when inorganic gardeners give them ammonium sulphate, or nitrate of soda, under a straw mulch, for this puts the potassium out of reach of their shallow roots, which are far more quickly affected than those of an apple or plum. The edges of the leaves fold downwards, and their margins turn brown and scorch at the edges. Comfrey under a mulch of grass mowings the following year is the best answer, or wood ashes, from tree prunings, rather than from softwoods, which could be high in calcium.

Red Currants
These too can suffer from potash shortage, which shows in very distinctive dark brown margins to the leaves, clearly marked and accompanied by some curling. The leaves can also have very much brighter red-brown margins, with more upcurling of the edges, from chloride injury, which can happen if too much potassium chloride is applied to correct the first complaint, although it is far more probably due to piling on wood ashes in large quantities, for despite their 'natural' reputation they hold enough salt (sodium

chloride) to make a beetroot blush. The answer is wilted comfrey under their mulch, or compost on the surface.

Gooseberries

The symptoms of potassium hunger are bluish-green leaves with purplish tinting that leads to grey-brown tips on leaf edges that curl downwards, followed by an early leaf fall and a poor crop. Gooseberries then need either a surface manure or compost, or wilted comfrey under a mowings mulch in the spring. They also suffer from magnesium lack, because some gardeners, in trying to make sure, give too much potassium. This brings pale green leaves with wide red bands at the edges, and early leaf fall as the bands fade to cream. You can try to correct this with an Epsom salts spray, or by watering the soil, but the major remedy is not to give your gooseberries extra potash on a clay soil. Only on sands are they likely to need it. Phosphorus deficiency, with leaves going dull purple and changing to red purple and falling early, is less common. To check how early is early in your area, look at your neighbour's gooseberries. If they are better fed, their leaves may be still working when yours have stopped from underfeeding.

Raspberries

Raspberries, loganberries and other fruits which have their fruiting canes cut out after harvesting can suffer from magnesium shortage, with yellow leaves showing veins still green and falling too early. Dark brown patches near the veins and at leaf margins which scorch and turn upwards mean that potassium is running low. Both deficiencies are easily corrected with Epsom salts, compost, or comfrey. If the leaves turn pale yellow all over, with red brown spotting, that means iron shortage, and 1oz of iron sulphate in a two gallon can (30g/10lt), watered over two square yards (2m²) in spring, should help.

Strawberries

Phosphorus, their most likely lack, shows in dull green leaves that turn purple, and poor growth. The best answer is to rotate your strawberry bed and start it off each time with plenty of bonemeal, for the next crop will get the benefit of the unexpended portion of the three years' rations. Potassium shortage is also possible, with dark green foliage and scorched leaf margins, and a shortage of iron, usually caused by too much calcium, means yellow leaves with very clear green veins. Epsom salts can clear these troubles as well as it does magnesium deficiency, which shows here as bright yellow elderly leaves with red tints in the middles and round the edges.

The old leaves of all strawberries are going to change colour as they wear out, showing thrift rather than disease. The time to think of mineral shortages is when it happens early. If a man throws up his bedroom window and shouts 'Fire!', he may not need the fire brigade; if his house is not on fire at all, he needs a psychiatrist!

Foliar Feeding

The safe and easy remedy for any suspected mineral shortage is to spray with one of the many seaweed foliar feeds, leaving it to the crop to take what is required and disregard the rest. Such preparations contain the following trace elements:

Aluminium	Copper	Molybdenum
Boron	Germanium	Nickel
Bromine	Iodine	Silver
Calcium	Iron	Sodium
Chlorine	Lead	Sulphur
Chromium	Magnesium	Vanadium
Cobalt	Manganese	Zinc

Do not attempt to use dried seawed to correct mineral deficiencies, because roots are less selective than leaves. Liquid seaweed is excellent as a foliar feed, but adding the whole collection of minerals to the soil in sufficient quantities to correct magnesium shortage, for example, will result in adding quantities of unrequired trace elements at far greater cost than using dolomite.

Foliar feeds provide perhaps the easiest way to correct deficiencies of boron, as well as magnesium, although there is not enough magnesium to cure a real 'lock-up' from too much chemical potassium. Spray in the spring, when the leaves are fully open, and again at midsummer. Better still make plenty of good compost and leaf-mould and use these. Then you will not need to spray at all.

12 Fertility for the Future

It was William Gilpin (1724–1804), author and illustrator of many books on the English countryside, who wrote, 'Land that is merely fertile is a barren prospect'. To him a landscape was a subject for an engraving, just as to so many of us it is something to photograph, or televise or film with Handel's 'Water Music' on the sound track. Yet if the land has not the fertility to go growing our food without becoming exhausted, humanity has no future.

Birds can be reminded of the danger in raiding orchards by loud reports from butane-powered alarm guns, but they need to have their learning reinforced at intervals of about a fortnight by shots from a fruitgrower with a gun, much as they come to ignore the sound of a railway train. The human memory is longer, and today the opportunity to read non-fiction paperbacks and watch science programmes allows us to look back more than a million years to the people of the Olduvai Gorge, well past 4004 BC, the date of the Creation, according to Archbishop James Usher. Yet, still, the 'foreseeable future' of the most far-sighted businessmen is only fifteen years long, and no politician of any Party appears to think as far ahead as thirty years, when North Sea Oil will run out.

We can envisage a future in which we shall sit in front of our television sets having 'information' flashed on the screen like tiny bright subtitles from silent films, but we seem unable to take in the idea that we cannot live by data alone, and we cannot eat electronics. Energy, food, water and pollution will rule our lives more and more as our numbers redouble. Within the lifetimes of babies now in their prams, there will be sixteen thousand million people sharing our planet.

No politician in any country, no ecologist, and not even the most far-sighted 'doomwatcher', seems to have considered the kind of sewage treatment problems that will have to be faced in the year 2000, much less the effect of converting the Baltic, the Mediterranean, the Red Sea, and even the North Sea into marine versions of Lake Erie and Lake Constance. Yet, the poisoning of the oceans by industrial pollution will become our major difficulty, as every country develops to the stage when it has general water sanitation, and industries that encourage more mouths to the acre, consequently increasing the numbers of fingers on switches, feet on accelerators, bodies to bathe, and minds to demand more and more from the world's depleted resources.

Of course the area of the oceans is enormous. But the PCBs (polychlorinated biphenyls) and a variety of highly persistent chemical wastes concentrate in the upper levels of what has become the sewage-grey sea; coated with oil slicks and poisoned with lead and cadmium. The top ten fathoms are the ones that matter, for there the phytoplankton float like free-living leaves, fixing nitrogen and gathering energy at the start of long marine food chains. Darken the water with inky effluents from the factories of the future, overfeed them with sewage, and we destroy one more living world of cycling and recycling. It is not a case of 'what the land loses, the sea gains', for we are poisoning shallows and estuaries, which are the breeding grounds of so many species of fish, with industrial wastes and factory farm residues that turn fertility into pollution.

The Living Filter System
There are many ways in which we can save both the soil and the sea. But all of them need time to build, and still more time to fight the prejudices of those who place higher value on short-term profit than on the future of the world we share with 200,000 more people every day. Perhaps the most complete and promising is the 'Living Filter System' developed by Professor William Sopper of Penn State University in Pennsylvania.[1]

Penn State is an American Oxford with more 'gown' than 'town', for it houses 30,000 undergraduates and staff, and 20,000 people to run shops and service industries. The University alone pumps 2 million gallons (9 million litres) of water a day, and, fed by an annual local rainfall of only 26in (65cm), the water table had fallen 60ft (18m) by 1962. As populations expand and water requirements rise, all the major cities of the world are running on an overdraft in their 'aquifers'—the term used by water engineers for the water-bearing strata into which they sink their wells—the American district of Baltimore holds the record for pumping the water table down by 150ft (45m).

The people of Penn State each consume 60 gallons (270lt) of water a day for personal needs, compared with Britain's 32 gallons (144lt). The stormwater is run straight from roofs and streets into Spring Creek, a tributary of the Susquehanna River. Consequently, the sewage, in addition to its freedom from the toxic metals added by industry, is also spared lead from petrol. Their 3 million gallons (13.5 million litres) of sewage a day is treated in an ordinary heated digestion plant, but when most of the sludge leaves the digesters it is mixed with the effluent leaving the settling tanks and pumped along four miles (2.5km) of piping to experimental areas of farm and forest land, where it is spread through spray irrigators. From the knowledge that has been gained since the experiment was started in 1962, it appears that 129 acres (52 hectares) can take the sludge and effluent from 10,000 people, giving the land 2in (5cm) of irrigation a week right round the year.

The worked-out farm taken over by Professor Sopper had grown mostly poverty grass (*Dathonia spicata*), but maize yields now achieved with wastewater (Professor Sopper's term for the effluent and sludge mixture) are reaching 116 bushels an acre 10m³/hectare) compared with 107 bushels (9.3m³/hectare from complete artificials with 2in (5cm) of well water. The wastewater averages 18.6 parts per million of potash, 19.9 p.p.m. of nitrogen and 8.5 p.p.m. phosphorus. A 2in (5cm) irrigation contained 10.08lb (4.56kg) potassium as K_2O, 8.702lb (3.94kg) phosphorus as P_2O_5 and 9lb (4.1kg) nitrogen. This adds up to less than the standard chemical fertilizer dressing, yet it secured an 8% higher yield.

The gain from irrigating lucerne was even more striking. With 5.42 US tons an acre (12.1 tonnes/hectare) of hay, compared with 2.27 US tons (5.1 tonnes/hectare) from complete artificials and well water, there was an increase of 138%. The reason for the greater efficiency of the plant foods in wastewater is partly the fact that much of the phosphorus and nitrogen were in a thin soup of methane bacteria, providing protein in an ideal form for rapid absorption by plant roots, soil bacteria, and fungi. The lucerne showed the larger increase, though both crops are greedy for available phosphorus, because lucerne is also greedy for zinc, which is always present in sewage, here again in forms that can be taken up quickly.

Every winter the portable aluminium pipes and sprinklers are moved from the farms growing grain and hay to forest areas, because the leaf-mould humus under the trees prevents the soil from freezing even in the hardest winters. Though fantastic domes and 'icebergs' form when the spray freezes, they trickle away without causing run-off when the thaw comes. The trees best suited to this system are the black walnut, grown as furniture timber, not for the nuts, and oaks, which showed an average of 83% increase in girth in five years compared with the control trees, which are only given plain water. White spruce doubled its height in the same period, but red pines did badly, because the boron from detergents used by the 50,000 people in Penn State added up to more than 1.1lb an acre (1.23kg/hectare), a level of toxicity at which symptoms begin in the more sensitive conifers. Broad leafed trees are therefore best for rapid growth under winter waste water.[2]

Professor Sopper takes the name for his method from the capacity of living soil on both farm and woodland to convert waste into drinking water fit to use direct from wells. It goes on the land holding 10 milligrams a litre of phosphorus—a level that filled Spring Creek with algae and killed the fish through eutrophication before the system was in use—but reaches the wells at 0.04mg with 0.5mg of nitrate—well below the 3.0mg of each which is the safe level for drinking water. Samples of the soil water taken at a foot (30cm) below the surface show only one coliform bacterium per 100 millilitres compared with 2,000 allowed by the American standard for safe swimming.

Still more important, though Penn State is using just as much water and the rainfall is no higher, the water table is slowly rising by about 14ft (4.3m) every ten years, despite the higher transpiration rate from better farm crops and faster growing trees. The energy to pump the wastewater along miles of PVC piping is provided by methane generated in the digesters, which is vastly less than the power that would be needed to carry the bulk of the liquid by tanker to the fields for spreading, or to dry and burn the concentrated sludge.

There is no climatic reason why the living filter system should not be applied in Britain. The use of forest land to take the winter effluent removes the difficulty that has been hardest for sewage farms to solve ever since the days of the agriculturalist John Joseph Mechi (1802–80)—the fact that farm crops in temperate climates dislike flooding with sewage in winter.

Fertility Flooding

At Penn State, the forests and farmland lie in indulating country, rather like a drier and hillier Surrey. The University of Arizona, however, stands on flat land, making flood irrigation impossible. There, experiments have developed a system for using only the effluent from the 17 million gallons (77 million litres) of sewage produced each day by the 220,000 people of Tucson, as they have to contend with a warmer and drier climate, and water requirements that double every ten years.[3] The effluent from their heated digestion plant is a clear liquid without odour, containing, on average, 65lb (29kg) nitrogen, 50lb (23kg) phosphorus as P_2O_5 and 32lb (14kg) potassium as K_2O, and the amount available is enough to cover an acre (0.4 hectares) 1ft (30cm) deep, the standard irrigation unit. (See Appendix 3k).

Among the grain crops grown experimentally at Tucson, the barley was not of first-class malting quality but the wheat was up to standard for milling and baking. In this case, the 112% increase in winter grazing from barley, 116% from wheat and 249% from oats, with the use of effluent, plus the gain in grain yields, is of less importance to the State of Arizona than the saving of water. In fact, the system of grazing grain crops through the winter and letting them come on to harvest, with the effluent or waste water transferred to pasture in summer, would be ideal for any dry, Mediterranean type climate like that in some parts of Australia, where very large sums are spent today in providing long outfall pipes to discharge the effluent far out to sea, right away from the thirsty land that needs the water so desperately.

A Tucson rancher has been growing barley on this system to keep four steers an acre (10 per hectare), starting at 500lb each (226kg) and gaining 2lb (0.9kg) a day live weight through the season, which ends when further grazing would injure the grain crop. The higher yield from the effluent, compared with the same plant foods in chemical form and the same amount of water, is due to the presence of trace elements in the effluent, and the organic forms in which the plant foods are supplied. There is a steady build-up of fertility, including potassium, and potatoes have turned out to be a usefully greedy break crop in the rotation.

Like Penn State, Arizona is using a heated digestion system which provides methane to power pumps and leaves only the beef tapeworm (*Taenia saginata*) as a possible pathogen—a very minor risk in countries where meat is rarely eaten uncooked and slaughterhouses are always under veterinary control.

In Australia, the famous Werribee Delta Works[4] has been using the 100 million gallons (450 million gallons) a day of sewage from the two million people in Melbourne, to irrigate 28,809 acres (11,700 hectares) of pasture. This makes possible heavy stocking, by Australian standards. In 1969, 52,356 sheep and 5,363 beef cattle were sold from this area. Throughout the 87 years since experiment began in 1893, there has been no sign of the build-up of toxic metals predicted by fertilizer pushers. The sewage flows into the works along a wide canal, then goes through a series of settling tanks, from which only the effluent is used. The solids settle out and are stacked to decay slowly and grow an assortment of local weeds, which seem indifferent to any toxic metals. The process is cheap, and trouble-free—except for the periodical swamping of the settling tanks by rain; most of the 18.93in (48cm) a year falls in the winter months. Protests arise when untreated sewage is discharged into the sea with the storm water at St Kilda, the local seaside resort.

The primitive but effective system is possible only because the Werribee Delta is low-lying and flat, so that gravity can take the effluent from field to field, flooding each in turn through sluices. The question of tapeworm eggs and pathogens is solved by allowing time to elapse before the pastures are grazed. Experiments are under way to find more efficient methods of handling the sewage from an ever growing city, but this sanitary engineer's equivalent of a James Watt steam-engine continues to pump water more cheaply than any modern replacement. The 'broken cycle' here is the solids, which accumulate slowly but surely. The plant foods they contain are relatively a minor waste compared with the effluent that goes on the pastures, as we saw in Chapter 8.

The Tanker Sludge System in Britain

Every day, 37 million gallons (167 million litres) of untreated sewage flow down the river Tyne carrying bacterial contamination far out to sea. The Tees receives industrial wastes and sewage from 500 separate outlets all the year round, the Severn takes raw sewage from 40% of the people of Wales, and every estuary in Britain is heavily polluted.[5] There are 148 local Authorities discharging sewage direct into the sea, and 200 seaside places where visitors can go paddling in what the report *Taken for Granted* calls 'visibly contaminated water'. There have certainly been improvements since 1970, but though we still use about 50% of our sludge on the land, we waste plant foods in all our effluent, and contaminate the seas with toxic metals and other industrial additions.

Though the Wanlip plant in Leicester, and Yorkshire Water Organics are the only two sewage concerns selling dried sludge to gardeners in Britain, there are many disposing of it as a liquid with about 4.4% dry matter. Of this 6.8% is nitrogen, 4.7% phosphorus, and 0.15% potash. One of the pioneers of this system is the West Hertfordshire Main Drainage Authority, which distributes 37 million gallons (167 million litres) a year of liquid called 'Hydig' with this analysis within a 40-mile radius of Rickmansworth.

One of many satisfied customers is Mr S. Reid of Iver, Bucks., who farms 85 acres (34 hectares) of poor, sandy land with a gravel subsoil, sludging it three times a year with 10,000 gallons an acre of Hydig. This allows stocking at the rate of three beasts of varied ages per acre (over seven per hectare). He buys 405 calves a year, suckles them on nurse cows and sells them as fat bullocks, beating factory farming on lower labour costs and lower capital investment. His 9 acres (3.6 hectares) of market garden crops and 5 acres (2 hectares) of mangolds, grown in rotation up and down his farm, profit from the fertility built up by the sludge and the heavy stocking. Clearly, it needs skill in balancing the demands of grazing mouths to prevent the grass from racing ahead on nitrogen and swamping the clover.

Hundreds of good farmers throughout Britain do not call themselves 'organic', but buy no chemical fertilizers, because farming with free fertility pays them better. They vary the system to suit their land, for it is appropriate for dairy cows or sheep, with kale, cabbage or potatoes as break crops, and wheat, oats or barley grazed in the spring to keep the straw short and avoid lodging (flattening of crops through weakness caused in the stems by excess nitrogen). So far, there have been no toxic metal disasters on tanker sludge farms, but inspectors from ADAS, aware of the possible danger, make routine tests to see that all is well.

At East Kilbride, near Glasgow, farmers pay for 2,000 gallon (9,000litre) tankers to pump 6,000 gallons an acre (67,000lt/ hectare) on their pastures in turn, using spray guns like giant lawn sprinklers. Their aim is to grow grass fast for hay, silage, and good grazing for cattle and sheep brought down from the hills to winter on the lowlands. Because they are paying for the sludge—and they must find it worthwhile—instead of having it spread free, as at Rickmansworth, they have worked out just how much produces the maximum effect.[6] Had Professor Sopper been selling his waste-water to canny farmers, he would have found that 10,000 people would supply sufficient to double the lucerne yield on many more than 129 acres (52 hectares).

Authorities in every country think of sewage as something to be got rid of as cheaply as possible on the minimum area. Yet sewage, in all its forms, is part of the income of the land, not its quickly-spent capital. We must therefore learn, through further research, how to spend it wisely over the maximum acreage, not to reduce the rates, but to reduce the drain on fertility of our soils.

The value of tanker sludge lies in its concentration. At Rickmansworth, they have 150,000 gallons of sludge a day, which is equivalent to 75 loads by 2,000 gallon (900lt) tanker. However, the drainage authority also uses several tankers holding 4,000 gallons (18,000lt) to deliver to distant farmers who have dug storage ponds so that they keep sludge available for spreading through their own tractor driven pumps in early spring, and on the straw and stubble after harvest, when everyone wants it. There is a night delivery service with extra drivers, to save buying more tankers. Mr Reid considers it important to check, even when it is his turn for a visit from the tanker after dark, that the black, tarry sludge is not sprayed on thickly enough to drown the worms, whose activity is all-important to good farmers who use tanker sludge.

If Rickmansworth tried to spread its effluent, as well as its sludge, it would need 13,850 journeys a day by the smaller tankers to spread the remaining 36,850,000 gallons, all year round, with an extra 13,850 every Leap Year, for the sewage flow never stops. This is just not possible, with fuel costs, traffic congestion, especially at weekends and Bank Holidays, and the labour. Yet the price of pouring our sewage effluent into our rivers and the sea, is wasted plant foods and pollution.

The Toxic Metal Problem

At Penn State, they use small sludge tankers to take concentrated sludge from the digesters to spread on their baseball and football fields, where the admission fees of spectators pay for all the students' amenities. They also use the sludge for experiments in growing forest trees on open-cast mining wastes, which are entirely without plant foods or humus. Britain is accustomed to considering only the relatively small quantity of sludge that contains the major part of the toxic metals, because these are heavier and sink to the bottom of settling tanks and digesters. In fact, treated sewage consists of a concentrate, and an enormously diluted solution of plant foods with far fewer heavy metals. The classic example of this is at Eye, in Suffolk, where 40,000 people used old-fashioned cesspools, which were pumped out infrequently by tanker. The concentrate went through a pressed cake process, before being composted with dustbin refuse. The sludge had only 2 p.p.m. of lead, compared with 1,200 for heavily industrialized Slough. Rural sludges are always low in lead, but 50 p.p.m. might have been expected. However, six months settling in cesspools produces the lowest average in Britain. If the tanker hoses ever managed to reach the very bottom of the cesspool to suck them clean, Eye might reach a higher level than Slough with the lead which has been accumulating since the 1930s. The level in the sludge at Penn State is 10 p.p.m. which is to be expected from this University town where lead from petrol in stormwater is not allowed to pollute the sewage.

Toxic metals are a distant threat, not an immediate problem on farm lands. Work at the Grassland Research Station at Hurley, Oxfordshire, has shown that 95% of the 2% of lead taken by grasses from the soil is returned in the manure of the animals grazing the grass and, of the 5% retained by the stock, most concentrates in their bones, which we do not eat. This explains why there has been no trouble from lead or even cadmium poisoning at sewage farms like Stoke Bardolph near Nottingham after a century of raising dairy cattle, and why they avoid raising pigs, which could eat soil.

The risk is that another century, with each year adding more lead, cadmium, mercury, copper, zinc, chromium and nickel than the soil acquired in the whole period between 1880 and 1940, might reduce some of our farmland to desert, as far as crops were concerned. The organo-chlorines break down in time, as do most pesticides, fungicides and herbicides, but metals remain in the soil. Because Authority thinks in the short term, but tries to hedge its bets, tanker sludge is officially approved, the farmers are satisfied, and the Water Authority Engineers are running the system well, but keeping an eye open for trouble. At the same time, research in this important field is minimal, and it is likely that the use of sludge will be 'phased out' during the next twenty years, in which case we shall burn our sludge expensively while still pouring our effluent into the sea.

The work of Professor Derek Bryce-Smith[7] on the effects of lead is of vital importance to the mental health of our children, but it relates almost entirely to the lead in petrol. It has, however, set back the use of sewage on the land by forty years, because both the petrol companies and their customers prefer to go on risking the brains of our children, and it is so much more convenient to blame sludge, just as smokers prefer to blame diesel smoke for lung cancer. The use of both sludge and effluent on the land offers a valid challenge to those who stand to profit from fast sales of the world's dwindling stock of fertilizer raw materials, and who insist that long-term starvation from soil exhaustion stares us in the face, unless we continue to pour pollution and fertility into the suffering sea. True, we have an instinctive prejudice against the risk of tapeworms, but there also exists the far stronger prejudice of large commercial firms against sewage sludges that are usually given away free and compete with the fertilizers they sell.

On the other hand, as world populations rise, the problem of sewage disposal will increase, and perhaps 500 of the 5,000 treatment plants in Britain alone are wearing out after over fifty years of service, and will need money spent on replacements and additions. In a democracy, the voice of the people can make itself heard. Therefore, we have to be aware of our need to fight for the fertility of our future. Tens of millions of pounds will in any case be spent. Let us fight to see that they are spent well.

Friends of Fertility

The Earth has Friends. So have many cathedrals and areas of natural beauty, and even slugs have a learned Society to care desperately about their strange love lives and their survival in a changing world. But so far there is no fighting organization to defend Fertility as it is defined in this book. However, it is to be hoped that one may grow out of the many and varied bodies in the Organic Movement, and the object of this chapter is to provide some practical suggestions for people who are concerned with campaigning as well as composting.

Every large sewage disposal plant has a laboratory where the effluents discharged into the sewers are tested to decide the rate that industries must pay for having their wastes treated. A large item is always BOD, or 'biochemical oxygen demand' and the highest payment in the London area for this service comes from a cake factory. There are hundreds of dedicated men and women to whom the challenge of the future is not Space but Sewage.

Though the present estimate of the time it will take for Britain's population to double is 116 years, and this might even fall, pollution depends on industrial activity, and this may double again and again in as little as ten years, producing potential disasters like that caused by the discharge of dimethyl mercury from the Chisso chemical factory into the bay that gave its name to Minamata disease.[8] If the effluent is of known danger, permission to discharge it in sewers may be refused, and the manufacturer must then pay to have it dumped in a 'safe tip' where the complex decay of mixed toxic chemicals can build up new levels of danger to filter through the soil. At present, laundries are still allowed to discharge whatever they like without question, because they began with plain soap and water. Nevertheless, they are now responsible for an ever-changing stream of detergents and their additives, dry-cleaning fluids, and other unknown materials, whose dangers we shall only know when evidence of death or disability can be brought home to those responsible. Any firm that discharged any waste before 1937 has the right to go on doing so, and it is now hard to establish exactly what they were discharging at that time, because of the absence of records.

To enforce the industrial effluent regulations would require many more chemists and inspectors. But the only way to make our sewage fit for continual use on the land without fear for the future is to stop industry pouring into it the toxic metals that mean permanent pollution, for once these, and the many (non-biodegradable) chemical compounds which contain man-made molecules that

Nature cannot take apart, have reached the sewage, they cannot be taken out without expensive and energy-consuming processes.

It is possible to extract almost any substance, at a price, and as the cost of cadmium, lead, mercury, and other metals, rises with the scarcity which will occur as rich ores are exhausted, it may well pay to do so, but at the expense of the manufacturer, who should treat his own effluent or shut down his process. The risk for every citizen of an industrial country is that scientific caution and bureaucratic reluctance to act will enable the dangerous dumping of industrial wastes to build up new Minimatas. In developing countries, the risk is higher still, as multi-national companies take advantage of the absence of regulations which are equal in force to those protecting the citizens of older states from processes of known danger. Younger, or poorer, administrations sanction the new factory and welcome the employment. They may be fortunate, if the factory produces wastes that merely pollute the sea after a short journey down a river estuary, but the dioxin disaster at Seveso in Italy is an example of the risk that can come when countries export their pollution problems to places where the controls are less rigorous.

To many people in Britain, pollution is a class issue, with middle-class conservationists attacking firms that create employment. However thick the smoke from the chimneys, and no matter what shade of dull, reddish-grey the river turns below the constantly disgorging outlet pipe, the foreman will argue that when the stink stops the town goes dead with unemployment. All ranks, from labourer to managing director, contend that if an extraction process is installed, the product will be undercut by competition from other countries without safety regulations. So we go on poisoning ourselves, as well as our children and grandchildren, because pollution is a political issue, and few politicians can think beyond the next by-election.

A hopeful field for research might be the treatment of sludges and effluents separately, starting with existing plants in favourable situations, and later building new ones in areas with expanding populations, or replacing others that are worn out. The two essential requirements are an area of farmland, ideally on sandy soil, to which the effluent could be pumped along lasting PVC piping, and an area of forest for the winter.

The most rewarding enterprise in Britain would be on the chalk land of Kent, Sussex, Buckinghamshire, Hampshire, Dorset and Wiltshire, where the effluent could grow barley, wheat, kale and pasture for dairy or beef cattle without imported fertilizers, and feed beech and ash woods through the winter for furniture timber.

There would be no more interference with amenities of townsfolk strolling in the new beechwoods of Buckinghamshire than there is with deer hunting in the forest of Pennsylvania from the sprinklers, which would be working only in winter, then moved back to the farms for the summer, away from the risk of vandalism.

The major gain would be in replenishing the chalk basin that supplies London's wells, for the higher water is above sea level, the more valuable it is. So many of our cities are situated on low ground beside rivers or the sea, that we may have to pump our effluent back to provide us with the living filters that could supply food, timber and water. It would not be economically or socially desirable to build heated digestion treatment plants to replace the existing seaside systems which waste fertility into the sea with tankers grinding up the hill against the summer weekend traffic, but pipelines laid right to the top of the downs would feed farms and woodlands in Sussex by the sea.

All this involves heavy engineering, built to last, a field in which Britain once excelled. Especially important are the dual-fuel engines that start with diesel oil and go over to methane when a coil heated by their cooling water has maintained the concentrated sewage in the digester at 90°F (32°C) for long enough to allow bacteria to take over. The engine then runs smoothly till its next overhaul.

To provide enough power to drive the effluent out to the farms, it might be necessary to reinforce the energy in the sewage with that from dustbin refuse, either by adding to the digester the pulverized paper, cardboard and food wastes that are compostable, or by pyrolysis, the making of a product resembling coal gas from the burnable fraction. In the first case, it would be necessary to restrict the inks of all magazines to those without the cadmium and lead.

We cannot tell what the household wastes of the future will be, but we can hope that all kitchen wastes will be composted, all possible paper salvaged, and only the minimum of recyclable refuse collected by the council, who will probably charge by the binful, as happens in Sweden and Denmark today, but will call only once a month, because there will be no decayable content. The replacement of lead additives in petrol by 10–15% of ethanol or methanol from sugarbeet or wood could be used to remove this dangerous form of pollution from the air.

Where an industry produced an effluent that could not be broken down and recycled, it would have to close down, or find a new way round the problem. It is here that the weapon of public concern could be effective. For example, a customer boycott of detergents (which consume almost as much of our shrinking store of good rock phosphates as the farmlands of the world, and contain toxic boron) in favour of ordinary soap, would be very helpful.

Conserving the Concentrate

The sludge direct from the digesters should be used where it would give the best value, as in Scotland, rather than disposed of in the smaller possible area. Because the nitrogen is readily available, and the build-up of lignins from regularly sludged land means a darker subsoil that warms up faster in spring, tanker sludge can solve a problem that preoccupies French organic farmers.

They insist that on clay soils, in cold springs, organic nitrogen in the soil becomes too slowly available to prevent grain crops suffering from lack of nitrogen at the tillering (branching) stage, which can result in a 50% reduction in the harvest. Therefore, they have insisted that a dressing of 30kg of Chilean nitrate of soda a hectare (27lb per acre) is organic, because it is essential. This is why the British 'inorganic' farmers within 40 miles (64km) of Rickmansworth excavate sludge ponds—because they want to spray on the Hydig at just the right time, rather than pay for far more than 30 kilos (66lb) of what is not so much a dressing of nitrogen fertilizer as the thin end of the wedge from the point of view of organic farmers taking a premium price for their grain.

At the other end of the season, the big demand is for drenching the straw broken up by a gadget on combines, so that it can be turned under with ample nitrogen to decay without robbery, providing humus instead of smoke, flames and ashes. If tanker sludge in a grain-growing area were reserved for these two purposes, its value would be spread over a huge acreage, offering perhaps a sustainable and pollution-free method of stockless farming, possibly with the grain crops undersown with trefoil for more humus, and a high-protein field bean as a break crop which would also provide a soya bean substitute for our climate.

Ever since 1968, Professor Barry Commoner of Washington has been warning of the dangers of nitrate fertilizers, which can wash from the soil into well water and be converted into poisonous nitrates by bacteria in the digestive system of babies under six months old. Infants have died from this in the United States, and water from wells in North Lincolnshire caused the symptoms in Britain in 1970.

The main effect is methaemoglobinemia, which is the inability of the red corpuscles in the blood to carry oxygen, producing cyanosis and, eventually, asphyxia. The World Health Organization estimate of the danger level is above 22.6 p.p.m., though the level that Water Authorities aim at is 11 p.p.m., and in the EEC there are moves to lower the level to 5.6 p.p.m. These are regarded with dismay by British water authorities, who are concerned at the vast sum it would cost to reduce our nitrate level to this point in the perpetual grain growing areas like North Lincolnshire, where such periods of drought as the summer of 1976 can build up large quantities of nitrates from chemical fertilizers that wash into the wells with the first good spell of rain.

In May 1980, the Anglian Water Authority was again shutting down wells between Lincoln and Grantham that went over the WHO limit after a dry spring. A pipe line has been laid to bring supplies from safe areas, and there are two plants in the Authority's area to bottle pure water for house-to-house delivery to families with young babies.[9]

All authorities insist that the use of farmyard manure, and especially the raw, uncomposted slurry that replaces the manure pile of factory farms, can also produce high nitrates in the soil, but the level in the soil water draining from Professor Sopper's effluent-fed farms was only 0.5 p.p.m.—far below even the EEC level. This is because plants take up their nitrogen in the form of small quantities of nitrates as it is released by bacteria that break down manure, by clover root bacteria, and others that live on humus in the soil and gather nitrogen from the air. Modern agriculture by-passes the bacteria with ready-made nitrates, especially nitrate of soda, nitrochalk, and a liquid ammonia squirted into the soil. Only a little of the nitrogen in sewage sludge or effluent is present as nitrate, but there is enough to start the grain crops off fast, and the rest is released slowly, together with the phosphorus, by the bacteria through the season.

It should be said that the value of grazing winter wheat in Arizona and on many British organic farms is to gain an early start in the process of branching from the base of the plants, referred to as tillering, as well as feeding the stock. This needs good fences or, preferably hedges, and skill in judging when the soil is dry enough to take the spreading hooves of the cattle, and how many beasts to put on the land for how long. These are the qualities that all good stock farmers need to preserve the fertility of their land.

Thinking Further Ahead
It is not just this year's crop that matters, nor even the next hundred years of cropping. The crops must go on through seed time and harvest for centuries to feed the children of our children's

children as long as the sun goes on shining. Because we have been given the ability to think ahead, we have the responsibility not to deny the joy of living to those who will exist thousands of years after we are dead.

Exponential growth is the blind doubling of cancer cells in a suffering body, the dead chemical reaction of acid and alkali, and the senseless fury of forest fire or nuclear explosion. We must replace the exponential growth of population with organic growth. This is the way that trees grow, from seed to seedling, sapling to forest giant. We grow similarly, and when we fall we must leave for recycling the experience we have drawn through the roots of our past, and thoughts we have received through leaves outspread to gather selectively the answers that are blown on the wind from the minds of others. We should leave the land of ideas more fertile than we found it.

1. HILLS, L. D. 'Putting Waste Water to Work' *The Ecologist* November 1975

2. SOPPER, W. E. 'Disposal of Municipal Waste Water through Forest Irrigation' *Reprint Series* 24 The Pennsylvania State University, University park, Pennsylvania

3. DAY, A. D., TUCKER, T. C., and VAVICH, M. G. (Arizona Agricultural Experimental Station, Tucson, Arizona) 'City Sewage for Irrigation and Plant Nutrients' *Compost Science* Autumn 1962

4. HILLS, L. D. 'Fertility or Pollution' *The Ecologist* November 1970

5. *Taken for Granted.* Report of the working party on sewage disposal. Ministry of Housing and Local Government, HMSO 1970

6. HILLS, L. D. 'The British System of Tanker Sludge Disposal' *Compost Science* November-December 1971

7. BRYCE-SMITH, D. 'Behavioural Effects of Lead and other Heavy Metal Pollutants' Chemistry in Britain 8/5 June 1972

8. TUCKER, Anthony *The Toxic Metals* Earth Island 1972

9. PATERSON, Stephen 'Fears over Nitrate Levels in Water' *Lincolnshire Echo* 30th May 1980

Appendix 1

The Soil Association Standards of Organic Husbandry

These standards are based on those agreed between The Soil Association, Walnut Tree Manor, Haughley, Stowmarket, Suffolk, and The Henry Doubleday Research Association of Convent Lane, Bocking, Braintree, Essex, nearly twenty years ago. Since then they have been modified and improved by the Soil Association Standards Committee, which employs its own farm inspectors both to approve new organic farmers and to see that existing farmers keep to the Standards.

Farmers and market gardeners who observe these standards are entitled to use the Soil Association symbol on their produce. This is a registered trademark. If produce with the label does not meet the standards, those responsible can be sued for infringing the patent, and the symbol is withdrawn from that farm or market garden. The basic problem for the consumer is to find the 'Symbol Quality' produce, which is grown to the following high standards, that are as precise as those for TT milk.

The aim of organic agriculture is to produce food of such quality and quantity as to promote health of the community and to maintain the soil fertility for future generations.

Soil fertility is a measure of the effectiveness of the living processes whereby inert materials and recycled organic matter are changed into more living forms using energy from the sun. An understanding of basic principles of plant nutrition is needed to find practical methods for promoting fertility in the individual soils of every farm and garden.

Plants are able to use energy directly from sunlight. From the air they obtain oxygen and carbon. The water drawn up through their roots provides hydrogen, the third constituent element of sugar, which is the primary energy source for animals and man. Plants need many other elements to grow, develop and bear fruit. They obtain nitrogen, calcium, phosphorus and potassium and many other minor, but no less essential, nutrients through the agency of living soil processes.

A complete, balanced and appropriate nutrition for plants, the requirements of which vary continuously (i.e. with temperature, stage of growth, length of day), can be provided only by managing the soil as a whole living system. We believe that produce from crops so nourished in turn helps to provide a complete and balanced nutrition for man and animals.

Organic husbandry may be considered under the following headings: Humus Husbandry; Soil Aeration; Soil Moisture; Balanced Mineral Availability; Crop Husbandry.

The following guidelines must be observed by those wishing to obtain a licence to label their produce with the Soil Association Symbol. The classes of applicable produce are cereals, vegetables and fruit; additional Standards dealing with animal products will be drawn up in due course.

Humus Husbandry

Humus is the complex material originating from decomposition of animal and plant residues by micro-organisms. Humus distinguishes a living soil from a dead one. What it does matters more than what it is.

It provides food for bacteria and fungi and a medium in which they can work. Different groups of microbes are vital for transforming organic residues to plant nutrients and fixing nitrogen from the air. We believe that microbes associated with the root are another group of special importance.

It encourages mycorrhizal association—channelling of nutrients into plant roots through fungal threads.

It changes the texture and improves the crumb structure of the soil. (See Soil Aeration.)

It holds moisture and so conserves water for the plant.

Quality of humus is as relevant as quantity. The carbon:nitrogen ratio is significant. For example a manure with sufficient straw to dung leads to better humus than dung applied on its own.

For maintaining and increasing humus content of the soil we recommend:

—Permanent pasture with seed mixtures incorporating a wide variety of grasses, legumes and herbs stocked with a variety of grazing animals.

—Rotations including mixed leys stocked with a variety of grazing animals.

—Green manuring.

—Sheet composting.

—Mulching.

—Yard manure from own farm.

—Slurry from own farm—spread on pasture or stubble and not on crops for human consumption.

—Compost from own plant material and animal manures made without additives or with only the following: herbal activators, seaweed preparations, ground and powdered rock and nitrogenous animal wastes.

The following may be used only after the source of supply has been approved in writing by the Standards Committee of the Soil Associations:

    Composted municipal waste

    Digested sewage sludge

    Brought-in manures

    Brought-in commercial vegetable waste, e.g. apple residues, coffee grounds, wool shoddy, banana stalks.

For minimizing wastage of humus we recommend that:

—Crop wastes should be recycled and not sold off, burned or otherwise destroyed.

—Soil inversion should be kept to a minimum. For example chisel ploughing is preferable to ploughing when soil conditions permit. Ploughing should be as shallow as practicable.

—Crop residues and manures should not be buried but used as a mulch or worked into the surface. Breakdown in the absence of air may lead to production of toxins.

—Soil should be kept covered by vegetation to protect the humus content from destruction by sunlight and rain.

Soil Aeration

Soil aeration is necessary to allow respiration of soil organisms. Moreover, substances produced by micro-organisms growing in the absence of air may be detrimental to plant growth.

First, practices for the removal of excess water from the topsoil are as follows:

—Water table adjustment by ditching.

—Tile draining, mole draining and subsoiling so that the water is maintained at the level of the watertable.

—Avoidance of soil pans and smearing, e.g. caused by heavy machinery, a rotavator used always at the same depth and wheel spin.

—Breaking up soil pans by subsoiling or deep chisel ploughing in dry conditions.

—Encouragement of increased numbers of soil fauna by humus husbandry to assist soil drainage and aerations, e.g. worms.

Secondly, soil aeration may be increased by improving soil structure by the following means:

—Plant roots on dying, if decayed by the right bacteria, leave passages in the soil.

—Most cultivations tend to increase air in topsoil but loss of humus through excessive air is a danger.

—The addition of organic matter, particularly when it leads to humus formation. (See Humus Husbandry.)

Soil Moisture

Soil moisture is necessary as plants absorb most of their nutrients dissolved in water and require water to prevent wilting. In temperate climates, irrigation on an agricultural scale is not normally an economic proposition but in intensive horticulture it may be.

Retention of water in topsoil depends again on structure. Loss of water by evaporation should be reduced by maintaining a soil cover as constantly as practicable. Subsoiling of dry clay soil produces fissures allowing improved root penetration. This also assists upward capillary movement of water from deep in the subsoil. Therefore, subsoiling may be a prudent alternative to drainage systems which remove water altogether. Emphasis should be on building up water retention in the soil, a characteristic much enhanced by humus.

Balanced Mineral Availability

Most soils have enormous reserves of all minerals needed for plant nutrition. In a humus-rich soil, well aerated and moist, micro-organisms release nutrients suitable for plant use. Since both plant and micro-organisms are interdependent and governed by identical climatic conditions, the rate of nutrient provision and the requirement of the plant are precisely matched. Moreover the nutrient provision is continuous and balanced. Such conditions can never be realized by the addition of water-soluble chemicals (e.g. NPK from the bag) which may cause excessive uptake of the limited range of nutrients so supplied. Excessive application of soluble chemicals may also cause 'disappearance' of trace elements. The practice of attempting to supply soluble chemicals direct to plants is therefore excluded from organic husbandry. The excessive use of some organic manures may also give an unbalanced mineral supply with similar detrimental effects. Practices from 'Humus Husbandry' ensure a return of some of the minerals removed by cropping. The availability of subsoil minerals is assisted by deep-rooting plants.

For soils in a low state of fertility, the necessary living systems may be encouraged by the addition of minerals and trace elements in suitable forms. Where soils are deficient in these they should be added. Brought-in organic manures specified for 'humus Husbandry' add minerals to the holding. These may be supplemented by the following:

—Slow acting powdered natural rocks, such as limestone, calcarium lithaneum (maerle), chalk, rock phosphate, granite or dolomite, kainite as mined, felspar and basalt. Also applications of up to 10cwt per acre (1.23 tonnes/hectare) of basic slag.

—Use of animal by-products such as hoof and horn meal, bonemeal, dried blood, wool shoddy, feathers, fish wastes, guano, etc., if free from soluble chemical additives and contaminants.

—Seaweed, in its natural state, liquefied, powdered, or as liquid extracts. Seaweeds are particularly valuable as a source of trace elements.

Crop Husbandry

Healthy plants grown in ideal conditions have a high degree of resistance to attack by diseases and pests.

Commercial conditions are never ideal, and some diseases and pests are always present. Incomplete or unbalanced nutrition of plants reduces their resistance. Repeated monocropping causes a build-up of diseases and pest which enjoy the conditions suitable to them.

Breeding genetically resistant varieties gives only temporary protection, until the offending organisms adapt or slightly different organisms build up. Plant breeding research for frequent genetic variation is expensive. The growing of a wide variety of crops in planned rotations together with the provision of complete and balanced plant nutrition should keep diseases and pests to an acceptable level. The idea of elimination of crop disease and pest organisms is unrealistic.

Present economic conditions make it necessary to restrict variety in rotations and so, even with good nutrition, pests and diseases tend to rise above acceptable levels. Crop protection methods must therefore be considered. Biological control by encouraging and even introducing natural predators of the disease organisms and pests can be effective. For example, ladybirds feed on a wide variety of aphids.

Biocides—chemicals which kill pest and disease organisms—are not selective and thus often kill useful predators reducing natural biological control. The use of sprays which make crops unattractive to pest and disease agents without killing them is therefore preferable. For example, it is suggested that the silica-based biodynamic sprays repel moisture on foliage, making it a less suitable habitat for fungi (e.g. potato blight). Liquefied seaweed preparations are not biocides but also help to protect foliage. Garlic extracts appear to have pest repellent effects.

When disease and pest damage are still above acceptable levels, only those biocides on the Soil Association's current permitted list may be used. The permitted list is under constant revision. New products and others not included on the list may be used only after written approval of the Soil Association Standards Committee or its authorized representative. Applications of permitted biocides should be made when day-flying insects (e.g. bees) are not working.

Weed Control
Weeds can be adequately controlled by the use of rotations and timely mechanical means, and in horticulture also by mulching. Some plants have the ability to restrict growth of others.

There is no satisfactory evidence that herbicides exist which do not contaminate the soil as a living environment.

Permitted List for Organic Farmers and Market Gardeners
This is the permitted list of products that may be used with the Soil Association Organic Husbandry Qualifying Standards. New products, resistant varieties and new applications appear and the list will be revised periodically. The numbers apply to the notes below.

A MANURES
1) Farmyard manure
2) Pig manure
3) Sheep manure
4) Horse manure
5) Goat Manure
6) Poultry manure
7) Slurry
8) Homeopathic preparations

B COMPOSTS
13) Composted organic animal and vegetable residues

14) Mushroom compost
15) Deeplitter compost
16) Municipal compost
17) Sewage sludge
18) Spent hops

C ANIMAL BY-PRODUCTS
25) Shoddy
26) Dried blood
27) Blood and bone
28) Bonemeal
29) Tannery wastes
30) Fishmeal

31) Hoof and horn
32) Dried animal manures
33) Guano

D MINERALS
37) Basic slag
38) Phosphate rock
39) Dolomite rock
40) Felspar rock
41) Ground chalk
42) Ground limestone
43) Ground basalt rock

E SEA PRODUCTS
49) Ground calcareous seaweeds
50) Seaweed meal
51) Seaweed foliar feeds

F HOMEOPATHIC SPRAYS
   AND PREPARATIONS
60) Biocides

G INSECT CONTROL
73) Pyrethrum, Rotenone
74) Derris
75) Garlic, herbal sprays and preparations
76) Quassia
77) Ryania
78) Nicotine
79) Homeopathic sprays and preparations
80) Diatomaceous earth

H FUNGUS CONTROL
96) Homeopathic sprays and preparations
97) Herbal sprays and preparations
98) Formaldehyde
99) Lime sulphur
100) Dispersable sulphur
101) Copper fungicide

J HERBICIDES
108) See notes

General

Compost/Manure to be acceptable must be produced from material grown or cultivated following Soil Association principles, or from material which is composted for at least three months and subject to these notes.

Organic fertilizers are effective not so much by what they contain but by what they do to the soil and its micro-biological life. Organic humus matter is highly important, together with the mechanical condition of the soil. To increase the earthworm and biological content are priority aims, as is the judicious use of the subsoiler/mole plough allowing aeration and so producing an increasing soil life.

Composting of materials is preferable to returning them neat to the soil. A carbon:nitrogen ratio of 30–35:1 (1 tonne straw to 2–3 tonnes fresh manure) should be aimed for. A minimum of 140°F (60°C) for several days with a maximum of 170°F (77°C) should be reached in the compost heap. A small amount of lime may be added to help decomposition and retain phosphate.

Sewage Sludge and Heavy Metals. Pathogens are present in sewage sludge especially raw untreated material. Most pathogens are destroyed by anaerobic sludge digestive processed and *digested sludge only should be used.* Risk of transmission of disease to animals and man is very low. Animals should not graze land treated with sewage sludge until at least five weeks have elapsed.

Sewage sludge is best composted and included with other materials in the heap. If it is used directly on land it must not be used on crops for direct human consumption. Application should be some time before sowing—at least one season's growth (harvest) before a crop intended for human consumption.

Most sludge contains heavy metals. These should be avoided as they are stable in the soil. The accumulation of toxic metals is likely to be less serious in soils with a high degree if humus content. Rural area sewage from small treatment works is less likely to have a high metal content. Accurate analysis of sludges is essential, and it is recommended that nitrogen from sewage sludge should not be greater than 150kg per hectare when applied to the soil.

The toxic effects of copper, nickel and zinc are cumulative and can be worked out with the help of ADAS Advisory Paper 10 (Permissible Levels of Toxic Metals in Sewage used on Agricultural Land) available from local Ministry of Agriculture.

Where no previous contamination with toxic metals, zinc equivalent maximum 250 p.p.m. (250mg per kg) in dry matter topsoil, and boron 4.4Kg/hectare.

Note that 250 p.p.m. = 500lbs (227kg) per acre (0.4 hectares) in soil. Further information will be added to the Permitted List when it becomes available.

The other metals causing human toxicity—cadmium, mercury and lead are a serious problem in sludge, especially cadmium because of its ability to translocate from the soil to the edible portion of plants. The level of cadmium in the soil should not exceed 3.3 p.p.m., lead 200 p.p.m. and mercury 2.5 p.p.m.

Our present protection lies in maintaining a high soil pH (6.0–6.5) to reduce cadmium availability and to err on the side of caution. A lowering of the pH of soils increases the risk of toxic effects from sewage sludges.

Lead is insoluble especially on alkaline soils, and when it is taken up by the plants it is retained in the roots; root crops therefore tend to be at greatest risk.

Mercury is absorbed from the soil into the root systems, but is not readily translocated to the edible portions of plants.

Notes on Permitted List

A MANURES

1–6) These will be of more value if composted before being spread. Steroid hormones and the so-called chemical hormones are *NOT* destroyed in composting. Antibiotics should be destroyed with composting, if satisfactory heating up to 170°F (77°C) takes place and heaps are turned to make sure contents are all thoroughly composted for three months.

2) Copper and zinc are incorporated in manufactured pig food and will be in pig manure from this source. Copper is highly toxic especially to sheep. (See above, note on Sewage Sludge and Heavy Metals.)

6) Growth hormones are incorporated in some manufactured poultry food and may be found in poultry manure from broiler units. Flash-dried deeplitter and poultry house muck is useful but frequently contains high

proportions of NH_3—toxic unless material weathered before direct application to plant. Better procedure is to compost. Not to be used on crops for direct human consumption unless previously cleared by OSC.

7) *Slurry* Carbon:nitrogen ration of 6:1 is too small and therefore use straw heaps sprayed with slurry. If this is impossible and slurry remains in lagoons, periodic aeration is recommended. Spread thinly and only in dry weather so that fresh manure is not immediately led towards roots. Spread on grassland immediately it has been cut or grazed. It should not be added in such quantities that it forms a cap and prevents aeration of top layers of the soil.

8) *Homeopathic Preparations* These preparations require considerable expertise and understanding of them is best sought from someone familiar with their use.

B COMPOSTS

13) Proprietary composts, e.g. John Innes, Jack Temple Compost and Levingtons contain added soluble fertilizers. Source of supply should be cleared with Soil Association first.

14) Beware of Gamma-BHC (persistent organo-chlorines). Source must be cleared.

15) See note 6, and note on Sewage Sludge and Heavy Metals.

16–17) Heavy metals are found in samples of sewage. Before using any product with sewage as an ingredient, obtain an analysis of heavy metal content. Digested sewage sludge contains approx. 6% nitrogen, 4% phosphate (P_2O_5), 0.3% potassium (K_2O) and is obtainable in semi-solid or pelleted (cake) form.

C ANIMAL BY-PRODUCTS

25) 3%–12% N shoddy from the woollen industry sometimes has glass/metal waste and Australian/New Zealand seeds in it. Seeds in the main produce large thistles.

26) 12%–13% N.

27, 28, 30, 31) Best applied before planting/sowing.

28) Source of phosphate 20%–24%. Steamed bonemeal is quicker acting.

29) Little value.

30) 7%–14% N. 9%–16% P_2O_5 (phosphate).

32) These should be watched for any additives, e.g. chemical hormones and steroids.

33) Source of potash.

D MINERALS

37) 9%–22% phosphate and about 25%–33% lime + trace elements. Sometimes contains added rock phosphate (Europhos). 6–10cwt per acre (750–1250kg/hectare) applied every three years. Small dressings yearly (2cwts per acre, 250kg/hectare) give better results and/or may be alternated with calcified seaweed and basalt rock dust. Apply autumn, winter or early spring. * Kainite and K Slag too highly soluble.

38) Finely ground produces 26%–33% insoluble phosphate. *Gasfa 301 only*. Up to 7cwt (875kg/hectare) per acre every 4th/5th year. Gasfa contains high proportion of calcium which might produce problems on high pH soils. (Superphosphate and triple superphosphate prohibited).
39) Source of magnesium.
40) Potash source.
42) Apply according to pH. A pH of 6.0 for grassland and 6.5 for cereals should be aimed for. Over-liming locks up trace elements and is to be avoided. Slaked or burnt limestone not recommended.

E SEA PRODUCTS
49) Up to 5cwt per acre (625kg/hectare) every 3 or 4 years. See also not 37. Not recommended on calcarious land.
50) Seaweed itself (*Laminaria*) most valuable up to 5–6 tonnes per acre (12.5–15 tonnes/hectare) on grassland and potatoes. Kelp 12%–16% K.
51) Contains trace elements and growth factors. These products must be checked for addition of soluble chemical fertilizers.

F HOMEOPATHIC SPRAYS AND PREPARATIONS
60) Applications of permitted Biocides should be made when beneficial day-flying insects (e.g. bees) are not working.

G INSECT CONTROL
73) Pyrethrum from the flower; Rotenone from the root of Pyrethrum. Photo-chemical—best applied in dull light/in the evening.
74) Must be kept clear of water as it will kill fish. Recommended for use as warble dressing—apply late autumn (November).
75, 78) Beware of taint.
80) *Diatomaceous Earth*. Active ingredients are 80% SiO_2 used as an insecticide in the form of a wettable powder for grain and seed storage. Trade name of Perma-Guard D.10 for prevention of damage by weevils and sawtoothed grain beetle, 7lb (3.3kg) of powder per tonne of grain.
Perma-Guard D20   Household insecticide.
Perma-Guard D.21   Plant insecticide.
Perma-Guard D.30   Livestock insecticide.
Possibility of use as antihelmintic e.g. parasites. Fed at rate of 1%–2% of total ration.

H FUNGUS CONTROL
98) Seed dressing and general fungicide wash, e.g. on seed boxes.
99) Is non-selective. It kills predators. Fruit crops.
100, 101) These chemicals are only temporarily allowed and are mainly to combat potato, tomato and vine blight. They will be replaced if and when organic alternatives or resistant crop varieties are found. They do not leave a residue on the produce. Copper fungicide at leaf stage only. No other fungicides.

108) No herbicides on crops for direct human consumption, and for other crops reference must be made to OSC.

No growth inhibitors.

No growth regulators + inhibitors, e.g., for standing corn, Cycocel.

No potato sprout inhibitors, e.g. Fusarex.

For further information, apply to The Soil Association.

Appendix 2
The Henry Doubleday Research Association

The Henry Doubleday Research Association began in 1955 out of a book, a bear and a tonne of lucerne seed. The book was my now long out of print *Russian Comfrey*, which began modern comfrey growing in all countries, and the HDRA grew out of the fan-mail it drew from farmers and gardeners all round the world.

In 1954 I sent the first modern comfrey to Canada, from Mrs Greer's field, and Mr A. H. A. Lasker, the Canadian seedsman who bought it, sent me a tonne of lucerne seed as a gift for my part in the epic struggle that got it across.

The lucerne was a variety barred to Britain by dollar shortage and about the most awkward possible present for a struggling gardening writer, for it hit Regulation 365, which then controlled food parcels and laid down that gifts must weigh no more than 22lb (10kg) and be 'for personal use only'. Such use would have required 50 acres (20 hectares) on which to sow the seed, and stock to eat it; but the £275 that a famous farm seedsman was willing to pay for it would be enough to start a research station.

Two MPs fought hard to get it through. There was a letter in the *New Statesman*, and an article in *Time and Tide*—but all in vain. Canada's gift lay at the London docks awaiting a British 'Boston Tea Party'—until a second generous gift arrived at the Regulation 365 barrier.

While the battle of the seed was raging, an American wild animal dealer gave a nice, tame black bear to an old friend in London, whose wife objected to its 'personal use' as a pet. Two hundredweight (100kg) of bear, breaking the weight restriction, sitting up to beg docker's sandwiches, and posing with Teddy-bear appeal for Fleet Street Photographers, soon crashed through the red-tape barrier. So it ambled to the children's corner of a zoo, closely pursued through the dock gates by a ton of lucerne seed.

With the money from selling the seed, I leased the Trial Ground at £10 a year when it was only about ¾ of an acre (0.3 hectares), paid for the fencing, the labour cost of planting the comfrey presented by the Comfrey Growers of Britain, and the publication of Comfrey Report No. 1, which is also out of print. From that small beginning we have grown, until in 1958 we became a Registered Charity of the type that gives away knowledge rather than money.

We would now be homeless had we not in 1961 appealed to our members (then only 470) and raised £1,500 towards the £2,500 needed to buy the freehold at building land price. Then a member of our Committee, the late Dr Sidney Osborn of Ipswich, lent us £1,000 interest free, to acquire the land for ever, with long triangle reaching down towards a bird sanctuary, making us just two acres (0.8 hectares). To our great regret, Dr Osborn died that winter, before we had begun paying back his loan, and left us the balance in his will. So, in part, our Trial Ground is a memorial to the doctor who bought the infant HDRA into the world, and to the generosity of our members in many countries.

I christened the Association after Henry Doubleday (1813–1902) who was a Quaker, like his forbears who sailed with William Penn to Pennsylvania. One of his descendants founded Doubledays, the American publishers, and his cousin Henry Doubleday of Epping made the first collection of butterflies for the British Museum. Henry Doubleday of Coggeshall introduced the hybrid he called 'Russian Comfrey' from Russia in the 1870s, in the hope that its protein, (called 'mucilaginous matter' in some of the early analyses) would replace the erratic supplies of gum arabic that were endangering his contract with the firm of De la Rue to supply gum for the later penny black stamps and some of the early colonial issues.

Unfortunately, gummy proteins do not stick stamps, Henry lost his contract, and his small gum factory failed. He appears to have introduced an F_1 hybrid of comfrey which produced up to 100 tonnes an acre in Britain, and to have spent the last thirty years of his life experimenting with it. It was his dream that the crop would not only feed horses, cattle, sheep, pigs and poultry, but also solve the problem of world hunger, when that vision came not from biologist Paul Ehrlich but from the Irish Potato Famine of the 1840s. After his death, his relations cleared up after 'poor Uncle Henry', the dedicated elderly batchelor, and burned the records of his work. As I was determined that my work on comfrey, which began in 1948, should not be tidied away and lost, I founded the Association and named it in his honour.

The work of the Association soon grew far beyond the agricultural, horticultural, medicinal and nutritional uses of comfrey, and it has gone on growing until today it is the largest body, in what is loosely called 'The Organic Movement', in Britain, and the third largest in the world. Its official objects are:
1) The improvement and encouragement of agriculture and horticulture generally.
2) Research into, and the study of, improved methods of organic farming and gardening.

3) Research into the utilization of Russian Comfrey in connection with the foregoing objects.

4) The encouragement of research and experiment in agriculture and horticulture by, and the dissemination of knowledge of the results of such research and experiment, among farmers, gardeners and schools.

It is a Research Association because a proportion of its members carry out experiments in their own gardens, as a hobby. These are designed to find cheap, simple, and effective answers to the problems of gardening using the fewest chemicals. Because this kind of research rarely has any prospect of finding anything to patent or sell, and is rarely carried out even by Universities, it is still possible for amateurs to step over the frontiers of science beside their garden paths. The design of the experiments is carried out at the Trial Ground, and though many start from 'old wives tales', still more often begin with a search through scientific papers by the HDRA staff, to find a possible way round an awkward pest problem.

Today, when as much as 80% of a gardening work can be adapted from other books, or, in the organic field, copied from those written for other countries with different pests, diseases, crops and climates, there is an ever-increasing demand for knowledge based on practical experience and sound research. In 1977, six hundred our of seven thousand members took part in this type of experiment, which can become an absorbing interest for any keen gardener. But experimenters form only a small percentage of an Association which anyone can join, for a subscription in 1980 of £8 a year or, for pensioners, £4 (though inflation and, especially, increases in postage rates, raise this slowly as time passes), and members range from complete beginners with their first garden, to PhDs in the varied subjects covered by our work. Most members, however, join in order to receive the Association's quarterly newsletter, and to benefit from its gardening advisory service, as well as to support what has been described as 'the growing point of the organic movement'.

The Trial Ground at Bocking, with three Open Days in July and August, has now become almost an organic mini-Wisley. Its resources include a library, available for research and study, which is mainly used at present by the four students a year who are the small number the Association has the space to train, trial plots that test out the many new systems of organic gardening, and experiments in the field of fertility, on which much of this book has been based.

The Association has a number of local groups spaced over the British Isles, three in Australia, one in New Zealand and one in India, which has just founded the first organic Farming Institute in a tropical country. A recent development is a vigorous campaign to preserve the vanishing vegetable varieties, which are just as important a part of our genetic heritage as our equally endangered wild life. 'Vegetable Sanctuaries', in which they can be preserved as though they were birds or wild flowers, are being started in Britain and eventually overseas, where the need is more urgent because so many more species are in peril.

The scope of the HDRA has extended beyond gardening, compost heaps

214

and companion plants, to population, pollution, diet and nutrition, because the concern of its members is for the Organic Movement as a whole. We grow, we change, we learn, we correct our mistakes and above all we think ahead, drawing the line between 'organic' and 'inorganic' between all that which we can enjoy out of the income of the good earth, and that which will harm those who will still need to use and love our land when we are gone.

Appendix 3
Trials and Reports

a) Test carried out at the HDRA Trial Ground (Summer 1975) to evaluate the effect of turning dried-out compost heaps.

Three heaps had dried out completely and harboured fire fang, white mycelia of the fungus found in poorly stacked manure (and a sign of failure). The three were rebuilt on 26th July, when all the material was forked out to allow replacement of the brick channels and forked back with alternate layers of fresh and sappy weeds. All three heaps were then hosed until damp and covered down with a carpet. The result was as follows:

Date	Internal temperature of compost heap (°F.)		
	Fertosan	Nothing	Seaweed
27th July	165 (74°C)	140 (60°C)	145 (63°C)
28th	174 (79°C)	165 (74°C)	182 (83°C)
29th	168	160	182
30th	166	158	178
31st	164	156	178
1st August	150	156	168
2nd	154	144	160
3rd	144	132	159
4th	136	125	150
5th	122	120	136
6th	118	120	135
7th	108	116	136
8th	82 (28°C)	82 (28°C)	90 (32°C)

Temperature records of three heaps after turning

The heap were watered again on 30th July, and took the extra moisture without any fall in temperature. All three kept well in step, producing excellent heating and a steady fall until the fungi took over. The seaweed had the edge on the other activators, but even the bin with nothing added managed respectable temperatures as the bacteria already in the heap woke up with the moisture and food in the added layers.

b)   The effects of selective weedkillers, a report of tests by Dr Denys Long, from *Selective Weedkiller Toxicity in Barley Straw* (HDRA, 1969).

A variety of extracts for testing on freshly germinated seedlings were prepared from chopped dry barley straw in the following ways:

1) 200g of straw was steeped in 2 litres of distilled water at 15°C for 12 hours and, after straining, the resultant fluid was evaporated without boiling to 1600ml.

2) 200g of straw was treated as above but at 60°C and then evaporated to 400ml.

3) 120g was steeped in 500ml methonal at 15°C for 12 hours and after straining, the liquor was evaporated to dryness before re-dissolving in 100ml distilled water.

4) 110g was similarly treated in methanol at 60°C, and the extract dissolved in 100ml water.

5) 80g were shaken for 8 hours in 200ml distilled water and allowed to stand for 4 days before straining off the aqueous extract.

6) Dry straw was milled through a 2mm screen and then moistened with distilled water to produce a soft paste.

Test beds for the six straw extracts and a control were set up with six small trays lined with filter paper and a seventh with a 5mm layer of straw paste. The filter papers and straw paste were well damped with distilled water and placed in a propagator. Areas of these beds were sown at different times with seeds of spinach, carrot, cress and mustard. In due course, all the seeds except the spinach had germinated and, when the seed leaves were fully open, five of the test beds were each soaked with one of the various extract solutions, the remaining test tray serving for control.

A small field test was also set up, in which a small patch of weeds was marked off containing mostly shepherd's purse (*Capsella bursa-pastoris*), Germander speedwell (*Veronica chamaedrys*), purple deadnettle (*Lamium purpureum*), and fine grasses. Throughout the period of observation, the weather was dry, and this area was kept damp with the water extracts 1 and 2.

None of the treated seedlings died and no effect could be observed in their early growth when compared with the control tray. Furthermore, the seedlings growing directly into the straw paste appeared to be unaffected. The weeds in the field test grew equally well and came to seedbearing.

Barley straw from fields treated with MCPA and Di-allate (Monsanto 'Avadex' for wild oat control) weedkiller in the month of May 1969 has been demonstrated to be sufficiently free of residual toxicity not to affect the vegetable seeds tested, or certain weeds. Since 1969 was a dry year, these findings would suggest that such straw would be quite harmless in a wetter year when the weedkiller would be more completely leached from the soil.

c) Potato yields from chopped and other composts.

	Plot No.	Yield (lb–oz)	Total Yield (lb–oz)
Chopped Compost	1	13–8	
	6	17–0	
	8	15–0	45–8
			(20.8kg)
Ordinary (Unchopped) Compost	3	28–0	
	5	24–0	
	7	24–0	76–0
			(34.4kg)
Artificial Fertilizer (Growmore)	2	27–0	
	4	28–0	
	9	27–0	82–0
			(37.2kg)

Comparison of potato yields from chopped and unchopped compost and a complete artificial fertilizer

d) HDRA tests on tough, woody garden waste broken down for composting by the Mighty Mac shredder.

In 1978 a heap was built on the Bocking Trial Ground using material shredded with Mighty Mac. This heap was planned to show what the shredder would do with material that could not otherwise have been composted, and at a time when all other heaps are slowing down for the winter. The material consisted of dried, fruited raspberry canes, grubbed over-age lavender and blackcurrant bushes, cherry prunings and a small apple tree, plus other garden refuse. The heap was built on 9th October in a New Zealand box with 3in (7cm) thick layers of shreddings covered with rotted manure and lightly watered. A second heap was made in a Huker bin. Two sets of temperatures were taken off each heap at the centre and on the outer boundary.

New Zealand Box	Outer	Inner	Huker Bin	Outer	Inner
11th October	110°F	145°F	11th October	110°F	120°F
12th	164	180	12th	155	174
13th	138	188	13th	140	176
14th	144	168	14th	140	174
15th	138	155	15th	130	166
17th	102	152	17th	112	146
18th	98	148	18th	84	128
19th	114	140	19th	86	128
23rd	—	140	23rd	—	130

Temperatures achieved by shredded material heaps

e) Comparative yields of potatoes grown with comfrey, compost and artificial fertilizers.

On 13th February three barrows of compost were rotary cultivated into the three compost squares and 3½lb (1.6kg) of Growmore into the artificials. As our standard plots are 7sq yd (about 6m²), this smallest size of packet does each one exactly. On Saturday 1st May, we planted 20 seed tubers of Record on each square, with 1lb (1.5kg/m) of cut comfrey for each foot of row on the comfrey square and 2lb (3kg/m) a foot on Square 3. We were late because a cold dry spring meant a slow start for everything. On 11th September we dug and weighed the crop, with the result shown below.

The plots are 'replicated', repeated so that no two come next to each other, to cancel out variations in soil fertility, on what is called a 'Latin Square replication'. This is the simplest system of all, and means that three treatments need nine plots, four need sixteen and so on. There are many, more complicated replications in use on large research stations, but this is the easiest for amateurs. It will be noticed that all the plots towards the top of the table are low and those at the bottom run higher, so that if the Growmore had been put at the top and the compost at the bottom the result would have merely measured the difference in the fertility, not in the treatments. The Growmore squares have had nothing but chemicals for three years, and in a dry season the lack of moisture-retaining power from the missing humus shows in a reduced yield.

Plot 7: Compost		Plot 8: Comfrey		Plot 9: Growmore	
Row 1	5lb 4oz	Row 1	5lb 12oz	Row 1	5lb 2oz
Row 2	7lb 6oz	Row 2	9lb 14oz	Row 2	6lb 14oz
Row 3	7lb 6oz	Row 3	8lb 14oz	Row 3	7lb 2oz
Row 4	8lb 8oz	Row 4	6lb 10oz	Row 4	7lb 12oz
Total:	28lb 8oz	Total:	31lb 2oz	Total:	26lb 14oz
	(12.9kg)		(14.1kg)		(12.2kg)

Plot 4: Comfrey		Plot 5: Growmore		Plot 6: Compost	
Row 1	10lb 4oz	Row 1	7lb 12oz	Row 1	12lb 2oz
Row 2	12lb 8oz	Row 2	8lb 14oz	Row 2	10lb 8oz
Row 3	13lb 2oz	Row 3	8lb 4oz	Row 3	12lb 1oz
Row 4	8lb 6oz	Row 4	8lb 9oz	Row 4	9lb 10oz
Total:	44lb 4oz	Total:	33lb 7oz	Total:	44lb 5oz
	(20kg)		(15.2kg)		(20kg)

Plot 1: Growmore		Plot 2: Compost		Plot 3: Comfrey	
Row 1	12lb 14oz	Row 1	12lb 4oz	Row 1	15lb 12oz
Row 2	10lb 10oz	Row 2	13lb 1oz	Row 2	15lb 10oz
Row 3	9lb 7oz	Row 3	11lb 10oz	Row 3	13lb 6oz
Row 4	13lb 9oz	Row 4	10lb 4oz	Row 4	13lb 2oz
Total:	46lb 8oz	Total:	47lb 3oz	Total:	57lb 14oz
	(21.1kg)		(21.4kg)		(26.2kg)

Totals: Comfrey 133lb   4oz (60.3kg)

         Compost 120lb   0oz (54.3kg)

         Growmore 106lb 13oz (48.5kg)

Potato yields on comfrey, compost and Growmore

f) Potato yields resulting from the use of compost, or compost and comfrey.

On each date, of the 96 plants, 8 with comfrey and 8 without were lifted.

	Compost and comfrey		Compost only	
	lb	oz	lb	oz
14 July	11	8	3	14
18 July	9	12	4	1
20 July	10	11	5	13
21 July	11	12	5	14
23 July	11	10	7	15
30 July	15	0	8	0
30 July	13	1½	5	8
4 August	15	2	9	12
4 August	16	4½	7	12
4 August	13	2	7	4
4 August	15	2	6	14
13 August	15	14	9	8
Total from 96 tubers	158	15	82	3
	(72kg)		(37.2kg)	

Potato yields

g) Comparative yields of onions grown with comfrey, compost and artificial fertilizer.

In September 1970, about a barrowload of wilted comfrey was dug into three squares of a bed of nine plots, each 7 square yards (about 6m²) on the HDRA trial ground; three other squares received a good barrowload of compost each, and the last three had 3½lb (1.6kg) of Growmore chemical compound fertilizer. The squares are as far as possible standardized at this size for ease of working out cwts. and acres in calculating from them. On 26th February 1971 the squares were all planted with onion sets which were lifted on 23rd August, with the following results:

Plot 7: Comfrey	*Plot 8: Growmore*	*Plot 9: Compost*
best dozen (oz.)	best dozen (oz.)	best doazen (oz.)
8, 7, 9, 11, 7½, 9, 6,	3, 2½, 4, 4½, 4½,	3½, 3¼, 3¾, 4¼,
7½, 9, 10, 6½, 8½	5¼, 4¾, 3¼, 3½,	4½, 4½, 3½, 3, 4¼,
	3½, 3¾, 4	3½, 4, 4½
Total: 17lb 8oz	*Total:* 7lb 12oz	*Total:* 12lb 12oz
(8.0kg)	(3.5kg)	(5.8kg)

Plot 4: Compost	Plot 5: Comfrey	Plot 6: Growmore
best dozen	best dozen	best dozen
8½, 8¼, 8¼, 10, 12½, 7¼, 10¼, 11, 10½, 11¾, 7¼, 7½	7, 5, 5½, 5, 12½, 10, 10, 7, 7, 5¼, 6¾,	3½, 4½, 2¾, 3, 2¾, 3¼, 3¾, 3, 3½, 3½, 3½, 3, 4,
Total: 18lb 0oz (8.2kg)	Total: 12lb 0oz (5.5kg)	Total: 10lb 8oz (4.8kg)

Plot 1: Growmore	Plot 2: Compost	Plot 3: Comfrey
best dozen	best dozen	best dozen
8, 8, 7, 9, 7½, 7½, 8¼, 6½, 6, 7, 7, 6½	5¼, 4½, 4, 4½, 5, 4½, 3, 2, 3, 3¾, 5¼, 3	8½, 10¾, 6, 12, 6½, 5¾, 5¾, 6½, 5¼, 7¼, 6¼, 8½
Total: 12lb 8oz (5.7kg)	Total: 16lb 0oz (7.3kg)	Total: 20lb 12oz (9.4kg)

Totals:		
Comfrey	... ...	50lb 8oz (22.9kg)
Compost	... ...	46lb 12oz (21.3kg)
Growmore	... ...	30lb 12oz (14.0kg)

Onion yields

h) Compost made from straw, with comfrey as sole activator.

In August 1979, a straw and comfrey heap was built in a New Zealand box on the Bocking Trial Ground. The material consisted of fifteen bales of wheat straw from the previous year's harvest, stacked in the open and partly decayed, and the comfrey cut from one quarter of an acre (0.6 hectares) grown for plant sales was built into the layers with no added manure, lime or any other activator. The heap was turned after three weeks, when it heated up again. The result was an excellent compost.

Days from building	Temperature °F	(= °C)
1	64	18
2	69	21
3	96	36
4	108	42
5	108	42
6	110	43
7	120	49
8	120	49
9	110	43
10	104	40
11	90	32
12	80	27

	Analysis %	F.Y.M. %	Indore Compost %
Ash	31.55		
Moisture	57.10	76.00	76.00
Nitrogen	0.45	0.64	0.50
Phosphorus	0.42	0.23	0.27
Potash	0.55	0.32	0.81

Comfrey-activated straw heaps: temperature and analysis

i) The use of sawdust as a mulch—a report by Mr Victor Ledoux.

Most organic gardeners are aware that sawdust is very useful as a surface mulch, but do not dare to use it because of the disastrous effects that follow when it is dug in. They agree that there is no danger of nitrogen starvation while the sawdust is on the surface, but they wonder what happens to the soil's carbon:nitrogen ratio as the worms work the sawdust deeper by the simple process of burying it under their casts. The following report should dispel their fears.

A mulch of about two inches of sawdust has been spread on part of my garden from the spring of 1951 to that of 1960, ten mulches in all.

Before application, the sawdust, which was of mixed hard and soft wood straight from a joinery, was allowed to mature slightly by being kept in open bins 5ft (150cm) square. About 1ft (30cm) of fresh dust was added to the bins every month till they were usually 4ft (120cm) high, though occasionally they rose to 5ft (150cm). The sawdust was thoroughly soaked as soon as received and allowed to mature for 10 months, ventilation being provided by vertical crow-bar holes 12in (30cm) apart. During the early months the heaps would warm up slightly.

For the first two years ½in (10mm) of compost was spread under every sawdust mulch so as to encourage worms and nitrogen fixing organisms. After this the usual heavy doses were applied to strips in turn. The second, third and fourth years Surbiton sludge was spread as recommended by the makers, since when only bonemeal (4oz per square yard or 150g/m²) has been given every year. When two crops of lettuce were taken off the same plot in succession the same year, the second crop was sometimes helped with dried blood.

The ground, never dug but simply hoed 3–4in (7–10cm) deep prior to sowing has been practically weed free. Lettuce, endives, corn salad, carrots, beetroot, peas, tomatoes and onions have constantly cropped heavily, even in those parts of the garden which were newly converted to sawdust mulches. In fact this year, 1961, tomatoes and peas have done very well on a plot which was not previously cultivated and was simply composted and covered with 8in (20cm) of raw sawdust. This treatment, however, ruined the marrows and cucumbers.

The following table shows the analysis of soil that has received 2in (5cm) mulches of sawdust every year for 10 years, which totals 20in (50cm) in all. Actually 14in (35cm) of soil have been built up, as shown by the fact that the clay subsoil is now at 24in (60cm), whereas it was at only 10in (25cm) when I acquired the garden. Down to 12in (30cm) deep the soil is very friable. The analysis of the top 2in (5cm) shows how sawdust has been transformed after 10 months' weathering on the surface of a biologically rich soil.

		As received %	Dry Soil %
Soil	Nitrogen	0.8	0.34
Top 2in (5cm)	Phosphorus	0.17	0.07
C:N ratio excluding			
lignins 11.1:1	Potassium	0.12	0.05
Soil	Nitrogen	0.3	0.2
4–12in (5–30cm) mixed	Phosphorus	0.06	0.04
C:N ratio 8.6:1	Potassium	0.04	0.02
Soil	Nitrogen	0.24	0.16
12–14in (30–35cm)	Phosphorus	0.043	0.03
C:N ratio 8.0:1	Potassium	0.025	0.017
Soil	Nitrogen	0.17	0.12
24–26in (60–65cm)	Phosphorus	0.08	0.017

Analysis of a sawdust mulched garden

The carbon:nitrogen ratios were measured without the lignins, which do not break down quickly by bacterial action, and so cannot rob the soil of nitrogen. This soil was safe at all levels and the fall in minerals on the way to the 2ft (60cm) level was a normal tail-off for a fertile soil.

j) Programme of tests carried out by the HDRA on the use of dried sludge and seaweed in making compost.

The seaweed started a quick bacterial increase, and the sludge released nitrogen and phosphate to keep it going at full speed for a long period. Compost heaps were set up on 5th June, containing as nearly as possible identical material with 4oz of the sludge and seaweed mixture spread on each square yard (150g/m²) of layer surface on one bin compartment, and 4oz a square yard (150g/m²) of dried sludge on the other. The temperatures fell only slowly during the following week, simmering the couch grass roots like long, thin potatoes and cooking weed seeds like rice.

The dry·mixture can be kept in a plastic container (we used a plastic dustbin) for scattering as the heap is built day by day, and if there were a manufacturer with a blending and bagging machine and enough enterprise to buy sludge and seaweed in bulk for wholesale marketing to garden centres, it would be a good activator to use in towns far from any organic manure. Fresh seaweed can be used, but the layers should be at least half ½in (12.5mm) thick, because of the moisture content.

| Date | Average internal temperature of compost heaps | |
	Sludge plus seaweed meal	Sewage sludge
7th June	120°F	100°F
8th	145	110
9th	155	120
10th	145	125
11th	150	120
12th	155	120
13th	147	126
14th	140	120
15th	137	117

Temperatures of sludge plus seaweed and plain sludge compost heaps

k) Tests carried out at Tucson, Arizona, to compare yields under irrigation with fertilizer, effluents and well water.
The experiments began in 1957 on four large plots each flooded 3–6ft (0.9–1.8m) deep at every irrigation to a total of three acre feet (0.33 hectare/metres). One had this much well water; the second had well water plus 100lb (45kg) nitrogen, 75lb (34kg) phosphorus as P_2O_5, with no potassium, in order to duplicate the standard dressing in the area when the grain crops were grown; the third had well water plus chemicals equivalent to the plant foods in the effluent; and the fourth was given effluent alone. The results are shown in the following table (tons are US tons 907kg):

	Well water	Well water + Fertilizer	Synthetic Effluent	Effluent
Winter Barley pasture	5.25 tons	8.45 tons	12.33 tons	11.14 tons
Winter Barley grain	1,621lb	2,619lb	2,704lb	3,032
Winter Oats pasture	3.13 tons	6.05 tons	8.32 tons	10.93 tons
Winter Oats grain	1,385lb	1,950lb	1,984lb	2,346lb
Winter Wheat pasture	4.14 tons	7.78 tons	9.46 tons	10.81 tons
Winter Wheat grain	1,075lb	1,664lb	1,807lb	2,201lb

[Tons are US tons of 2,000lb or approx. 0.9 tonnes.]

Grain and pasture yields with fertilizers and effluent

PF